Data Communications
Testing and Troubleshooting

D1284983

HOWARD W. SAMS & COMPANY
HAYDEN BOOKS

Related Titles

For the retailer nearest you, or to order directly from the publisher, call 800-428-SAMS. In Indiana, Alaska, and Hawaii call 317-298-5699.

Data Communications Testing and Troubleshooting

GILBERT HELD

HOWARD W. SAMS & COMPANY

A Division of Macmillan, Inc.
4300 West 62nd Street
Indianapolis, Indiana 46268 USA

© 1989 by Gilbert Held

FIRST EDITION
FIRST PRINTING—1988

All rights reserved. No part of this book shall be reproduced, stored in a retrieval system, or transmitted by any means, electronic, mechanical, photocopying, recording, or otherwise, without written permission from the publisher. No patent liability is assumed with respect to the use of the information contained herein. Although every precaution has been taken in the preparation of this book, the publisher and author assume no responsibility for errors or omissions. Neither is any liability assumed for damages resulting from the use of the information contained herein.

International Standard Book Number: 0-672-22616-2
Library of Congress Catalog Card Number: 88-62901

Acquisitions Editor: *James S. Hill*
Development Editor: *James Rounds*
Manuscript Editor: *Katherine Stuart Ewing*
Illustrator: *Wm. D. Basham*
Cover Art: *Meridian Design Studio*
Indexer: *Gilbert Held*
Technical Reviewer: *Nick Lombardo*
Compositor: *Shepard Poorman Communications Corporation*

Printed in the United States of America

Trademark Acknowledgments

All terms mentioned in this book that are known to be trademarks or service marks are listed below. In addition, terms suspected of being trademarks or service marks have been appropriately capitalized. Howard W. Sams & Company cannot attest to the accuracy of this information. Use of a term in this book should not be regarded as affecting the validity of any trademark or service mark.

Digital Dataphone Service is a trademark of AT&T.

Kilostream service is a trademark of British Telecom.

OMNINUX and Racal-Milgo are trademarks of Racal-Milgo, Inc.

*This book is dedicated
to the time when real GLASNOST occurs,
the Berlin Wall is removed,
and citizens of all countries obtain
the right to practice their religion
and the ability to emigrate if they so desire.*

Contents

Acknowledgments

The development of a book is a long and involved process that requires a large amount of patience, understanding, and support.

Because this book was developed between full-time employment and family obligations, the latter unfortunately sometimes suffered while I took the time required to develop the manuscript that resulted in this book. Thus, I would especially like to thank my family for their patience and understanding.

Although family support is critical for successfully developing a manuscript, many other persons made important contributions in cooperation and help. I would like to thank Mr. Jim Hill of Howard W. Sams for supporting this book, Mr. Joseph Savino of Frost & Sullivan, Inc., for enabling me to conduct a series of seminars in Europe that formed the basis for this book, and Mrs. Carol Ferrell who once again converted my handwritten manuscript into a form suitable for publication. Lastly, I would like to extend my appreciation to Katherine Stuart Ewing for her fine editing as well as her work in ensuring that the nontrivial task of putting a book through production became a simple task.

Chapter 1

Introduction

As THE TITLE OF THIS BOOK IMPLIES, its objective is to introduce the reader to the related fields of data communications testing, troubleshooting, and capacity planning. To achieve this objective, I constructed the book in a modular fashion, placing special emphasis on a review of measurements and data channel parameters for those readers requiring background information about these. Therefore, readers familiar with data communications measurements and data channel parameters can skim through or skip the initial chapters in this book.

From chapter 2 on, I include a series of review questions at the end of each chapter. I encourage you to work these questions, then before reading succeeding chapters, to compare your answers to the answers included at the end of this book.

Rationale

The investigation of three important and related areas in data communications forms the basis for this book.

Concerning testing, the well-known "Murphy's Law" states that in any given situation, all that can go wrong does. By learning what and how to test, you can develop a procedure for scheduled testing that isolates problems before they become major. Examples of testing that may prevent the occurrence of major problems include the identification of marginal circuits and the switchover of primary to secondary logic on certain communications equipment.

If you identify marginal circuits and inform the appropriate communications carrier of the situation, you may be able to rectify the problem before the circuit fails. Similarly, if you can identify that the primary logic on a communications device failed and that the equipment effected cut-over to secondary logic, you can probably prevent an interruption of communications service by replacing the failed primary logic and resetting the device. Replacing the primary logic is necessary because the failure of secondary logic after a failure of primary logic renders the device inoperative.

The second area I focus on in this book is troubleshooting the communications network. In this era of divestiture, the successful and reliable operation of a data communications network is primarily the responsibility of the user and not the communications carrier or carriers. Because most networks have communications equipment and facilities obtained from many vendors, you must be able to isolate the cause of a communications failure. To do so requires that you have a background in and knowledge of communications parameters and measurements as well as knowledge about the performance of various tests designed to isolate the transmission impairment. Therefore, in this book, I immediately discuss the interrelationship of testing and troubleshooting.

The last focal area of this book concerns capacity planning. A well-known adage says that the data transmission requirements of a network's communications users grow to exceed whatever bandwidth the network analyst provides. Although this may not always be true, it does present two important capacity-related areas that network analysts must consider if they are to be effective. If a communications system has excessive capacity, there is a high probability that the organization is spending more money than necessary on equipment, facilities, or a combination of the two. Conversely, if capacity is insufficient to satisfy the end users' requirements, the organization's productivity may suffer because of extended response times or the inability of persons to access corporate computer and information resources.

End users complaining about excessive capacity is about as rare as encountering ancient fossils on a public rhw beach. Conversely, as surely as the sun rises in the East, you can depend on the same end users complaining whenever they encounter excessive response times or when they cannot easily access the organization's network. Because many instruments originally developed for testing and troubleshooting provide information about the utilization of equipment and facilities, this book examines how you can use such devices for capacity planning. In addition, in this book, I review the fundamental concepts of traffic engineering, which provides the mathematical basis for sizing such common networking devices as multiplexers, concentrators, and front-end processor ports.

Objective

By establishing a foundation of knowledge concerning the interrelated fields of data communications testing, troubleshooting, and capacity planning, this book should help network analysts to operate and maintain networks. Because of the pervasiveness of the data communications field and the multitude of available equipment and facilities, this book can neither cover every conceivable situation nor provide insight into every device that you can use in a network. What this book does is provide a foundational knowledge of procedures and methods that you can follow, along with many examples of the isolation and correction of transmission impairments that I have encountered while managing a large scale communications network.

Chapter 2

Basic Measurements

IN THIS CHAPTER, we review the basic measurements associated with data communications facilities. You need to know these measurements to operate certain types of equipment, to compare measurements to parameters associated with different types of carrier facilities, and to determine reason(s) for a deterioration in communications service.

Power Ratios

One method used to categorize the quality of transmission on a circuit is to state the ratio of power received to power transmitted. The gain or loss of power on a circuit is given by the equation

$$B = \log_{10} \frac{P_O}{P_I}$$

where:

B = power ratio in bels

P_O = output or received power

P_I = input power

Here, the bel is the unit that results from taking the logarithm to the base 10 of the ratio of power out to power in. One reason that we use the logarithm to the base 10 is that the response of the human ear to changes in volume is logarithmic. Because of the following logarithm relationship,

$$\log_{10} \frac{1}{X} = -\log_{10}X$$

if the output or received power is less than the input power, this condition indicates a power loss. Similarly, if there is more output power than input power, there is a power gain, which we note by either the presence of a plus sign or the absence of a minus sign.

Although the bel, named for Alexander Graham Bell, was initially used for communications power measurements, a more precise unit of measurement was required as communications systems evolved. This requirement was satisfied by the decibel (dB), which is one-tenth of a bel. You can compute dB gains and losses with the following formula:

$$dB = 10 \log_{10} \frac{P_O}{P_I}$$

To illustrate the use of the decibel for measuring power gains and losses on a transmission system, consider the transmission line illustrated in Figure 2-1. If we assume that the line has a 10 milliwatt (mw) power input, and a dB meter records a power output of 1mw, what is the dB loss? Using the formula for dB,

$$dB = 10 \log_{10} \frac{1}{10} = -10 \log_{10} 10 = -10$$

Input Power 10mw

dB Meter = 1mw

Figure 2-1. Transmission line with 10dB loss.

Thus, the circuit illustrated in Figure 2-1 has a 10dB loss. Table 2-1 presents the values of 14 common logarithms to help you compute power gain and loss measurements.

Table 2-1. Common Logarithm Values

Log	Value	Log	Value
Log 1	0.000	Log 8	0.903
Log 2	0.301	Log 9	0.954
Log 3	0.477	Log 10	1.000
Log 4	0.602	Log 20	1.301
Log 5	0.699	Log 30	1.477
Log 6	0.778	Log 40	1.602
Log 7	0.845	Log 100	2.000

Another reason for the use of a logarithmic unit in measuring power gains and losses is the reduction of arithmetic to addition and subtraction in a transmission system because of the properties of logarithms. As an example, consider the transmission system illustrated in Figure 2-2, where a 10dB signal enters an amplifier that provides a 5dB gain. Because of the properties of logarithms, the output signal level is +10dB +5dB or 15dB. Assuming a line loss of 7dB, a dB meter placed at the output side of the transmission line would read 8dB. Thus, the output is equal to the input plus the gain minus the loss.

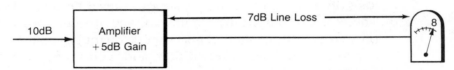

Figure 2-2. dB gains and losses are added algebraically.

Signal-to-Noise Ratio

The signal-to-noise (S/N) ratio, a well-known communications measurement, is the signal power divided by the noise power on a circuit. Use this ratio to categorize the quality of a circuit. The S/N ratio is measured in dB.

A high S/N ratio is desirable because it maximizes the signal's capability of being correctly interpreted at a receiver. On most conditioned leased lines, a signal-to-noise ratio between 23dB and 26dB is normally encountered, resulting in the signal power being between 200 and 400 times that of the level of noise on the circuit. Although a high S/N ratio is better than a low S/N ratio, too much power on an analog circuit can adversely affect telephone company amplifiers. Thus, telephone companies, as well as the Post Telephone and Telegraph (PTT) organizations that regulate and provide communications services in foreign countries, specify the transmit level of signals to be carried over their facilities.

Reference Points

To standardize testing and measurements requires the use of reference points. In the case of the decibel, 0dB is equivalent to a 1:1 power ratio and serves as a reference point for dB measurements.

In telephone operations, the reference level of power is 0.001 watt (1mw). This level of power represents the average amount of power generated in the transmitter of a telephone during a voice conversation. Thus, by using a 1mw power level, telephone company personnel obtain a reference level for comparing gains and losses in a circuit. For convenience, 1mw of power is considered equal to 0dB. To ensure that no one forgets that 1mw is the reference level, the letter *m* is attached to the power level. Thus,

$$\text{dBm} = 10 \log_{10} \frac{\text{Signal power in milliwatts}}{1 \text{ milliwatt}}$$

Compared with dB, which is used to express the amount of gain or loss, dBm is used to denote the power level because of a gain or loss. Therefore, 0dBm means 1 milliwatt, and absolute power levels are expressed as XdBm, where X is a numeric quantity. Table 2-2 compares the relationship between dB and dBm and their power or S/N ratio for 23 common dB and dBm values.

As analog circuits are routed through telephone company facilities, the gains and losses along each segment of the route are added algebraically. Thus, a −20dBm loss on a circuit followed by a +6dBm gain results in a −14dBm total loss.

In addition to using a reference power level, telephone companies use a standard frequency for testing voice circuits. In North America, we use 1004Hz, which results in a testing device supplying 0dBm of power to a circuit at 1004Hz frequency. In actuality, because 0dBm is 1mw, 1mw of power at 1004Hz is used as the reference power level. In Europe and most other countries outside of North America, the standard frequency for testing voice circuits is 800Hz; however, 0dBm of power is still used.

Transmission Level Point

The transmission level point is the power in dBm that should be measured when a specific test tone signal is transmitted at some location that is selected as a reference point. In North America, the transmission level point is referenced as the TLP, and a 0dBm, 1004Hz signal is transmitted at the reference point. In Europe, the transmission level point is known as the dBr (decibel reference), and a 0dBm, 800Hz signal is transmitted at the reference point.

To understand the use of the TLP, consider Figure 2-3, where a test instrument is connected to the terminator block on a circuit. At point A, we assume that a reading of −12dBm is expected when a 0dBm signal is applied to the terminator block. In this situation, point A would be a −12TLP.

Table 2-2. Relationship Between dB/dBm, Gain/Loss, and Power Measurements

dB/dBm	Output/Input Ratio
0	1.0:1
1	1.2:1
2	1.6:1
3	2.0:1
4	2.5:1
5	3.2:1
6	4.0:1
7	5.0:1
8	6.4:1
9	8.0:1
10	10.0:1
13	20.0:1
16	40.0:1
19	80.0:1
20	100.0:1
23	200.0:1
26	400.0:1
29	800.0:1
30	1,000.0:1
33	2,000.0:1
36	4,000.0:1
39	8,000.0:1
40	10,000.0:1

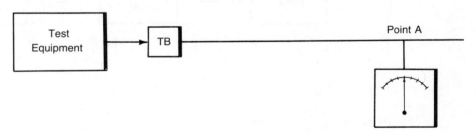

Figure 2-3. Measuring the TLP.

Zero Transmission Level

To reference the TLP back to the test tone level, a unit of measurement known as the dBm0 (decibel milliwatt zero transmission level) is used, where

Zero transmission level = actual measurement − test tone level

Thus,

$$dBm0 = dBm - TLP$$

Here, dBm0 is a measurement that shows the departure of a system from its design value. As an example of the use of the transmission level point, assume that the TLP is 12, whereas the actual dBm is measured as 10. Then,

$$dBm0 = dBm - TLP$$

or

$$dBm0 = 10\text{-}12 = -2$$

This tells us that the system is 2dBm under its design goal. Figure 2-4 provides a comparison of the TLP, measured dBm, and dBm0 for a transmission system that consists of a circuit routed from a termination block at a customer's premises through two telephone company amplifiers. Although the dBm0 throughout the system is shown at a constant −9, in actuality the departure from the design goal varies in a random manner in spite of efforts by the communications carrier to make it approach zero.

	Block	18dB Loss	20dB Amplifier	10dB Loss	6dB Amplifier
	*	*	*	*	*
TLP (dBr):	13	−5	+15	+5	+11
Measured dBm:	4	−14	+6	−4	+2
dBm0:	−9	−9	−9	−9	−9

Figure 2-4. Measurement comparison.

Noise Measurement Units

The noise level at any point in a transmission system is the ratio of channel noise at that point to a predefined amount of noise that is selected as a
reference level. This ratio is usually expressed in decibels above reference noise, or dBrn, which is an arbitrary level that represents the lowest
noise level an average telephone listener can hear.

For noise measurements, the dB scale is shifted so that −90dBm becomes the noise reference level, as illustrated in Figure 2-5. As shown,
0dBrn is set arbitrarily equal to 90dBm.

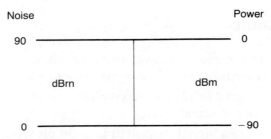

Figure 2-5. Noise and power relationship.

Meter Utilization

When a meter is used to measure noise, a "C-message" filter is used between the meter and the line. The filter is used to remove the 1004Hz
component of the test signal and the power line frequencies (60Hz and
its harmonics), leaving only the noise. When the C-message filter is used
in noise measurements, the units are called *decibels above referenced
noise C-message weighted,* which is abbreviated dBrnc.

As with power measurements, a transmission level point is used to
provide a reference level for noise where:

C-message weighted zero level = actual noise level − test tone level

Here, the C-message weighted zero level is abbreviated as dBrnc0.
Thus,

$$dBrnc0 = dBrnc - dBm$$

Levels

Levels of a circuit is a term normally used to reference the signal or noise intensity and is usually measured in dBm. This measurement is used to indicate whether too much or too little power is present, a critical measurement because either condition can cause signal distortion. If levels are too high, amplifiers in a circuit path become overloaded, resulting in an increase in crosstalk or intermodulation. Conversely, if levels are too low, the signal may be inaudible so that it either is received incorrectly or not at all.

Review Questions

1. The received power on a circuit was determined to be one-hundredth of the transmitted power. What is the power ratio in dB?

2. A signal of 12dB entered an amplifier with a gain of 7dB. What is the output signal level?

3. A 1mw signal is applied to a circuit with the resulting output determined to be .01mw. What is the power level of the circuit?

4. The noise on a circuit was measured as 30dBrn. What is the equivalent power level?

5. If the TLP at a location in a transmission system is 16 and a meter shows that the actual dBm is 14, what is the zero transmission level at that location and what does it indicate?

Chapter 3

Basic Data Channel Parameters

IN THIS CHAPTER, we examine the basic parameters of analog circuits and the transmission impairments that can occur on such circuits. Using this information as a base, we can examine the methods used to improve channel characteristics that, in turn, reduce transmission impairments.

Bandwidth

Bandwidth is a measurement of the width of a range of frequencies, such that

$$B = f_2 - f_1$$

where:

B = bandwidth

f_2 = highest frequency

f_1 = lowest frequency

Figure 3-1 illustrates the bandwidth of a telephone channel compared to the audio spectrum heard by the human ear. Here the bandwidth passed through the telephone channel is the range of frequencies between 300Hz and 3300Hz, or 3000Hz. Because the data transmission rate is proportional to the bandwidth of a channel, the telephone company network was constructed so that the data rate obtainable on a telephone channel had a finite limit.

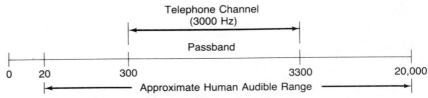

Figure 3-1. Bandwidth of a telephone channel.

Passband

The band of frequencies passed through the telephone channel is more commonly known as the channel's passband. In our discussion, the passband is defined more formally as a contiguous portion of an area in the frequency spectrum, which permits a predefined range of frequencies to pass. Thus, the passband of a telephone channel permits the frequencies between 300 and 3300Hz to pass.

To understand the rationale for using a passband, you need to know something about the design goals of early telephone systems. To economize on the number of lines needed to interconnect telephone company offices, telephone engineers decided to limit by high-pass and low-pass filters the passband of each telephone channel. The low-pass filter attenuates all high frequencies at and above a cutoff frequency (f_0), as illustrated in Figure 3-2A. Thus, all high frequencies at and above the cutoff frequency cannot flow through a low-pass filter. The high-pass filter illustrated in Figure 3-2B operates roughly the reverse of the low-pass filter, permitting all high frequencies at and below the cutoff frequency (f_0) to pass through the filter while attenuating the low frequencies. By using low-pass and high-pass filters and by adjusting the cutoff frequencies of the filters, a passband is created.

At each telephone company central office, frequency division multiplexers originally were designed to take the passband of each telephone channel that required routing from that central office to a distant office. The multiplexers shifted the passband in frequency onto a common long distance circuit, which was used to transmit many simultaneous voice conversations. Figure 3-3 illustrates the frequency division multiplexing of voice conversations.

In Figure 3-3, the shaded areas between passbands (P_1, P_2, etc.) represent guard bands used to prevent a frequency drift that results in one conversation affecting another conversation.

At the distant office, the passband was shifted back in direction and magnitude to reconstruct the original signal. Then the reconstructed

HOWARD W. SAMS & COMPANY

Bookmark

DEAR VALUED CUSTOMER:

Howard W. Sams & Company is dedicated to bringing you timely and authoritative books for your personal and professional library. Our goal is to provide you with excellent technical books written by the most qualified authors. You can assist us in this endeavor by checking the box next to your particular areas of interest.

We appreciate your comments and will use the information to provide you with a more comprehensive selection of titles.

Thank you,

Vice President, Book Publishing
Howard W. Sams & Company

COMPUTER TITLES:

Hardware
- ☐ Apple 140
- ☐ Macintosh I01
- ☐ Commodore I10
- ☐ IBM & Compatibles I14

Business Applications
- ☐ Word Processing J01
- ☐ Data Base J04
- ☐ Spreadsheets J02

Operating Systems
- ☐ MS-DOS K05
- ☐ OS/2 K10
- ☐ CP/M K01
- ☐ UNIX K03

Programming Languages
- ☐ C L03
- ☐ Pascal L05
- ☐ Prolog L12
- ☐ Assembly L01
- ☐ BASIC L02
- ☐ HyperTalk L14

Troubleshooting & Repair
- ☐ Computers S05
- ☐ Peripherals S10

Other
- ☐ Communications/Networking M03
- ☐ AI/Expert Systems T18

ELECTRONICS TITLES:
- ☐ Amateur Radio T01
- ☐ Audio T03
- ☐ Basic Electronics T20
- ☐ Basic Electricity T21
- ☐ Electronics Design T12
- ☐ Electronics Projects T04
- ☐ Satellites T09

- ☐ Instrumentation T05
- ☐ Digital Electronics T11

Troubleshooting & Repair
- ☐ Audio S11
- ☐ Television S04
- ☐ VCR S01
- ☐ Compact Disc S02
- ☐ Automotive S06
- ☐ Microwave Oven S03

Other interests or comments: _____

_____

Name_____
Title _____
Company _____
Address _____
City _____
State/Zip _____
Daytime Telephone No. _____

A Division of Macmillan, Inc.

4300 West 62nd Street Indianapolis, Indiana 46268

22616

Bookmark

BUSINESS REPLY CARD

PERMIT NO. 1076   INDIANAPOLIS, IND.

FIRST CLASS

POSTAGE WILL BE PAID BY ADDRESSEE

HOWARD W. SAMS & CO.

ATTN: Public Relations Department

P.O. BOX 7092

Indianapolis, IN 46209-9921

NO POSTAGE
NECESSARY
IF MAILED
IN THE
UNITED STATES

HOWARD W. SAMS & COMPANY

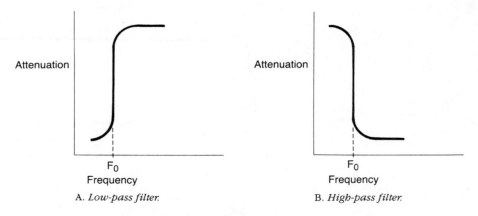

A. *Low-pass filter.*

B. *High-pass filter.*

Figure 3-2. Low-pass and high-pass filter operations.

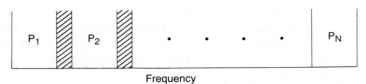

Frequency

Figure 3-3. Frequency division multiplexing.

passband was routed to the other party on the long distance telephone call. Because the passband was constructed to permit all voice tones except for very low and very high frequencies to be passed, the use of filters is unnoticeable to the human ear. In economic terms, however, the use of the passband was very noticeable, because a voice conversation now required approximately one-sixth the bandwidth of a nonfiltered conversation. Thus, with filters, the telephone company was able to multiplex six times more voice conversations between offices in a 20KHz bandwidth than were possible when the company transmitted a 20KHz signal for each voice conversation.

By using electrical filters, which are also known as loading coils, the passband of a telephone channel takes on the characteristics of an amplitude-frequency response curve as illustrated in Figure 3-4.

At the low and high cutoff frequencies, the signal strength is attenuated to render inaudible the frequencies that are slightly past the cutoff frequencies.

In examining the amplitude-frequency response of a telephone channel, note that under ideal conditions, the passband has zero attenuation

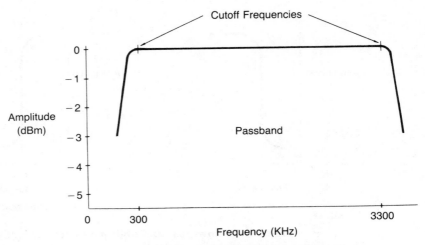

Figure 3-4. Passband of a telephone channel.

and is not affected by using filters on the circuit. In actuality, as one moves from the center of the passband toward either cutoff frequency, attenuation begins to increase. This explains why most modems are designed to use one or more carrier frequencies that are at or near the center of the passband.

Channel Capacity and Modulation Techniques

In 1928, Nyquist described the relationship between the bandwidth of a channel and the maximum signaling rate that could occur on that channel. The signaling rate, which was also known as the baud rate, was determined to be

$$B = 2W$$

where:

    B = baud rate

    W = bandwidth in Hz

The Nyquist relationship states that the rate at which data can be transmitted without intersymbol interference occurring must be less than or equal to twice the bandwidth in Hz. Thus, an analog circuit with a bandwidth of 3000Hz can only support baud rates at or under 6000 signaling elements per second. Because an oscillating modulation technique, such as amplitude, frequency, or phase modulation, halves the achievable signaling rate, modems can operate only up to 3000 baud. To achieve a high data transmission rate, therefore, a modem must increase the amount of information each baud (signal change) contains. This can be accomplished by such techniques as dibit and tribit encoding.

In dibit encoding, two bits are used to generate a phase change. Thus, because every phase shift represents two bits, the bit rate is twice the baud rate. In tribit encoding, three bits are used to generate a phase change so that the bit rate is three times greater than the baud rate.

Table 3-1 lists one of the more commonly used sets of phase changes employed by modems using dibit encoding. Modems using this encoding technique examine the composition of bits two at a time, shifting the phase of the carrier signal to correspond to the dibit value. The receiving modem measures the phase shift and generates the pair of bits assigned to the denoted shift.

Table 3-1. Phase Modulation Example

Dibits	Phase shift
00	0
01	90
10	180
11	270

The plotting of all possible phase shifts that can be generated by a modem is known as the modem's constellation pattern. Figure 3-5 illustrates the signal pattern of a modem that is capable of generating the phase shifts listed in Table 3-1. Note that the signal points are equidistant from one another, which reflects modem designers' desire to minimize the effect of an unintended phase shift or other transmission impairment shifting a signal point far enough that it causes the receiving modem to misinterpret an invalid signal point as a valid one.

As modem designers strove to obtain higher data rates under the constraint of the Nyquist relationship between bandwidth and baud rate, they developed more complex modulation techniques that packed more bits into each signal change. Among these techniques was one known as quadrature amplitude modulation (QAM) in which the amplitude and phase of a signal was varied, based on the composition of four bits of data to be modulated.

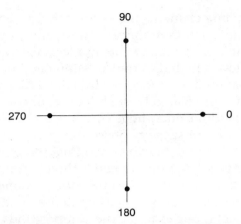

Figure 3-5. Dibit encoding signal pattern for 2400bps modem.

Figure 3-6 illustrates the constellation pattern of modems designed to follow the Consultative Committee for International Telephone & Telegraph (CCITT) V.29 standard for operations at 9600bps. In comparing the constellation patterns of the 2400 and 9600bps modems illustrated in Figures 3-5 and 3-6, note that the modem with the higher operating rate has the denser constellation pattern.

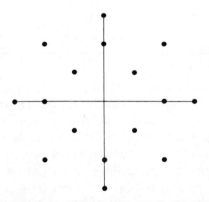

Figure 3-6. CCITT V.29 16-point constellation pattern.

In general, as transmission rates increase, modem constellation patterns become denser, with a reduction in the distance between signal points. Because a fixed amount of transmission impairment or signal distortion has a higher probability of causing a point in a dense constellation pattern to be misinterpreted than a point in a less dense pattern, in general, the density of the constellation pattern is proportional to its susceptibility to signal distortion. Thus, engineering techniques designed to pack more bits into each signal change resulted in constellation patterns that became both more complex and generally more susceptible to signal distortion.

Shannon's Law

The Nyquist relationship governs the maximum signaling rate. Claude Shannon developed a theory dealing with the maximum data transmission rate, in bits per second, obtainable on a circuit. Shannon's work at MIT in 1949 resulted in the description of a relationship between the maximum bit rate capacity of a channel of bandwidth W and its signal-to-noise ratio as follows:

$$C = W \log_2(1 + S/N)$$

where:

C = capacity in bits per second

W = bandwidth in Hz

S = signal power of the transmitter

N = power of the thermal noise

Experimentation found that a "near perfect" channel would have a signal-to-noise ratio of 30dB, which is equivalent to the signal power being 1000 times that of the noise power. Thus, according to Shannon's Law, the maximum data transmission capacity became

$$
\begin{aligned}
C &= W \log_2(1 + S/N) \\
&= 3000 \log_2(1 + 10^3) \\
&= 3000 \log_2(1001) \\
&= 3000 \times 10 \text{ (approximately)} \\
&= 30000 \text{bps}
\end{aligned}
$$

Current Transmission Rate

At present, the highest data transmission rate obtainable on voice grade analog circuits is roughly 19200bps, and although modems have advanced rapidly over the past few years, a further one-third improvement is possible within the constraints of Shannon's Law.

Impairments and Corrective Measures

Although many factors can affect the quality of a transmitted signal, the four key factors are attenuation distortion, envelope delay, signal power level, and noise. In this section, we examine the factors affecting data transmission, the methods used to measure different impairments, and the use of different devices to reduce or minimize the effect of different types of impairments.

Attenuation Distortion

Attenuation is the loss in signal strength as the distance between a transmitter and receiver increases. Electronic signals that carry information are made up of an array of frequencies, with a specific amplitude associated with each frequency. Ideally, all the frequencies across the passband of a telephone channel should undergo the same amount of attenuation as illustrated in Figure 3-7A. Unfortunately, high frequencies lose their strength more rapidly than low frequencies, as illustrated in Figure 3-7B, which results in the distortion of signals that include high frequency components.

Across a voice channel or cable used to directly connect two devices, the degree of amplitude distortion versus frequency affects the operation of modems and the reception of digital pulses. As an example of the former, consider a frequency shift keying (FSK) modem that places two separate tones on the line, one to represent a mark and the other to represent a space. Although the frequencies used to represent mark and space are located near the center of the passband, one tone is higher in frequency than the other. If the amplitude-frequency response across a voice channel deteriorates, the degree of deterioration affects the tone used to represent one binary condition before it affects the tone used to represent the second binary condition.

When digital signals are transmitted directly on a cable—say, between a terminal and a computer—the amplitude-frequency response across the cable affects the signal. This is because the attenuation of a cable increases at a rate in decibels that is proportional to the square root of the frequency, causing more attenuation to occur at high frequencies than at low frequencies. Because a square wave is the sum of weighted sinusoidal waves, as shown in Figure 3-8, the high frequency energy that served to shape the corners of a square wave is lost more quickly than the energy of the fundamental wave. As a result of this action, the corners of digital pulses begin to deteriorate first. Because attenuation increases in

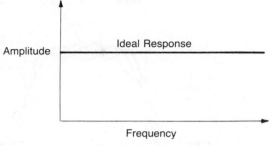

A. *Ideal amplitude-frequency response.*

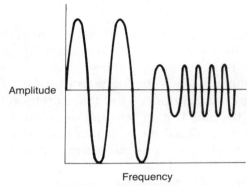

B. *Effect of attenuation distortion.*

Figure 3-7. Frequency attenuation.

direct proportion to the length of a cable, increasing the distance between a terminal and computer port results in a point being reached where the level of distortion makes the digital pulse unrecognizable at the receiver.

Measurements

In North America, a 1004Hz test tone at 0dBm is used as a reference frequency to measure attenuation distortion and to adjust the active line components of voice frequency leased lines at the time they are installed. The actual frequency response loss depends on the type of voice frequency (VF) line installed—unconditioned or conditioned. At present, AT&T offers two categories of conditioning, known as C conditioning and D conditioning. Several types of C conditioning are tariffed to

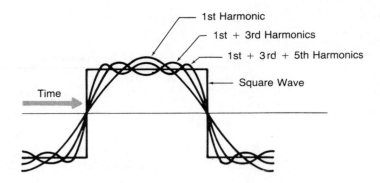

Figure 3-8. Square wave characteristics.

provide various degrees of control over attenuation and envelope distortion. In comparison, D conditioning is available in two types and is designed to limit noise and harmonic distortion.

Table 3-2 lists the limits in dB of the frequency response loss for a basic (unconditioned) and four common types of C conditioned AT&T circuits, plus British Telecom's Keyline analog service that is offered in the United Kingdom. Note that a negative value in the table is less loss or a gain, whereas a positive value is more loss, or simply a loss.

Table 3-2. Bandwidth Parameter Limits—Frequency Response Loss

Channel/ Conditioning	Frequency Range	Limits in dB
Basic	300-500	−3 to +12
	500-2500	−2 to +8
	2500-3000	−3 to +12
C1	300-1000	−3 to +12
	1000-2400	−1 to +3
	2400-2700	−2 to +6
	2700-3000	−3 to +12
C2	300-500	−2 to +6
	500-2800	−1 to +3
	2800-3000	−2 to +6
C4	300-500	−2 to +6
	500-3000	−2 to +3
	3000-3200	−2 to +6
C5	300-500	−1 to +3
	500-2800	−.5 to +1.5
	2800-3000	−1 to +3

Table 3-2. (cont.)

Channel/ Conditioning	Frequency Range	Limits in dB
British Telecom Keyline	300-500	−2 to +6
	500-2800	−1 to +3
	2800-3000	−2 to +6

Note: + means more loss

C1 and C2 conditioning are applicable for point-to-point and multi-point channels. C3 conditioning is applicable for access lines and trunks associated with a Switched Circuit Automatic Network or Common Control Switching Arrangement. C4 conditioning is for point-to-point and three- and four-point multidrop lines, whereas C5 conditioning is only applicable for a point-to-point channel.

In Europe, a test tone of 800Hz is used as the common reference frequency to measure attenuation distortion. Several CCITT recommendations cover attenuation distortion. CCITT recommendation G.132 specifies that no more than 9dB of attenuation distortion is acceptable between 400Hz and 3000Hz, based on a test tone of 800Hz, which is the maximum variation that can be expected from the reference level of 800Hz over the voice spectrum. A second CCITT recommendation, M.1020, covers the permissible signal loss over the frequency range for 4-wire international leased lines. Figure 3-9 illustrates the permissible signal loss specified by CCITT recommendation M.1020. Compare Table 3-2 to Figure 3-9 and note that M.1020 is the same as British Telecom's Keyline service. In Figure 3-9, as in Table 3-2, a positive dB means more loss, whereas a negative dB is less loss.

Adjusting Attenuation Distortion

Attenuation equalizers are used to adjust the attenuation distortion found on a typical circuit into an acceptable range of amplitude-frequency response limits. Such equalizers are designed to introduce a variable gain at frequencies within the passband. This variable gain serves to compensate for the difference between high and low frequencies and the increased attenuation at the edges of the passband. Figure 3-10 illustrates how attenuation equalizers can be used on a circuit to correct attenuation distortion.

The process of installing and adjusting attenuation equalizers de-

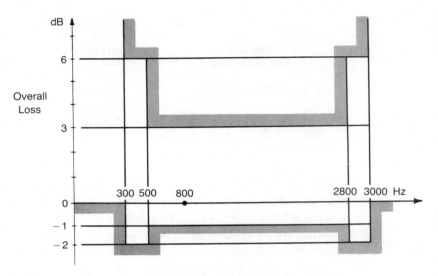

Note: Below 300Hz and above 3000Hz, the loss is not less than
0.0dB but is otherwise unspecified.

Figure 3-9. Attenuation distortion (CCITT M.1020).

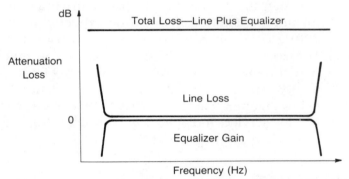

Figure 3-10. Using an equalizer to correct attenuation distortion.

pends on the type of circuit conditioning, if any, obtained for a leased
line. Because calls over the switched telephone network are routed dif-
ferently based on call destination and network activity at the time of the
call, fixed attenuation equalizers cannot be used on this network. In
place of equalizers, many modems contain built-in automatic and adap-
tive equalization circuits that first send training signals between each modem, then adjust the modem's equalization circuits to best compensate
for the distortion on the circuit.

Delay (Phase) Distortion

As a signal propagates down a transmission medium, its phase, amplitude, and frequency can be affected. To understand the effect of phase changes, let us first examine a distortionless channel through which all frequencies pass at the same speed. When data is transmitted over a distortionless channel, the frequency and phase of the signal have a constant linear relationship, as illustrated in Figure 3-11A. Unfortunately, the shift of phase with respect to frequency is normally nonlinear in most transmission media, resembling the curve illustrated in Figure 3-11B. Some frequencies are delayed more than others during transmission, which can result in the distortion of the original signal. Although the human ear is insensitive to a signal delay varying by frequency, this delay can adversely affect data transmission.

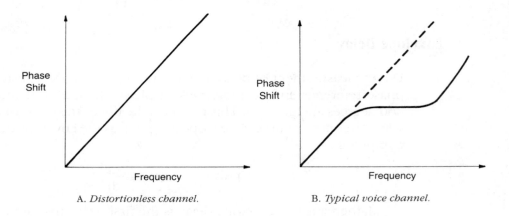

A. *Distortionless channel.*   B. *Typical voice channel.*

Figure 3-11. Relationship between phase and frequency.

Because of the nonlinear relationship between the harmonics of complex signals, they propagate through a transmission medium at different velocities, which causes a degree of received signal distortion. This is illustrated in Figure 3-12. When a large degree of distortion occurs, the late arriving energy of one pulse can interfere with the start of the following pulse, resulting in intersymbol interference. As an example of the effect of delay distortion, consider the received data illustrated in Figure 3-12A. In this situation, the degree of delay distortion resulted in the generation of several false pulse rises, each of which could be misinterpreted as a binary one condition, as shown in Figure 3-12B.

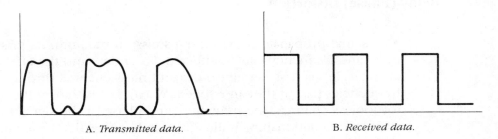

A. *Transmitted data.*   B. *Received data.*

Figure 3-12. Delay distortion.

Phase delay is measured at a particular point by dividing the phase by the frequency, resulting in the change of phase versus frequency. Thus,

$$\text{Phase Delay} = \frac{\theta}{F}$$

Envelope Delay

Direct measurement of phase delay is not practical because an absolute phase reference and keeping track of phase changes over multiples of 360 degrees are required. This results in the use of the slope of the phase versus frequency curve. This slope is known as the envelope delay and is computed as

$$\text{Envelope Delay} = \frac{d\theta}{dF}$$

Mathematically, envelope delay is the first derivative of phase delay. The shape of the envelope delay curve, obtained by measuring delays at different frequencies, reflects the degree of change in the slope of the phase versus frequency curve. This delay change varies based on the transmission distance and the type of conductor used for transmission. Figure 3-13 illustrates three typical voice channel envelope delay curves based on the length of the circuit.

Some of the most common sources for envelope delay distortion are the filters used by telephone companies to restrict the passband of the voice channel in order to maximize frequency division multiplexing efficiency. These filters delay frequencies approaching the cutoff frequency more than frequencies far removed from the cutoff frequency, which results in the occurrence of envelope delay distortion.

As an example of the possible effect of envelope delay on data transmission, consider a transmission system that uses frequency shift keying

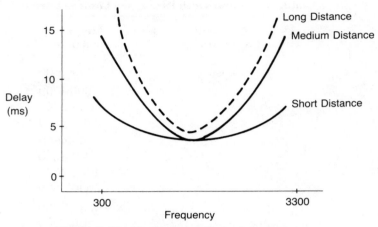

Figure 3-13. Typical envelope delay curves.

(FSK) modems, where one frequency represents a mark and a second frequency represents a space. Suppose that the signaling rate of the modem is 1000 baud, resulting in each tone used to represent a mark or space having a duration of one millisecond. If the relative envelope delay between the mark and space frequencies equals or approaches one millisecond, the two frequencies become superimposed at the receiver, in effect, obliterating the mechanism by which the receiving modem determines the state of the signal.

Table 3-3 lists envelope distortion delay bandwidth parameter limits for six common types of leased lines. As with attenuation distortion, the CCITT has promulgated recommendations about group delay distortion.

Figure 3-14 illustrates the CCITT M.1020 4-wire internal leased line group delay distortion recommendation. In comparing the British Telecom Keyline bandwidth parameters listed in Table 3-3 to the CCITT M.1020 recommendation illustrated in Figure 3-14, note that the group delay distortion limits are identical. Note also that the group delay under the shaded area in Figure 3-14 is the permissible delay distortion.

Delay Equalizers

Although all communications circuits exhibit a degree of delay, it is important to flatten the delay time across the passband. Doing so reduces the potential of intersymbol interferences because it prevents one part of a signal from arriving before the other part.

Table 3-3. Bandwidth Parameter Limits—Envelope Distortion Delay

Channel/ Conditioning	Frequency Range	Limits in dB
Basic	800-2600	1750
C1	800-1000	1750
	1000-2400	1000
	2400-2600	1750
C2	500-600	3000
	600-1000	1500
	1000-2600	500
	2600-2800	3000
C4	500-600	3000
	600-800	1500
	800-1000	500
	1000-2600	300
	2600-2800	500
	2800-3000	3000
C5	500-600	600
	600-1000	300
	1000-2600	100
	2600-2800	600
British Telecom Keyline	500-600	3000
	600-1000	1500
	1000-2600	500
	2600-3000	3000

A delay equalizer can make delay times approach a linear value. In Figure 3-15, the delay equalizer introduces a delay roughly the inverse to that exhibited by the channel, resulting in a relatively flat delay across the passband.

Noise

A third major source of transmission impairments is channel noise, which includes such random disturbances as power hum, thermal noise, impulse noise, and crosstalk. In comparing the effect of noise on voice versus data transmission, the ability of people to comprehend what is said before an interruption means that voice conversations have less susceptibility to a given level of noise. In comparison, noise that results in just one bit in 1000 being received in error results in the entire data block

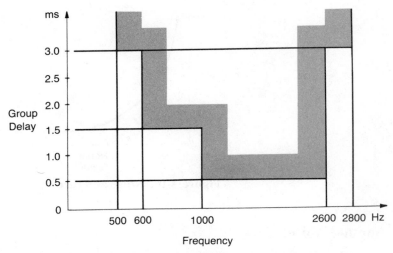

Figure 3-14. Group delay distortion (CCITT M.1020).

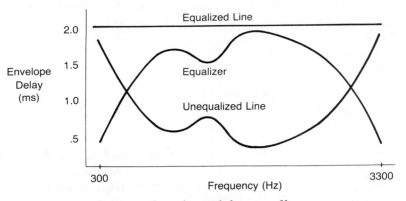

Figure 3-15. Using a delay equalizer.

being retransmitted when error correction is accomplished by block re-transmission.

The level of noise in a circuit determines the level of the transmitted signal that must be used to obtain a minimum acceptable signal-to-noise ratio at the receiving end of a transmission path. If the noise level increases at a higher rate than the signal level, the throughput on a circuit is adversely affected. As illustrated in Figure 3-16, the increase in the noise level compared with the signal level causes a higher bit error rate on the channel. This, in turn, causes additional retransmissions to occur, which lowers the total throughput on the channel.

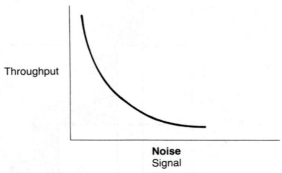

Figure 3-16. Noise and throughput.

Impulse Noise

Impulse noise is irregular spikes or pulses of short duration and relatively high amplitudes. This type of noise is noncontinuous, with random time intervals between spikes or pulses, as illustrated in Figure 3-17.

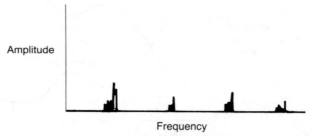

Figure 3-17. Impulse noise.

Sources of impulse noise include old electromechanical telephone company switching equipment, electrical storms, and the operation of machinery. When impulse noise occurs within the audio frequency range, it sounds similar to a random series of clicks or bursts of static.

The effect of impulse noise on voice is marginal because the impulses are of relatively short duration. Their effect on data can be considerable, depending on the transmission rate, because the signal duration is proportional to the data rate. That is, a high data rate has a smaller signal duration than a lower transmission rate. Because impulses are of short duration, they do not affect a longer signal at a low data rate to the degree that they can affect a shorter signal at a higher data rate.

Circuit Objectives

With respect to impulse noise, the performance measurement of leased lines involves counting the number of impulses that exceed a predefined reference level during a predefined interval of time. AT&T has defined limits on the number of impulses that are permitted to exceed a specified threshold during a 15-minute interval. Fifteen counts are permitted in 15 minutes at a −6dB threshold above a 1004Hz test tone, 9 counts are permitted at −2dB above 1004Hz, and 5 counts are permitted at +2dB above 1004Hz. As an example of the AT&T circuit objectives, assume the measured value for a received 1004Hz test tone is −16dBm. Then, a threshold set at −22dBm (−16−6) should not permit more than 15 impulses in a 15 minute period.

Two additional circuit objectives that warrant mention are the CCITT recommendation Q.45 and British Telecom's Keyline service. CCITT recommendation Q.45 for a 4-wire international exchange is 5 counts in 5 minutes at a threshold level of −35dBm0. British Telecom Keyline circuit objective is for no more than 18 impulse noise counts in 15 minutes at a threshold level of −21dBm0.

Thermal (White) Noise

Thermal or white noise occurs in all transmission systems as a result of the movement of electrons, power line induction, and cross modulation from adjacent circuits. This noise in the audio spectrum is heard as hiss, similar to what one hears when tuning between FM stations.

Compared with impulse noise, thermal noise is characterized by a near uniform distribution of energy over the frequency spectrum. Figure 3-18 illustrates the effect of thermal noise at different frequencies across the passband of a circuit. This noise usually has a minimal effect on data transmission because it boosts all signals by approximately the same amount. Because of this, the average thermal noise expected on a circuit is used to set the lower limit for the sensitivity of a receiving station.

Jitter

The unwanted change in phase or frequency of a transmitted signal is known as phase jitter. Although of little consequence in voice transmission because the human ear is insensitive to small phase and frequency changes, phase jitter can seriously affect data transmission.

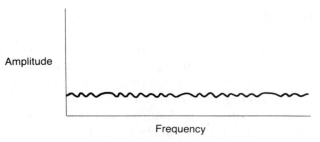

Figure 3-18. Thermal (white) noise.

Phase jitter normally results from noise or other types of undesired signal interference. To understand the effect of phase jitter on data transmission, assume that an FSK modem is used on a circuit. Because a receiving device re-creates squarewaves by "watching" for the transitions in an incoming signal, any distortion that moves its point of zero transition results in the re-creation of a pulse shifted in time. When a significant amount of jitter occurs, the received data is misinterpreted.

Figure 3-19A shows the effect of phase jitter on a sinusoidal signal. Figure 3-19B illustrates the effect of phase jitter on the re-creation of a digital signal.

The percentage of jitter is the maximum variation in the transition time divided by the time it takes to transmit two bits and multiplied by 100. Thus, the percentage of jitter shown in Figure 3-19B becomes:

$$\% \text{ Jitter} = \frac{A \times 100}{2B}$$

Under CCITT M.1020, a limit of up to 15x peak-to-peak phase jitter is permitted.

Line Conditioning

In the United States the most common voice grade private line used for data transmission is the type 3002 circuit. This circuit may be unconditioned, or the user's organization can request that the telephone company add line conditioning.

Line conditioning or equalization is the method primarily used to compensate for the attenuation distortion (amplitude-frequency response variations) and envelope delay that occurs on a circuit. The communications carrier accomplishes compensation by adding fixed equalizers at the time the circuit is installed. These equalizers correct dis-

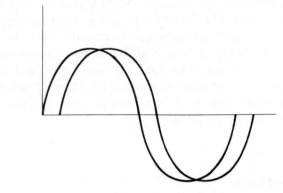

A. *Phase jitter on analog signal.*

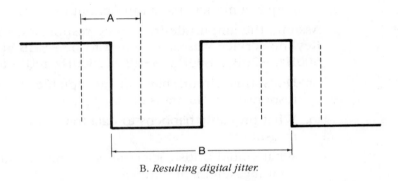

B. *Resulting digital jitter.*

Figure 3-19. Analog phase jitter and resulting digital jitter.

tortions caused by attenuation distortion and envelope delay and are adjusted by telephone company personnel to provide an approximate equal and opposite signal attenuation and envelope delay to the circuit's characteristics.

Five common types of C conditioning are available from AT&T. C1 and C2 conditioned lines can be ordered for point-to-point, multipoint, and switched line configurations. C3 conditioning is similar to C2 conditioning but is only applicable to private switched networks that have a maximum of four trunks and two access lines in tandem. C4 conditioning is applicable for multidrop circuits and can be ordered for two-, three- and four-drops. C5 conditioning is similar to C2 conditioning but is only applicable for point-to-point circuits and is primarily intended for overseas circuits.

The parameters associated with C conditioning affect attenuation distortion and envelope delay but do not control noise and harmonic distortion. The latter two causes of signal impairments can be alleviated by D conditioning, which is available in two types—D1 and D2.

D1 conditioning is available for point-to-point circuits, whereas D2 conditioning can be used on two- or three-drop circuits. D conditioning is used to minimize noise and harmonic distortion, which are critical for the transmission of data because they can interfere with the accurate reproduction of pulses.

Review Questions

1. Given a baud rate of 2400 signals per second and a dibit encoding technique, a modem has a throughput of _____ bps?

2. Assume the amplitude-frequency response on British Telecom's Keyline service was determined to be $-3dB$ at 300Hz, $-3dB$ at 500Hz, $-2dB$ at 800Hz, $-3dB$ at 2800Hz and $-4dB$ at 3000Hz.

   a. Does this circuit have an acceptable amplitude-frequency response for data transmission?

   b. What probably happens to data transmitted on the service just measured?

   c. What would British Telecom do to this circuit if you gave them your measurement findings?

3. As the percentage of peak-to-peak phase jitter increases, which constellation patterns become more susceptible to erroneous interpretation—Figure 3-5 or 3-6? Why?

Chapter 4

Analog Testing

I N THE PAST, most organizations that transmitted data over analog telephone facilities relied on the communications carrier to do analog testing. If a circuit became inoperative or if technical control center personnel suspected that a communications problem resulted from an impairment on the analog side of the network, they called their AT&T representative for help.

Because of the divestiture of AT&T, a circuit that was formerly the responsibility of one communications carrier now may be the responsibility of several carriers. In addition, the response of each communications carrier to a reported problem may vary considerably. Therefore, technical control center personnel who want to maintain their organization's network by examining key characteristics of the lines they use have to become familiar with analog testing.

Many organizations need to be capable of testing analog circuits, so this chapter first reviews the causes of signal degradation, including an examination of the parameters that affect data transmission on analog circuits. Using this information as a base, we then investigate the utility of several tests that can denote the condition of analog circuits, which permits the organization to report failing circuits to the appropriate telephone company before the circuit becomes completely inoperable.

Signal Degradation

When a voice frequency (VF) communications facility is used for the transmission of data, many factors can result in signal degradation. Measuring various analog line parameters may reveal the sources of signal degradation, and corrective action then may be possible. Testing of analog facilities also can be used to verify a requested level of circuit conditioning and when the conditions as measured warrant such action, request remedial action from the communications carrier.

Table 4-1 lists 11 parameters that affect data transmission on an analog channel and the methods used to control those parameters. As mentioned in chapter 3, equalizers can be used by the communications carrier to alleviate the effect of attenuation distortion and envelope delay distortion on C conditioned lines. Similarly, D conditioning can be installed on leased lines to minimize the effect of the noise, which serves to enhance the signal-to-noise ratio and to minimize harmonic distortion.

Table 4-1. Analog Channel Parameters

Parameter	Method of Control
Attenuation Distortion	Conditioning
Envelope Delay Distortion	Conditioning
Signal-to-Noise Ratio	Conditioning
Harmonic Distortion	Conditioning
Impulse Noise	Carrier Specifications
Frequency Shift	Carrier Specifications
Phase Jitter	Carrier Specifications
Echo	Carrier Specifications
Phase Hits	Not Controlled
Gain Hits	Not Controlled
Dropouts	Not Controlled

Impulse noise, frequency shift, phase jitter, and echo primarily are controlled by carrier specifications. When the range of the parameter falls outside the carrier specification, the communications carrier may be able to perform some remedial action to correct the problem. As an example, impulse noise may be limited by shielding or by the rerouting of a circuit. Phase jitter, which can be caused by noise or signal interference, may be alleviated in a similar manner.

Information covering phase hits, gain hits, and dropouts that are not controlled by the communications carrier may provide the carrier with information that it can use to correct a malfunction of its equipment. Phase hits are sudden, uncontrolled changes in the phase of a received signal, whereas gain hits are sudden, uncontrolled increases in the received signal level. Dropouts are sudden, large reductions in the signal level that last more than a few milliseconds. Sunspot activity can adversely affect these parameters. The failure of an amplifier in the circuit route is another possibility that can cause an abnormal condition. By having the capability of testing an analog circuit and comparing observed readings to the communications carrier's specifications, the technician may be able to request that the carrier perform remedial action when such activity is warranted.

Testing the Channel

Several types of analog tests can be done to provide some knowledge about the quality of the circuit for data transmission. To obtain meaningful test results, a reference frequency and a selected impedance level are used. The test frequencies used are 1004Hz in North America and 800Hz in Europe, with most analog test sets capable of generating a sine wave at those frequencies. When testing is conducted on a 4-wire circuit, an impedance of 600 ohms is used, whereas testing on most 2-wire circuits uses 900 ohms.

Circuit Loss Test

A circuit loss test is one of the most common measurements that can be made on a VF line. This test is also known as a power line or line loss test because it is used to determine the amount of energy lost during a transmission. Because energy loss can result in a received message becoming distorted, this test can be used to show the potential severity of signal degradation.

In a circuit loss test, a test tone of 0dBm at either 1004Hz or 800Hz is placed on the line, and a dB meter is used to record the received signal strength. Because the reception of any signal shows continuity, this test also can be used to verify the continuity of a circuit.

Figure 4-1 illustrates how circuit loss can be measured on 2-wire (Figure 4-1A) and 4-wire (Figure 4-1B) circuits. On a 2-wire switched telephone network connection or leased line, two analog test sets are required to measure circuit loss. One test set is used to generate the test frequency. The second test set includes a dB meter to measure the strength of the received signal. On a 4-wire circuit that terminates in a telephone company 42A connector block and 829 channel interface, a test tone at 2718Hz can be used to connect the transmit pair to the receive pair of wires at the distant end. Then one test set can be used, because a 1004Hz 0dBm test tone sent on the transmit side of the line is looped through the 829 and back to the receive side of the line. This enables the dB meter of the test set to monitor the signal level.

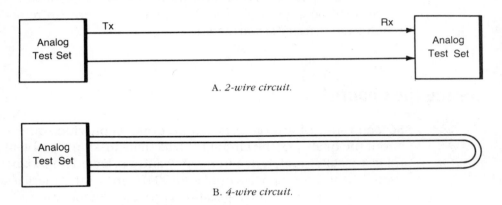

A. *2-wire circuit.*

B. *4-wire circuit.*

Figure 4-1. Measuring circuit loss.

Telephone company personnel in North America use a circuit loss test at circuit installation time, with line components being adjusted to obtain a 16dB attenuation at a 0dBm 1004Hz test tone. After installation, the loss measurement on an AT&T circuit should be 16dB ± 4dB during circuit loss measurements. If the results of a circuit loss test fall outside of the 12 to 20dB range, either excessive attenuation or excessive amplification is occurring, which can result in the failure of modems attached to the circuit.

Gain/Slope Test

The gain/slope frequency response test is used to obtain an indication of the loss that is occurring over the passband of a channel, including the "corners" of the channel formed by telephone company filters. This test is used to obtain an indication of the loss at discrete test frequencies.

In the gain/slope test, attenuation is measured at 404, 1004, and 2804Hz. Next, the differences in attenuation between the pairs of readings at 404Hz and 1004Hz and 1004Hz and 2804Hz are computed to obtain an indication of the "corners" of the circuit's frequency response. As an example, assume the dBm loss at the three test frequencies is measured as follows:

Frequency (Hz)	Loss dBm
404	20
1004	12
2804	24

The two slope values are calculated as −20-12 or −8dBm and −24-12 or −12dBm.

By plotting the three test frequency measurements and computing the two slope values, a representative picture of the loss over the passband is obtained, as shown in Figure 4-2.

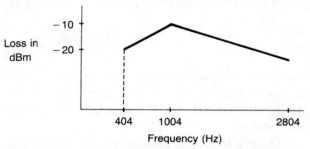

Figure 4-2. The gain/slope frequency response test.

As Figure 4-2 indicates, the differential loss at 404Hz is an 8dBm slope, whereas the differential loss at 2804Hz is a 12dBm slope. In this example, the gain/slope test provides an indication of the corners of the frequency response concerning the −12dBm point at 1004Hz. Because the larger the slope, the poorer the response; the flatter the curve, the better the frequency response. A slope that becomes large at the corners of the frequency response can adversely affect modems that use a broad range of frequencies for carriers, with a resulting decrease in the throughput of such modems.

Stepped Frequency Response Test

To obtain a more accurate picture of circuit loss across the passband, measurements can be taken at a sequence of frequencies. Typically, a stepped frequency response test involves taking readings in 100Hz increments from 200Hz to 3500Hz. The results of these readings then can be used to obtain a more accurate graph of attenuation versus frequency for the circuit being tested. As with the gain/slope test, the flatter the curve, the better the circuit can carry frequencies in the passband.

Signal-to-Noise Ratio Test

The signal-to-noise ratio test can be used as an indicator of transmission line quality. Because this test shows the signal power with respect to noise power, it is more significant than simply measuring the background noise on a circuit.

In a signal-to-noise ratio test, a test tone at 800Hz or 1004Hz is first applied to the circuit and both the noise level and signal level of the tone are measured together. Next, a notch filter is used to remove the 800Hz or 1004Hz test tone component of the received signal, leaving only the noise component to be measured.

When the signal level is very high compared with the noise level:

$$\frac{S + N}{N} \cong \frac{S}{N}$$

Thus, the preceding measurements permit the determination of signal-plus-noise and noise to be used to approximate the signal-to-noise ratio. For unconditioned lines, an S/N ratio of 24dB or greater is considered acceptable.

During the late 1980s, several commercial firms conducted tests of different types of modems to measure their levels of performance over a circuit that had different simulated signal-to-noise ratios. Figure 4-3 illustrates the generalized results of these tests for three modems manufactured by one vendor. When modems from one vendor were compared with a modem operating at a similar speed and manufactured by a different vendor, the curves varied slightly, suggesting that some modems have a better level of sensitivity to varying signal-to-noise ratios than other modems. In addition, as shown by the generalized chart displayed in Figure 4-3, modems operating at a higher data rate have a higher sensitivity to noise and require a greater signal-to-noise ratio to operate correctly.

Impulse Noise Tests

An impulse noise test is used to measure voltage spikes that are much larger than the average background noise level. Because communications carriers set limits on the number of impulses that can occur during a predefined period of time, this test can be used to determine whether a circuit is within the carrier's specifications for the occurrence of impulse noise.

Table 4-2 lists AT&T limits on the number of impulses allowed in a 15-minute interval, based on a defined threshold above a 1004Hz test tone.

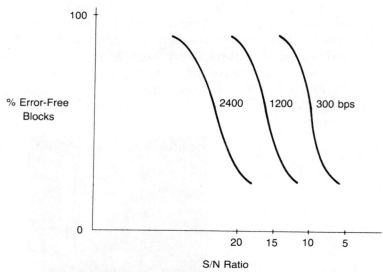

Figure 4-3. Error-free blocks versus signal-to-noise ratio.

As an example of the use of Table 4-2, assume that the measured value for the received 1004Hz test tone is −12dBm. Then, a threshold of −18dBm (−12−6) should allow no more than 15 counts in any 15-minute period. To do an impulse noise test when the threshold is −18dBm, the analog test set would be set to −18dBm and its counter would be set to zero. Depending on the type of test set used, a timer could be set to 15 minutes or the operator could manually time the test, then observe the impulse count at the end of the time period.

Table 4-2. Bell System Impulse Noise Limits

Threshold Above 1004Hz Test Tone Power	Number of Impulses Allowed in 15 Minutes
−6dB	15
−2dB	9
+2dB	5

Circuit Quality Monitor Test

A circuit quality monitor test uses an oscilloscope to observe a polar plot of the circuit's signal amplitude versus signal phase. This test results in a display of the "eye pattern" of the circuit's signal.

Figure 4-4 illustrates three oscilloscope patterns that show the effect of noise on a circuit. In Figure 4-4A, successive signal points in a 16-point constellation pattern are bunched together, with the phase and amplitude of each point relatively fixed. As noise increases on a channel (Figure 4-4B), successive signal points begin to disperse from their fixed locations. Finally, the large shifts in successive signal points due to phase jitter (Figure 4-4C) result in some received signal points being misinterpreted.

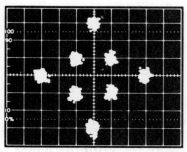

A. *Transmission signal on a good-quality, voice-grade channel.*

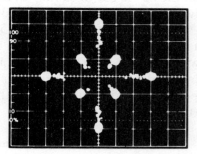

B. *Transmission on a noisy channel.*

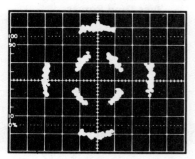

C. *Transmission signal with phase jitter.*

Figure 4-4. Oscilloscope patterns.

Envelope Delay Test

The purpose of this test is to measure the transmission delay over the passband. Envelope delay is measured on an end-to-end basis and can be used to determine whether a line is properly conditioned or whether an unconditioned line meets the carrier's specifications.

In an envelope delay test, the circuit to be measured is swept from 500Hz to 3000Hz and a zero reference is established at the point of minimum delay, which is usually 1800Hz. Then envelope delay is measured at 300Hz, 500Hz, 600Hz, and every 200Hz to 3000Hz. The resulting measurements then can be compared with the specifications of the communications carrier.

Figure 4-5 illustrates the graph of a typical envelope delay curve. If the curve begins to approach long delay times within the voice channel passband, the telephone company probably will have to adjust the delay equalizers on the circuit being tested.

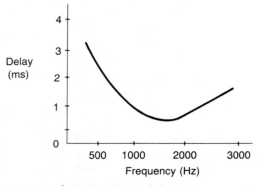

Figure 4-5. Envelope delay curve.

Test Measurement Recording

Many organizations maintain circuit record cards on which they post the results of one or more analog tests. Figure 4-6 illustrates a typical circuit record card that you can use as a guide for the development of such a card. You may want to add additional measurements based on the availability of test equipment or tailor Figure 4-6 to best meet your operational requirements.

Circuit Number _____   Date _____

800/10004Hz loss _____

Gain/Slope Test

Freq	Level	Freq	Level	Freq	Level
404	_____	1004	_____	2804	_____

Stepped Frequency Response Test

Freq	Level	Freq	Level	Freq	Level	Freq	Level
300	_____	1100	_____	1900	_____	2700	_____
400	_____	1200	_____	2000	_____	2800	_____
500	_____	1300	_____	2100	_____	2900	_____
600	_____	1400	_____	2200	_____	3000	_____
700	_____	1500	_____	2300	_____	3100	_____
800	_____	1600	_____	2400	_____	3200	_____
900	_____	1700	_____	2500	_____	3300	_____
1000	_____	1800	_____	2600	_____	3400	_____

Impulse Noise Test

Threshold Above Test Tone Power	Number of Impulses Recorded in 15 minutes
−6dB	_____
−2dB	_____
+2dB	_____

Envelope Delay Test

Point of Minimum Delay _____ Hz

Freq	Delay	Freq	Delay	Freq	Delay
300	_____	1200	_____	2200	_____
500	_____	1400	_____	2400	_____
600	_____	1600	_____	2600	_____
800	_____	1800	_____	2800	_____
1000	_____	2000	_____	3000	_____

Figure 4-6. Circuit record card.

Review Questions

1. A gain/slope test was conducted on circuits X and Y. The slope values for each circuit were determined to be

Circuit	*Slope Values (dBm)*
X	8, 12
Y	4, 6

Which circuit has less loss over the passband?

2. As an envelope delay curve approaches the slope of a narrow parabola, intersymbol interference can be expected to _____?

3. Assume the following signal level versus frequency readings were obtained on two circuits. Which circuit has the better response?

Frequency Hz	Signal Level dBm	
	Circuit X	Circuit Y
500	−20	−28
1000	−15	−24
1500	−15	−20
2000	−16	−16
2500	−16	−20
3000	−20	−24
3500	−35	−35

The Digital Interface

In THIS CHAPTER, we focus our attention on the digital interface between data terminal equipment (DTE) and data communications equipment (DCE). The signal characteristics of the RS-232-C/V.24 conductors are examined, permitting us to review several cabling tricks that can be used to economize wiring within a facility. Using the preceding information as a base, we conclude this chapter by analyzing the control signal indicators and how those indicators can be used for troubleshooting several types of digital interface-related problems, some of which may be due to the improper implementation of a cabling trick.

The Interface

Terminals and computer ports are examples of equipment that is called data terminal equipment or DTEs. Equipment falling into this category has in common the feature of transmitting data on pin 2 and receiving data on pin 3 of the 25-conductor RS-232-C/V.24 interface. Modems and other communications devices are called data communications equipment or DCEs. The point where the DTE connects to the DCE is known as the digital interface or point of demarcation.

The RS-232-C/V.24 physical interface standard cables are typically 6, 10, or 12 feet in length with "male" connections on each end. This standard is illustrated in Figure 5-1.

Although the RS-232-C/V.24 standard covers the maximum cabling distance between DTE and DCE and the function and operation of the 25 conductors that can be contained in the cable, it does not govern the ca-

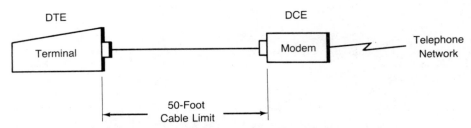

Figure 5-1. The V.24/RS-232-C physical interface.

bling of DTE to DTE or DCE to DCE. When the standard was first promulgated, it was intended to cover communications whereby terminals would be connected to modems and was not envisioned as a standard for connecting terminals directly to computers or to govern the output of one modem into another modem. As networks grew in complexity, technicians developed cabling tricks by strapping, crossing, or disabling conductors in cable linking devices to obtain operational compatibility between devices. Even when connecting DTE to DCE, similar cabling tricks may become necessary because many manufacturers use only certain conductors at the physical interface, whereas other manufacturers may require different conductors to be activated to operate their devices. By understanding the signal characteristics of the physical interface, you can fabricate the appropriate cable to make most devices operate.

Signal Characteristics

The voltage level on the conductor or interchange circuit determines its state. Figure 5-2 illustrates the voltage ranges for RS-232-C/V.24 conductors, which are more formally called interchange circuits.

As shown in Figure 5-2, voltages between +3 and +15 result in the state of the conductor being considered ON. This state is equivalent to a logic 0 or SPACE condition. Voltages between −3 and −15 result in the state of the conductor being considered OFF. This state is equivalent to a logic 1 or MARK condition. Voltages between +3 volts and −3 are considered to be in a transition region, and the state of the conductor is neither ON nor OFF.

When in doubt, you usually can determine the type of device by examining the voltage level on pins 2 and 3 when the device is not transmitting data. This is because the RS-232-C/V.24 standard states that the transmitter is always at a logic 1 (−3 to −15 volts) when the device is not

```
+15V -------------------------------------------------------------
                                               Positive Range ON Function
 +3V -------------------------------------------------------------
                                               Transition Region
 -3V -------------------------------------------------------------
                                               Negative Range OFF Function
-15V -------------------------------------------------------------
```

Figure 5-2. Interchange circuit voltage ranges.

transmitting. Thus, if the device is a DTE, it has a voltage between −3 and −15 volts on pin 2 when not transmitting, whereas a DCE would have that voltage range on pin 3 when not transmitting. Although a voltmeter could be used to do the preceding test, in actuality, a breakout box is used more commonly to examine the digital interface. The use of a breakout box is described in detail in Chapter 6.

Conductor Overview

Table 5-1 lists the RS-232-C/V.24 interchange circuits grouped by circuit category. Each of the 25 conductors falls into a ground, data, control, or timing category, as shown by the upper right column headings in the table. For the last three categories, the From DCE and To DCE subheadings show the defined standard flow of control signals or data. As an example of the use of these subheadings, consider pin 2's row, which has an X placed in the To DCE column. This shows that transmitted data flows to the DCE, or from DTE to DCE. Similarly, the X in the From DCE column for pin 3's row shows that received data flows from the DCE to the DTE.

The interchange circuits listed in Table 5-1 can be referenced in one of several ways. They can be referred to by their pin number, interchange circuit letter designator, CCITT numeric identifier, circuit description, or by an acronym descriptor. Although the acronym descriptors are not listed for the circuits contained in Table 5-1, the use of the acronyms is probably the most common method of referring to RS-232-C/V.24 circuits. This is because—compared with other mechanisms that can be used to identify the interface conductors—acronyms, such as TD for transmitted data are much easier to remember and use in conversations

Table 5-1. V.24/RS-232-C Circuits by Category

Pin No.	Interchange Circuit	CCITT Equivalent	Description	Gnd	Data From DCE	Data To DCE	Control From DCE	Control To DCE	Timing From DCE	Timing To DCE
1	AA	101	Protective Ground	X						
7	AB	102	Signal Ground/Common Return	X						
2	BA	103	Transmitted Data			X				
3	BB	104	Received Data		X					
4	CA	105	Request to Send					X		
5	CB	106	Clear to Send				X			
6	CC	107	Data Set Ready				X			
20	CD	108.2	Data Terminal Ready					X		
22	CE	125	Ring Indicator				X			
8	CF	109	Received Line Signal Detector				X			
21	CG	110	Signal Quality Detector				X			
23	CH	111	Data Signal Rate Selector (DTE)					X		
23	CI	112	Data Signal Rate Selector (DCE)				X			
24	DA	113	Transmitter Signal Element Timing (DTE)							X
15	DB	114	Transmitter Signal Element Timing (DEC)						X	
17	DD	115	Receiver Signal Element Timing (DCE)						X	
14	SBA	118	Secondary Transmitted Data			X				
16	SBB	119	Secondary Received Data		X					
19	SCA	120	Secondary Request to Send					X		
13	SCB	121	Secondary Clear to Send				X			
12	SCF	122	Secondary Received Line Signal Detector				X			
9	—	—	Reserved for Data Set Testing							
10	—	—	Reserved for Data Set Testing							
11	—	—	Unassigned							
25	—	—	Unassigned or (DTE Timing)							

when troubleshooting the digital interface. Later in this chapter when I review each conductor in detail, I list for general reference the acronym descriptor and pin number of the conductor after its name.

Figure 5-3 illustrates an example of the control signal sequence, called handshaking, that normally occurs on a 2-wire, half-duplex transmission system. Before transmission occurs, the computer and terminal each provide a data terminal ready (DTR) signal to the attached modem associated with each DTE device. This signal is used to prepare each modem to operate on the circuit. Similarly, each modem provides a data set ready (DSR) signal to the DTE connected to the modem. This signal shows that the modem is powered on and ready to operate.

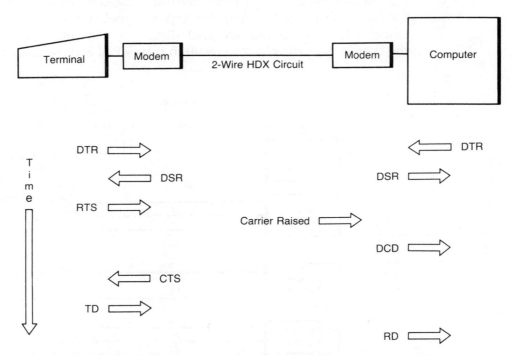

Figure 5-3. V.24/RS-232-C control signal sequence example.

When the terminal prepares to transmit data, it sends its request to send (RTS) signal, which results in the modem attached to the terminal sending a carrier tone to the remote modem. That modem receives the carrier tone and sends a data carrier detect (DCD) signal, which is passed to the computer port. The modem connected to the terminal then sends a clear to send (CTS) signal to the terminal, which informs the terminal's control circuits that transmission can occur. This is followed by the terminal transmitting data (TD) on pin 2, which is modulated by the remote modem and demodulated by the modem connected to the computer at the central site. At that location, the modem passes received data (RD) on pin 3 to the computer.

Asynchronous Operations

To understand the signals required to connect an asynchronous terminal device to a low speed modem, consider Figure 5-4. Note that only 9 of 25 conductors are required in this example because pin 7 (signal ground) is strapped to pin 1 (protective ground). This tells us that a careful examination of conductors required for cables should be attempted because a 25-conductor cable can cost two to three times the cost per foot of 9-conductor cable. Although this may not appear significant for short cable distances, when you connect terminals directly to computer ports, acquiring the correct type of cable can result in substantial economic savings.

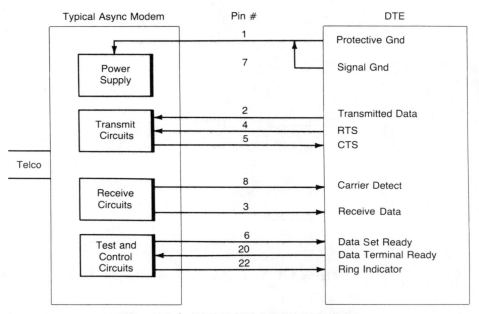

Figure 5-4. DTE-DCE interface example.

The functions of the 10 interchange circuits illustrated in Figure 5-4 are described in the following.

Protective Ground (GND, Pin 1)

This interchange circuit is normally electrically bonded to the equipment's frame. In some instances, it can be connected also to external grounds as required by applicable regulations.

Signal Ground (SG, Pin 7)

This circuit must be included in all RS-232 interfaces because it establishes a ground reference for all other lines. The voltage on this circuit is set at 0V to provide a reference for all other signals. Although the conductors for pins 1 and 7 can be independent of one another, typical practice is to "strap" pin 7 to pin 1 at the modem. This is known as tying signal ground to frame ground, and an example of its use is shown in Figure 5-4.

Transmitted Data (TD, Pin 2)

The signals on this circuit are transmitted from a terminal device to the modem. When no data is being transmitted, the terminal maintains this circuit in a marking or logical 1 condition. This is the circuit over which the actual serial bit stream of data flows from the terminal device to the modem, where it is modulated for transmission. When two DTEs are connected, pins 2 and 3 must be reversed. Otherwise, data transmitted on pin 2 never appears as received data at the other device.

Request to Send (RTS, Pin 4)

The signal on this circuit is sent from the terminal to the modem to prepare the modem for transmission. Before sending data, the terminal must receive on pin 5 a clear to send signal from the modem.

Clear to Send (CTS, Pin 5)

This interchange circuit is used by the modem to send a signal to the attached terminal. The signal shows that the modem is ready to transmit. By turning this circuit OFF, the modem informs the terminal that it is not ready to receive data. The modem raises the CTS signal after the terminal initiates a request to send (RTS) signal.

Carrier Detect (CD, Pin 8)

Commonly called received line signal detector (RLSD), this circuit's signals are used to show the terminal that the modem is receiving a carrier signal from a remote modem. The presence of this signal is used also to illuminate the carrier detect light-emitting diode (LED) indicator on modems equipped with that display indicator. If this light indicator goes out during a communications session, the session has ended owing to a loss of carrier.

Receive Data (RD, Pin 3)

Data, after demodulation by a modem, is transferred over this interchange circuit to the attached terminal. When the modem is not sending data to the terminal, this circuit is held in the marking condition. When two DTEs or two DCEs are to be connected, the flow of data on pins 2 and 3 must be cross-connected. That is, pin 2 of one DTE or DCE must be connected to pin 3 at the other end of the cable and vice versa.

Data Set Ready (DSR, Pin 6)

Signals on this interchange circuit are used to show the status of the data set connected to the terminal. When this circuit is in the ON (logic 0) condition, it serves as a signal to the terminal that the modem is connected to the telephone line and is ready to transmit data. Because the V.24/RS-232-C standard specifies that the DSR signal is ON when the modem is connected to the communications channel and not in any test condition, a modem using a self-testing feature or automatic dialing capability passes this signal to the terminal after the self-test is completed or after the telephone number of a remote location is successfully dialed.

Data Terminal Ready (DTR, Pin 20)

This circuit controls the modem's connection to the telephone line. An ON condition prepares the modem to be connected to the telephone line, after which the connection can be established by manual or automatic dialing. If the signal on this circuit is placed in an OFF condition, the modem drops any telephone connection in progress, providing a mechanism for the terminal device to control the line connection.

Ring Indicator (RI, Pin 22)

This interchange circuit shows to the terminal device that a ringing signal is being received on the communications channel. This circuit is used by an auto-answer modem to "wake-up" the attached terminal device.

Figure 5-5 summarizes the relationship of seven key control signals between a pair of asynchronous modems.

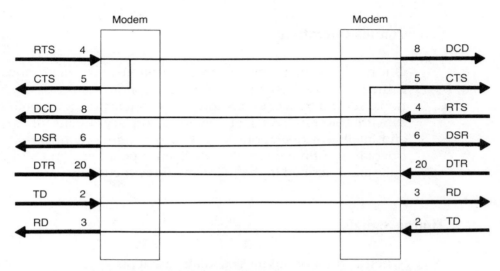

Figure 5-5. V.24/RS-232-C asynchronous control signal summary.

In examining the control signals illustrated in Figure 5-5, start at the top of the modem on the left. When a request to send (RTS) signal is received, a carrier tone is placed on the line, which results in the modem at the right presenting a data carrier detect (DCD) signal to the attached DTE. The modem at the left raises its clear to send (CTS) signal, which is sent to the DTE attached to that modem. Similarly, when a DTE attached to the right modem has data to send, it raises its RTS signal, which results in that modem placing on the line a carrier tone that is received by the left modem. That modem then starts its DCD signal. After putting the carrier on the line, the right modem starts its CTS signal, which is passed to the DTE attached to it.

If the DTE attached to the left modem is to send or receive data, the modem must present a high voltage on pin 6, which is a data set ready (DSR) signal, in response to the terminal's data terminal ready (DTR) signal. Thereafter, data transmitted from the DTE to the left modem on pin 2 is modulated onto the carrier tone to the right modem, where it is de-modulated and passed as received data to the DTE attached to the mo-dem on pin 3. The reverse situation occurs when the DTE attached to the right modem transmits data on pin 2, which results in the left modem sending the data to the DTE attached to it on pin 3. Later in this chapter, we examine how the indicators on modems may be used to isolate the cause of transmission problems.

Synchronous Operations

One major difference between asynchronous and synchronous modems is the timing signals required for synchronous transmission. Two addi-tional key differences are an optional secondary channel, built into some synchronous modems, that requires secondary circuits for its operation, and intelligent operations, which also require secondary circuits. The operation of timing signals, intelligent operations, and secondary cir-cuits are described in the following three sections.

Timing Signals

When a synchronous modem transmits, it places a square wave on pin 15 at a frequency equal to the modem's bit rate. This timing signal serves as a clock from which the terminal synchronizes its transmission of data onto pin 2 to the modem. Thus, pin 15 is called transmit clock (TD CLK), or more formally, transmission signal element timing (DCE). DCE means that the communications device supplies the timing.

Whenever a synchronous modem receives a signal from the telephone line, it places a square wave on pin 17 to the terminal at a frequency equal to the modem's bit rate. The actual data is passed to the terminal on pin 3. Because pin 17 provides receiver clocking, it is known as receive clock (RD CLK), or more formally, receiver signal element timing (DCE).

In certain cases, a terminal device, such as a computer port, can pro-vide timing signals to the DCE. In such situations, the DTE provides a clocking signal to the DCE on pin 24. DTE is given the formal name of transmitter signal element timing (DTE).

Figure 5-6 summarizes the clocking signal relationship between a pair of synchronous modems. The relationship of clocking and data cir-cuits is easy to visualize because the acronyms identify the pairing of clocking to data circuits.

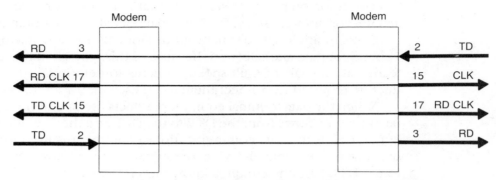

Figure 5-6. Synchronous modem clock signal summary.

Intelligent Operations

Three interchange circuits can be used to change the operation of an attached communications device. One circuit functions to determine that a deterioration in a circuit's quality has occurred, whereas the other two circuits change the transmission rate to reflect the circuit quality.

Signal Quality Detector (CG, Pin 21)

Signals on this circuit are transmitted from the modem to the attached terminal whenever there is a high probability of an error in the received data because the circuit's quality is falling below a predefined level. This circuit is maintained in an ON condition when the signal quality is acceptable and turned to an OFF condition when there is high probability of an error. Many modems illuminate a CG indicator to denote that a circuit is in a marginal condition. When a modem is used in a network management system, this circuit can be used to set an alarm condition that automatically informs the operator when the circuit is in a marginal condition.

Data Signal Rate Selector (CH/CI, Pin 23)

When an intelligent terminal device, such as a computer port, receives an OFF condition on pin 21 for a predefined period of time, it may be programmed to change the data rate of the attached modem, if the modem is capable of operating at dual data rates. The terminal device provides an

ON condition on pin 23 to select the higher data rate or range of rates or an OFF condition to select the lower data signaling rate or range of rates.

Some multiple speed synchronous modems also use unassigned pins 11 or 25 for data rate selection. Because of this, you need to examine the technical manuals of multispeed modems to determine the cable conductors required to connect them to DTEs.

When the data terminal equipment selects the operating rate, the signal on pin 23 flows from the DTE to the DCE and the circuit is known as circuit CH. If the data communications equipment is used to select the data rate of the terminal device, the signal on pin 23 flows from the DCE to the DTE, and the circuit is known as circuit CI.

Secondary Circuits

In certain instances, a synchronous modem is designed with the capability to transmit data on a secondary channel simultaneously with transmission on the primary channel. In such cases, the data rate of the secondary channel is normally a fraction of the primary channel's data rate.

To control the data flow on the secondary channel, the RS-232 standard employs five interchange circuits. Pins 14 and 16 are equivalent to the circuits on pins 2 and 3, except that they are used to transmit and receive data on the secondary channel. Similarly, pins 19, 13, and 12 perform the same functions as pins 4, 5, and 8, used for controlling the flow of information on the primary data channel.

Cabling Tricks

As previously mentioned, the RS-232-C/V.24 standard was developed to connect DTEs to DCEs and does not cover such common situations as the cabling of a terminal to a computer port. In addition, although the standard defines 25-conductor operations, usually a lesser number of conductors is required to cable two devices together. In this section, we examine a variety of cabling tricks, which, when done properly, can make incompatible devices compatible or permit the user to economize on cabling costs. By understanding these common cabling techniques, problems occurring from their improper use can be avoided easily.

The Null Modem

A null modem is a special cable designed to eliminate the need for modems when interconnecting two collocated data terminal equipment devices. DTEs transmit data on pin 2 and receive data on pin 3, so one should never connect two such devices with a conventional cable because the data transmitted from one device would never be received by the other. For two DTEs to communicate with one another, a connector on pin 2 of one device must be wired to connector pin 3 on the other device.

Figure 5-7 is an example of the wiring diagram of a null modem cable, showing how pins 2 and 3 are cross-connected and illustrating the configuration of the control circuit pins on this type of cable.

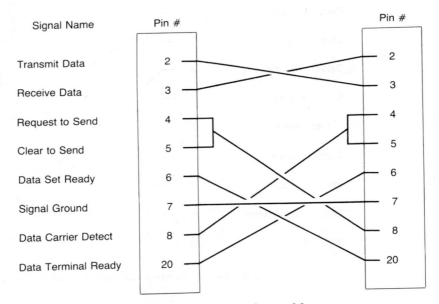

Figure 5-7. Null modem cable.

The cable configuration illustrated in Figure 5-7 works for most data terminal equipment interconnections. However, a few exceptions exist, one of which occurs when a terminal device is to be cabled to a port on a mainframe computer, port selector, or similar DTE that operates as a "ring-start" port. This means that the port must obtain a ring indicator (RI, pin 22) signal. In this situation, the null modem must be modified so that data set ready (DSR, pin 6) is jumpered to ring indicator (RI, pin 22) at the other end of the cable to initiate a connect sequence.

Because synchronous terminals require a transmit and receive clock, a cable capable of providing such signals must be used to connect two synchronous DTEs. Figure 5-8 illustrates the conductor wiring required to construct a synchronous null modem cable. In this situation, one DTE provides clocking to the other DTE by connecting pin 24 at one end of the cable to pins 15 and 17 at both ends of the cable. Thus, clocking provided by one terminal on pin 24 results in the generation of TD CLK and RD CLK at both sides of the cable.

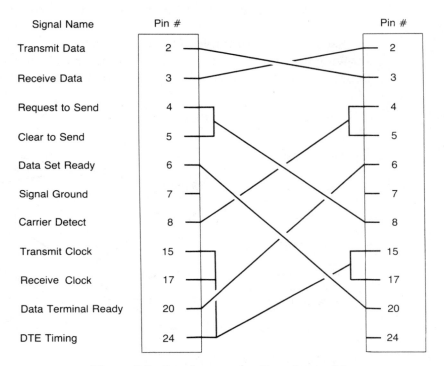

Figure 5-8. Synchronous null modem cable.

3-Conductor Cable

A general purpose 3-conductor cable can be used to connect two devices when hardware flow control is not required and a modem will not be controlled.

Figure 5-9 illustrates the use of a 3-conductor cable for DTE to DCE and DTE to DTE or DCE to DCE connections.

When a DTE is to be connected to a DCE, conductors 2 and 3 are passed straight through the cable. By tying pin 4 to pin 5 on each side of

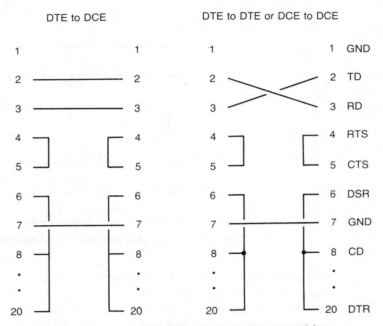

Figure 5-9. General purpose 3-conductor cable.

the cable, RTS raised causes CTS to be raised. Similarly, tying pin 20 to pins 6 and 8 on each side of the cable causes DTR to raise DSR and CD. In examining the 3-conductor cable on the left side of Figure 5-9, note that in addition to ground (conductor 7), only conductors 2 and 3 are required.

When a DTE is connected to another DTE or two DCEs are connected, a similar 3-conductor cable may be used, as illustrated in the right portion of Figure 5-9, by crossing conductors 2 and 3, tying pins 4 to 5, and joining pin 20 to pins 6 and 8 on each side of the cable.

Figure 5-10 illustrates a 5-conductor cable that can be installed between a DTE and DCE (modem) when asynchronous control signals are required. In this instance, 5 conductors are needed because DCD and DTR have to pass between the DTE and DCE.

By fastening multiple heads to each cable, using 3- and 5-conductor cabling can permit, as an example, the interconnection of up to three devices using 9-conductor cabling and up to eight devices using 25-conductor cabling. This technique can also result in much aggravation under certain situations. Specifically, when the conductors are unshielded or a cable is spliced and the conductors are not reshielded, multiple transmissions through one conductor may result in crosstalk from one transmis-

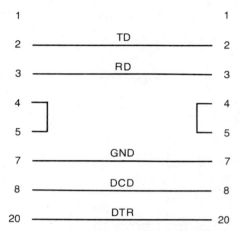

Figure 5-10. General purpose 5-conductor cable.

sion affecting another transmission. Because the degree of crosstalk depends on the total number of conductors in use at a particular time, crosstalk problems are random and result in intermittent transmission problems that can be difficult to isolate. Thus, although using 3-and 5-conductor cables can result in significant economic savings compared with routing separate cables between devices, without proper shielding, significant problems can arise.

Troubleshooting with Control Signal Indicators

Figure 5-11 illustrates a typical front panel display that is commonly found on many asynchronous modems. By examining the state of illumination of the indicators many communications problems can be isolated and resolved.

The MR or modem ready indicator illuminates when power is supplied to an external modem. On occasion, personal computer users have connected the modem's power converter to one wall outlet and computer to a second power receptacle. If the modem outlet's circuit breaker should switch for some reason, the computer would have power but the modem would not. In this situation, simply looking at the MR indicator may provide an indication of the cause of the problem.

Two additional indicators that can be used to determine easily correctable problems are the high speed mode (HS) and auto answer (AA) indicators. For multispeed modems, the illumination of the HS indicator

| HS | AA | CD | OH | RD | SD | TR | MR | AL |

Legend:

HS—High Speed Mode

AA—In Auto Answer Mode

CD—Carrier Detect Signal Received

OH—Modem Took Control of Telephone Line to Establish Data Link

RD—Receive Data Flashes When Data Bit Received from Telephone Line

SD—Send Data Flashes When Data Bit Is Sent by DTE Connected to Modem

TR—Terminal Ready ON When Modem Receives Data Terminal Ready Signal from Attached DTE

MR—Modem Ready Indicates Modem is ON

AL—Analog Loopback is ON When Modem Is in Analog Loopback Self-Test Mode

Figure 5-11. Asynchronous modem indicators.

shows that the modem is operating at its highest data rate. Thus, if this indicator is not illuminated, the attached terminal or personal computer has not placed the modem in its highest data rate, which probably results in the terminal or computer operator reporting a "slow response time" problem to technical control center personnel. In this situation, the adjustment of a terminal switch setting or software program parameter may be all that is required to fix the problem.

When the AA indicator is illuminated, the modem is placed in its automatic answer mode of operation. Because the frequency assignment of many modems is such that an originate mode can only operate in tandem with an answer mode modem, placing the modem in answer mode and dialing a modem at a computer center normally precludes the establishment of communications. This is because most modems at computer centers are designed to receive calls, and their frequency assignments are set to the answer mode frequency, so the frequencies of the calling and called modems are incompatible for transmission. Here the solution is to disengage the local modem from automatic answer mode, in effect making it into an originate mode modem.

The carrier detect signal illuminates when the carrier tone is received from the remote modem. If communications appear to be broken, the operator should examine the illumination of the CD indicator. When the CD is lit, the communications path to the distant device is still operative, and a response delay could be the result of a heavy workload on the computer system causing a processing delay.

The OH indicator illuminates when the modem takes control of the telephone line, which is similar to your picking up the handset of a telephone. If the modem does not appear to be dialing and the OH indicator is not lit, it is highly probable that the modem is unplugged from the telephone line, an easily corrected situation.

The send and receive data indicators illuminate or, more correctly, flash as a data bit is sent to the modem or received from the telephone line. By examining these indicators, you may be able to determine whether a terminal has failed, because the illumination of the RD indicator without terminal printing or display suggests that the terminal is not receiving or displaying data passed to it by the modem. Similarly, if the SD indicator fails to illuminate while you press keys on the keyboard of a terminal attached to a modem, either the modem is not receiving the data because of a cabling problem or the modem is inoperative.

The terminal ready indicator shows that the modem is receiving a DTR signal. If this indicator is not illuminated, the attached terminal or computer port may not be operational and should be checked. Finally, the illumination of the AL indicator occurs when a modem is in a self-test mode of operation. In this situation, the modem is not operational and cannot modulate data presented to it by a DTE. Here, take the modem out of its self-test mode to resume normal operations.

Using Modem Circuit Indicators

Examining the circuit indicators or lamps on the front panel can isolate many of network failures. As an example of the use of modem indicators, consider the network segment illustrated in Figure 5-12. If no data is received at the computer for the following network configuration, what is causing the impairment?

The seven potential causes of the transmission impairment can include the terminal, modems, computer, cables between DTEs and modems, and the leased line connecting the terminal to the computer. By examining the modem indicators at each end of the circuit, you may be able to isolate the cause of the problem.

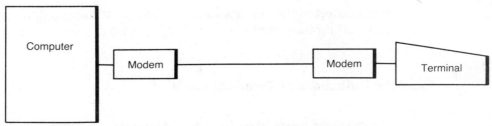

Figure 5-12. Inoperative network segment.

Examining Modem Indicators at Computer Site

First, check the CD indicator. If it is ON, there is continuity, and one modem hears the carrier tone output by the modem at the opposite end of the circuit. If the CD indicator is not illuminated, a break in the circuit may be causing a loss in continuity, the modem's receiver may be defective, or the modem's CD circuit may have failed.

Next, check the DTR indicator. If the DTR indicator is not illuminated, the computer port may not be activated, the modem could be defective, or the AC power source to the modem could be disconnected.

If the DTR indicator is ON, then check the DSR indicator. If the DSR indicator is OFF, the modem may be in a test mode or is defective. If the modem is in a test mode and has a test mode indicator, that indicator should also be examined to verify that this is the cause of the problem. The solution then is to place the modem back in its operational mode.

Also check the TD indicator because this circuit by itself or with other indicators can provide additional information about the operational state of the modem. If the line connecting the computer to the terminal is a polled circuit, the TD indicator should flash on periodically when data in the form of polls is transmitted from the computer port to the modem. If the TD indicator is OFF and the line is a polled circuit, either the indicator has failed or, more probably, the computer is causing the problem.

If transmission on the circuit between the computer and the terminal is half duplex, the RTS and CTS indicators should be ON whenever the TD indicator is ON. If the RTS indicator is ON and the CTS indicator is OFF, the modem has probably failed and is not transmitting data to the remote terminal.

Another indicator that warrants examination is the receive signal quality (RSQ) indicator contained on the front panel of many synchronous modems. When this circuit is illuminated, the circuit quality has deteriorated to the point where it is too poor to pass data. In this situation, calling the telephone company is probably justified.

Examine Indicators at Terminal Location

Examine also the modem indicators at the terminal location to help isolate the cause of the transmission impairment. Again, if the CD indicator is ON, there is continuity. If the CD indicator is OFF, either the line has failed, the modem's receiver is defective, or the modem's CD circuit has failed. If the CD indicator is ON, check the RD indicator when the computer is polling the terminal on the circuit. If the RD indicator is ON but the DTR indicator is OFF, the terminal is not servicing the data it is receiving.

Next, check the DTR indicator when data is keyed at the terminal. If the DTR indicator is OFF, either the modem is not cabled correctly to the terminal or the modem is defective. If the DTR indicator is ON, check the DSR indicator. If that indicator is OFF, the modem is in a test mode of operation or the modem is defective. Finally, check the TD indicator when data is keyed at the terminal. If the DTR and CTS indicators are on but the TD indicator is OFF, the terminal is probably defective. If the RTS indicator is ON and the CTS indicator is OFF, the modem has most likely failed and is not transmitting data to the computer.

Based on the preceding, modem indicators obviously can help in isolating network problems. Unfortunately, not all modems have indicators. Some that don't are internal modems, which are installed inside the system unit of personal computers. When key modem indicators are missing from the front panel of a modem or an internal modem is used, the state of the conductors between the modem and the attached DTE can be observed by using a breakout box. The operation and utilization of different types of breakout boxes and other communications test equipment are discussed in chapter 6.

Review Questions

1. A remote terminal user accesses a computer center, but only transmits a few minutes before being disconnected. Each time this situation occurs, the user notices that the modem's RSQ lamp first flashes, then becomes solidly lit before the DCD goes OFF. What is the probable cause of the problem?

2. A remote personal computer user dials a computer center, then complains about slow data transmission. When asked to report the status of the indicators on the modem attached to his or her personal computer, the user says the HS lamp is OFF. What could be causing the slow data transfer?

Chapter 6

Diagnostic Hardware and Digital Testing

T HE NEED TO TEST and troubleshoot data communications equipment and line facilities is the driving force behind the development of a variety of diagnostic hardware. Although the operational capabilities of diagnostic equipment vary considerably among different devices and within similar devices manufactured by different vendors, such equipment normally provides the data communications user with at least one of three key abilities: to monitor a communications line, to observe the status of the conductors at the physical interface, or to transmit patterns of data and observe the response of equipment and facilities to such test patterns.

In this chapter, we examine the operational characteristics and utilization of nine distinct types of network diagnostic hardware. This examination is designed to provide background information that can be used in determining the most appropriate types of devices to acquire, based on your organization's network structure and the types of communications problems that may arise. The following list itemizes the types of diagnostic hardware that are examined in this chapter. In general, the sophistication of the diagnostic hardware cataloged in the following list increases nearer the end of the list. The protocol analyzer usually is considered the most sophisticated and expensive type of diagnostic hardware that can be purchased to help the network technician in testing and troubleshooting data communications hardware and facilities.

Types of Network Diagnostic Hardware

Cable analyzer/tester

Breakout box

Pattern generator

Bit error rate tester

Modem test set

Block error rate tester

Error-free second tester

Line monitor

Protocol analyzer

Cable Tester/Analyzer

The cable tester/analyzer is a device designed to test the conductors in a data communications cable. Normally, the ends of the cable to be tested are connected to each end of the cable tester, then the operator initiates the test.

Types

Some cable testers automatically send a short duration signal in conductor pin sequence whenever the operator presses a key on the device. Other cable testers permit the operator to program the sequence of conductors to be tested. Devices that are programmable are most useful when the technician has many nonstandard cables to check, because programmable devices reduce test time and the repetitive process of entering a certain pin sequence to be used for the test.

Operation

When the signal is transmitted from one end of the cable tester, a light emitting diode (LED) illuminates to show the conductor under test. At the receive side of the cable tester, a second row of LEDs is used to show a conductor continuity, tie, or short. As an example of the use of a cable tester, assume the transmit side of the device causes the LED associated with pin 2 to illuminate. If pin 3 lights at the receive side of the device, pins 2 and 3 are crossed. Similarly, pin 2's LED illuminating at the receive side of the cable tester suggests that the pin 2 conductor is wired straight through the cable, whereas no LED being illuminated suggests a short on the pin 2 conductor.

Because a conventional cable tester requires both ends of the cable to be fastened to the device, such a tester is impractical to use by itself when a cable has been previously installed. In this situation, one can remove the cable and fasten both ends to the tester, use two testers (which can result in excessive walking if the cable is routed a long distance), or obtain a "bounce-back module." The latter is an option sold by many cable tester manufacturers that permits an installed cable to be easily tested with one cable tester by one person. As the name implies, the bounce-back module is designed to receive the conductor test voltages transmitted by the cable tester and echo them back to that device. Normally, a cable tester can be purchased for less than $250, with a bounce-back module costing an additional $50 to $100.

Breakout Box

The breakout box is a portable hand-held tester primarily used for examining the condition of the conductors at the physical interface level. This examination can be between data terminal equipment (DTE) and data communications equipment (DCE), two DTEs, or two DCEs.

Breakout boxes range in scope from simple monitoring devices to units that permit the operator to change the state of one or more conductors or to patch one conductor to another. Most breakout boxes are designed for use on RS-232 interfaces, with other breakout boxes designed for use with a wideband V.35 interface or a Centronics parallel printer interface. Regardless of its ultimate use, the breakout box is one of the most powerful tools for testing and troubleshooting communications.

In this section, we first review the basic functions and operations of several types of RS-232 breakout boxes. Then, after obtaining a basic understanding of the functions and use of these devices, we examine several of the more practical uses of breakout boxes, which makes the famous credit card slogan "don't leave home without it" most appropriate for this category of equipment.

Overview

The breakout box was originally designed to provide a visual indicator of the state of the conductors at the physical interface. The simplest type of breakout box is passive, providing several light emitting diodes (LEDs) whose illumination or lack of illumination corresponds to the voltage level on a conductor. A passive breakout box provides the capability of monitoring either all or a subset of the interface conductors while passing all leads through as is. To examine the operation and utilization of breakout boxes, we focus our attention on devices designed for use on an RS-232 interface, although discussions contained in this section that do not refer to specific conductors are appropriate also to breakout boxes designed for use on other types of physical interfaces.

Figure 6-1 illustrates a schematic diagram of a low cost, passive, RS-232 breakout box. One end of the breakout box normally contains a "male" DB 25-P plug connector. The opposite end of the breakout box contains a "female" DB 25-S socket connector.

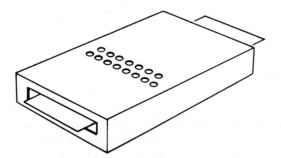

Figure 6-1. Passive breakout box.

In the RS-232 standard, DTEs and DCEs are supposed to have female DB 25-S connectors, whereas the cable connecting DTE to DCE has male DB 25-P connectors on each end. Thus, in most situations, the breakout box can be easily inserted into either end of the cable connection between DTE and DCE. This is illustrated in Figure 6-2. Figure 6-2A shows the standard cabling of DTE to DCE, whereas Figure 6-2B shows how the breakout box can be inserted between one of the devices and the cable. In actuality, the breakout box can be inserted between the DTE and a cable connector as illustrated, between the DCE and a cable connector, or between DTE and DCE.

To ease the breakout box's insertion between devices, many manufacturers incorporate two short flat ribbon cables to tie separate connectors to each end of the device. Although not normally incorporated into low cost, passive, breakout boxes, flat ribbon cables are commonly used with more expensive breakout boxes for additional flexibility in inserting the device between a DTE and a DCE.

Some of the more expensive breakout boxes, such as the Datacom Northwest Model 1000, have dual gender connectors attached to each end of the flat ribbon cable that is connected to the device. The use of

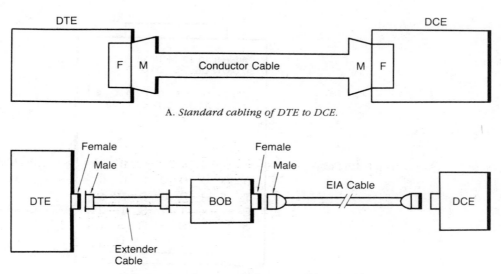

A. *Standard cabling of DTE to DCE.*

B. *Breakout box inserted between DTE and cable.*

Figure 6-2. Using the breakout box.

dual gender connectors ensures that the technician using the breakout box always is able to insert it into a network segment, regardless of the type of cable end or device connectors encountered.

Types of Passive Breakout Boxes

Passive breakout boxes provide the user with the capability to monitor either all or a subset of the conductors at the physical interface. Some low-cost devices only provide the user with the capability to monitor pins 2, 3, 4, 5, 6, 8, and 20. These are the key data and control leads used with most asynchronous transmission applications. Other passive breakout boxes include two rows of interface circuit probe points and an additional LED display labeled TEST, with a patch point wired to the TEST LED. This conjunction leads to the spare LED.

Figure 6-3 illustrates a schematic diagram of a passive breakout box designed to monitor eight interface leads at one time. The TEST LED provides the operator with the capability to monitor any other lead. The design of the passive breakout box illustrated in Figure 6-3 is based on economy, because LEDs normally cost more than probe points. By reducing the number of LEDs, the size and the complexity of the breakout box are reduced. Typical retail cost for a device similar to that illustrated in Figure 6-3 ranges from $75 to $100.

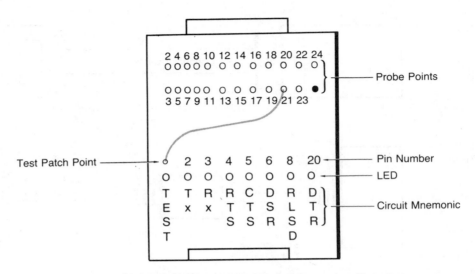

Figure 6-3. Passive breakout box with test patch point.

The status of any conductor can be displayed on the TEST LED by using a "mini-patch" cord. In Figure 6-3, the ring indicator (pin 21) circuit status is displayed at the TEST LED because the pin 21 probe point is patched to the test patch point.

Single Versus Multistate Monitoring

When a single row of unicolor LEDs is included in the breakout box, the device is considered a single state monitor. This is because of the definition of the RS-232 standard for data and control signals. In the RS-232 standard, a positive voltage at or greater than +3 volts and fewer than or equal to 15 volts is defined as a "logic 0" or SPACE. A negative voltage at or fewer than −3 volts but fewer than or equal to −15 volts is defined as a "logic 1" or MARK. Here, voltages between the logic 0 and logic 1 delimiters are considered a transitory state, as illustrated in Figure 6-4.

When only one set of LEDs is used in a breakout box, the LEDs normally illuminate in response to a positive voltage, denoting a logic 0 or signal SPACE. The absence of illumination on the LED suggests a negative voltage or a transitory voltage. Only when the LED is illuminated, therefore, can the user of the breakout box be assured of the state of the signal on the conductor the LED is designed to denote.

The use of a second row of LEDs changes the breakout box into a tri-state unit. This type of device normally uses red and green rows of LEDs,

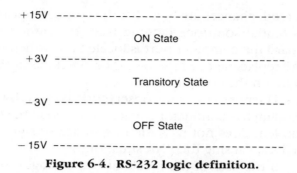

+ 15V --

ON State

+ 3V --

Transitory State

− 3V --

OFF State

− 15V --

Figure 6-4. RS-232 logic definition.

with a pair of LEDs assigned to each conductor to be monitored. Normally, breakout boxes are designed to illuminate red LEDs when a positive voltage is present. Green LEDs are illuminated when a negative voltage level occurs. Thus, if neither LED is illuminated, the monitored conductor is in a transitory condition.

As an alternative to the use of dual rows of green and red LEDs, some breakout boxes employ a single row of LEDs that can be illuminated in either color. Although this type of device is functionally equivalent to a breakout box that uses two separate rows of LEDs, color-blind persons cannot use the device effectively. Thus, breakout boxes using dual rows of LEDs should always be selected if any technicians in an organization are color-blind or color vision impaired.

Some breakout boxes are constructed with dual pairs of red and green LEDs. One pair of LEDs is used on the DCE side of the interface. The second pair of LEDs is used on the DTE side of the interface.

Passive Device Utilization

Because a passive breakout box can only monitor the condition or state of interface conductors, its role is limited to the examination and verification of control signal conditions. As an example of a possible utilization of this device, consider a dial-in modem connected to a computer port. Suppose that one or more persons complained that the only response to dialing the switched telephone network number of the line connected to the modem was constant ringing—the classic "ring no answer" (RNA) communications problem. By inserting a passive breakout box between the modem and the computer port, the breakout box's operator usually can determine the cause of the ring no answer problem.

Before receiving a call, the computer port normally has pin 20 (data terminal ready) raised or in the ON condition. If this condition is not observed, chances are high that the computer port is the RNA culprit, with potential solutions ranging from the removal and reinsertion of the board the computer port is located on, which is known as reseeding, to the replacement of the board or checking of the communications software on the computer.

The next step in the observation process is to determine whether the modem has conductor 6 (data set ready) in the ON condition. If not, the modem does not pass the ring indicator signal when an incoming call arrives, causing the RNA situation.

If the user of the breakout box arranges for an associate to dial the modem while observing the control signals, the absence of pin 6 (data set ready) or pin 22 (ring indicator) being ON means that the modem is probably the RNA culprit. Possible solutions to this problem can range from the reseeding of a board in the modem to refastening connectors or replacing a modem board or the entire modem.

If both the data set ready and ring indicator signal are high, apparently the computer port is not correctly responding to the modem, suggesting that the computer port and possibly the communications software operating on the computer should be examined. In many instances, the computer operator has deactivated one or a group of "lines," either due to a standard operating procedure or for testing, but has not issued an appropriate command to put the line back into service. For such situations, a request to operations to "reactivate line XXX" can be noted from a compliance standpoint; once done the data terminal ready signal should appear. By providing a window to observe the state of control signals, the passive breakout box can be a valuable instrument in solving communications related problems.

Active Breakout Box

Compared with a passive breakout box, an active device contains patch and cross-connect probe points for both DTE and DCE sides of the device. In addition, an active breakout box contains a set of switches that can be used to break open the data and control lines of the physical interface. Because of this property, these switches are commonly called breakout switches.

Some active breakout boxes are battery powered. Other devices are powered from the line they are monitoring. At the high end of this product category, several breakout boxes, such as the Datacom Northwest Model 1000 illustrated in Figure 6-5, include positive and negative voltage sources that can be used with jumpers or mini-patch cords to simulate control signals. Products in this category normally sell for $275 to $350.

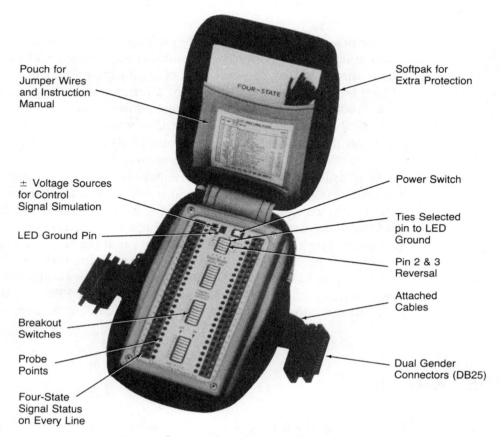

Pouch for Jumper Wires and Instruction Manual

Softpak for Extra Protection

± Voltage Sources for Control Signal Simulation

Power Switch

LED Ground Pin

Ties Selected pin to LED Ground

Pin 2 & 3 Reversal

Attached Cables

Breakout Switches

Probe Points

Dual Gender Connectors (DB25)

Four-State Signal Status on Every Line

Figure 6-5. Datacom Northwest Model 1000.

The following table lists seven key features of the Datacom Northwest Model 1000 breakout box. I previously commented on the use of the four rows of 25 LEDs per row, so in the following list, I focus attention upon the remaining features.

Key Features of Datacom Northwest Model 1000

100 LEDs in four separate rows

Positive and negative voltage sources

50 probe points

2 pairs of dual gender connectors

Breakout switches for each conductor

Pin 2 and 3 reversal switch

Positive and negative voltage sources

The positive (+) and negative (−) voltage sources are included in the Model 1000 to permit operators to simulate any of the RS-232 conductor signals that they may require. This control signal simulation is accomplished by first patching one end of a jumper wire supplied with the Model 1000 to the appropriate voltage source. Then, the operator can connect the opposite end of the jumper wire to one of the 50 probe points on the device. Each probe point is associated with a conductor signal on the appropriate side of the breakout box.

As an example of the use of the voltage sources and probe points on the Model 1000, consider the operator who wants to observe the reaction of a device to the presence of a ring indicator signal but who does not have a dial-network circuit over which a call can be made. By connecting the Model 1000 to the RS-232 port on the device, then patching a jumper wire from the positive voltage source to the probe point associated with pin 22 (ring indicator), the operator can simulate the occurrence of that signal. Then, by observing the other LEDs on the Model 1000, the operator can note the response of the device to a ring indicator signal.

Probe Points

As shown in both Figure 6-5 and the list entitled "Key Features of Datacom Northwest Model 1000," the Datacom Northwest Model 1000 has two rows of 25 probe points, which totals 50 probe points. These probe points can be used for patching and simulating RS-232 data and control signals at either side of the device.

The patching capability of the Model 1000 is all-inclusive, permitting the operator to use a jumper wire to connect any signal or data conductor on one side of the device to any other signal or data conductor on the same or opposite of the device. To understand the purposes of using probe points, consider an operator who is working with a "ring-start" communications device, such as a port on a port selector.

If the operator desires to directly connect a terminal to the port selector, no ring indicator signal occurs because the connection bypasses the switched telephone network. In this situation, the technician examines other control signals turned on by the terminal and determines the effect of jumping one of the terminal control signals to the ring indicator signal.

By using the probe points on the Model 1000, the technician could, as an example, first cable the Model 1000 to a port on the port selector. Then the technician could use one jumper wire to patch a positive voltage to the data terminal ready (DTR) probe point to simulate that control signal without cabling the terminal to the port selector port. Next the technician could jumper the DTR probe point to the RI probe point, in effect forcing the ring indicator signal to become active whenever a DTR signal is present. If the Model 1000 operator then notes the flashing of an LED on either pin 2 or pin 3, the port selector probably was activated by forcing the RI signal high and is beginning to transmit a sign-on message to a "pseudo" terminal simulated by the Model 1000.

The LED may flash either on pin 2 or pin 3 because the port on the port selector could be configured as either a DTE or a DCE. If configured as a DTE, data is transmitted on pin 2, whereas if the port is configured as a DCE, data is transmitted on pin 3.

Once the required jumpering is noted, the Model 1000 operator can use the information to fabricate an appropriate cable. For the previous example, pin 20 (DTR) would be jumpered to pin 22 (RI) in a cable, to ensure that each time a directly connected terminal was turned on, the port selector would receive the required ring indicator signal.

Dual Gender Connectors

The dual gender connectors on each of the two cables attached to the Model 1000 ensure that the device can be connected to any standard RS-232 connector without requiring the operator to search for an adapter. To understand the utility of dual gender connectors, consider the RS-232 cabling standard where DTEs and DCEs are supposed to be built with female socket connectors, whereas cables connecting the devices are supposed to have male connectors on each cable end to permit the cables to be fastened to each device. In actuality, many DTEs and DCEs do not conform to the connector standard and the resulting cable connecting the two devices, a DTE to a DTE or a DCE to a DCE, may have cable connectors different from that standard.

By including both male and female connectors on each end of the cable connected to the Model 1000, this breakout box can be inserted into every type of device, whether connected to standard or nonstandard cable connectors. Thus, the inclusion of dual gender connectors alleviates the need to search for a cable adapter or "gender mender" device required by other breakout boxes that have only one connector on each cable.

Breakout Switches

The 25 breakout switches on the Model 1000 can be used to break open the data and control lines when the left side of each switch is pushed down. When examining the operation of two devices, the breakout switches are valuable for enabling and disabling data and control signals. By using these switches, a technician can easily examine the effect of changes in control signals of one device on another without requiring the actual operation of the primary device.

As an example of the utility of breakout switches, consider the previous example, where a terminal is to be directly connected to the port of a port selector. To examine whether the port selector recognizes a drop of the DTR signal as a disconnect request, the Model 1000 operator could simply flip the DTR breakout switch to drop that control signal. Then, either by examining the port selector console or the interface on the port of the port selector, the operator is able to determine whether the absence of DTR causes the port selector to disconnect the terminal. If the operator is examining the port interface, he or she first notes some activity on either pin 2 or pin 3, depending on whether the port is configured as a DTE or DCE, causes the green LED associated with that pin to illuminate. This occurs because the RS-232 standard states that a transmitter is always at a negative voltage when not transmitting.

Pin Reversal Switch

The pin reversal switch enables the Model 1000 operator to easily reverse pins 2 and 3 in an RS-232 test application, such as when attempting to connect two DTEs or two DCEs. In comparison, other breakout boxes require the operator to use two jumper wires to patch the probe points of pin 2 to pin 3 and pin 3 to pin 2.

Utilization

The patching and control signal simulation capability of active breakout boxes enables them to be used in a variety of situations where a passive device may be of little or no use. To consider the versatility of the active breakout box, we examine its utilization in several typical communications areas.

Suppose that a communications port on a personal computer is directly cabled by snaking the cable through a conduit to the computer room where it is connected to a port on a protocol converter. After loading a communications program and entering its terminal emulation mode, data entered from the keyboard fails to be displayed on the computer's monitor. There are several possibilities: the communications cable was crimped when snaked through the conduit, the software was configured incorrectly, or the protocol converter is not operating correctly. The elimination of these possible problems can be used to isolate the impairment. By using an active breakout box as a loop-back plug, the technician obtains a mechanism to check the cable.

Figure 6-6 illustrates the use of an active breakout box as a loopback plug. By inserting the device between the cable and the protocol converter port and appropriately using breakout switches and jumpers or mini-patch cords, the active breakout box can be used to check the continuity of conductors in the cable.

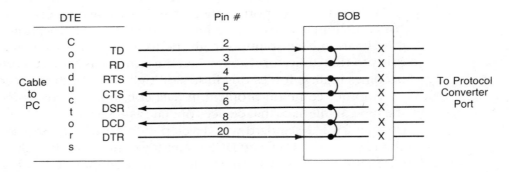

Legend: X—Breakout Switch in Open Position

Figure 6-6. Using a breakout box as a loopback plug.

As shown in Figure 6-6, transmit data is patched to receive data, request to send is patched to clear to send and data terminal ready is patched to both data set ready and data carrier detect. Then the breakout switches on the breakout box for each of the previously mentioned circuits are placed in the open position to disable any signals emanating from the port on the protocol converter.

Although the use of the breakout box in the previously described situation only confirms whether the personal computer is functioning as a terminal, the breakout box could also be connected directly to the computer's communications port. If characters are echoed back to the computer's display when the breakout box is connected to the computer's communications port but no characters are echoed when the device is inserted between the cable and the protocol converter port, the technicians can safely assume that the cable is defective.

Interface Modification

An active breakout box probably finds its primary use in the area of interface modification. By using the patching capability of the device, technical control center personnel can determine special cabling requirements needed to make compatible devices with incompatible control signals.

Consider the direct connection of a terminal device to a port selector that operates as a ring-start device. This means that the port selector must receive a signal on pin 22 (ring indicator) if it is to be placed in operation. Because a directly cabled terminal does not provide a ring indicator signal, the technician could insert an active breakout box between the cable and the port selector port connector and by using jumpers or mini-patch cords, attempt to derive the required signals before fabricating a cable. In this situation, one solution might be to jumper or patch data terminal ready to ring indicator. Then, when the terminal is powered on and DTR becomes high, it forces ring indicator high, starting the port selector.

Another common problem in data communications is determining the type of interface that devices operate as—DTE or DCE. Although the original RS-232 standard was developed to govern the serial data interchange between DTE and DCE operating equipment, in today's modern communications environment, it is quite common to have DTEs connected to DTEs and DCEs connected to DCEs. In such situations, technicians must first determine the type of each device to be cabled together (DTE or DCE) and the conductor flow requirements, then fabricate the appropriate cable to make compatible the incompatible devices.

Returning to the previous example about the cabling of a personal computer to a protocol converter, another problem that can cause incompatibility is if the protocol converter port is configured as a DTE device. To verify this, the technician can connect a breakout box to the port of the protocol converter. Because the RS-232 standard specifies that a transmitter is always a logic one (negative voltage) when not transmitting, the green LED associated with pin 3 on a three-state breakout box illuminates if the protocol converter port is configured as a DCE. If the port is configured as a DTE, the green LED on pin 2 illuminates. Assume that the green LED on pin 2 is illuminated, showing that the protocol converter port is configured as a DTE.

Some protocol converters can be programmed via a configuration port, so it might be possible to simply change the port to a DCE port to obtain compatibility with the DTE operating personal computer. If this is not possible, the technician must determine the control signals and data path connections required to develop a null modem cable for connecting DTE to DTE. This can be accomplished by either examining the manuals of the protocol converter and the personal computer's asynchronous communications adapter to determine their control signal requirements or by using a breakout box to determine the required control signals.

The technician can connect the breakout box to the protocol converter port to note the control signal outputs of that device. This is accomplished by noting which red LEDs illuminate because when at rest, they generate a positive voltage. Next, the technician can verify the control signal inputs to the protocol converter port by patching pins 2 to 3 and 3 to 2, which connects the transmit data and receive data conductors of the personal computer to the appropriate transmit and receive conductors on the protocol converter port. This is done because it was previously determined that the protocol converter port is configured as a DTE, and conductors 2 and 3 must be reversed for two DTEs to operate.

Once pins 2 and 3 are reversed, the technician can apply a negative voltage (control OFF) to each potential input and note the results. This can be accomplished by placing one end of a mini-patch cord into the negative voltage source on the breakout box, then patching the opposite end of the patch cord to each potential input source. If the protocol converter port stops operating when a negative voltage is applied on a conductor, a control input has been located that is used by the device. Similarly, the control inputs to the personal computer's asynchronous communications adapter can be determined in order to develop a DTE-DTE wiring chart. Then the technician can use the breakout box to verify the null modem conductor assignments. Figure 6-7 illustrates the use of an active breakout box configured as a modem eliminator cable to verify the conductor cabling before the required cable is fabricated.

Cable Verification

Through the utilization of an active breakout box, the pin connections of a cable can be examined. If the cable has not been installed, each end of the cable can be connected to the breakout box, and the operator can

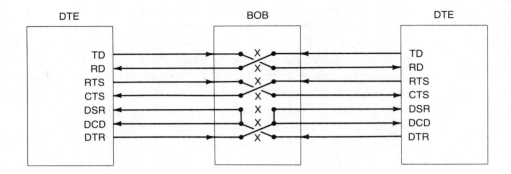

Legend: X—Breakout Switch in Open Position

Figure 6-7. Using an active breakout box as a null modem cable.

apply either a positive or negative voltage to each of the conductor probe points on one side of the device, then examine the LEDs at the other side of the breakout box. In this manner, bridging, opens, and continuity of conductors can be noted.

As an example of the use of an active breakout box to do cable testing, assume one end of a mini-patch cord was connected to a voltage source probe point. If the operator patches the other end of the cord to pin 2, and the LED associated with pin 3 on the other side of the device illuminates, pins 2 and 3 are reversed. Similarly, if the operator patched the other end of the cord to pin 20, and pins 6 and 8 illuminated on the other side of the breakout box, DTR is tied to DSR and DCD.

If a cable is already installed, it is usually too difficult to remove it for testing. In such situations, an active breakout box can be placed at one end of the cable and a passive device at the other end. Then one person can patch a positive or negative voltage to each conductor probe and walk back and forth to the other end of the cable to note the results for each probe point voltage application, or two people can help one another, with one person changing the patch from the voltage source to each conductor probe point while the second person records the results.

As shown, the breakout box is a very useful and practical piece of network diagnostic hardware. Because of its low cost and high level of assistance in testing and troubleshooting, it is quite common for most technicians to carry one in the same manner that engineers used to wear slide rulers. Although other types of communications test equipment, including line monitors and protocol analyzers, are being manufactured with built-in breakout boxes, this is more of a testament to the versatility of the standalone unit than its possible replacement.

Pattern Generator

A pattern generator is a data communications testing device that enables an easily recognizable test message to be transmitted to local or remote DTEs or DCEs. By transmitting a test message and observing the response to the message, the pattern generator operator can verify the quality of a circuit or cable and the operation of communications equipment and terminal devices that may be connected on the circuit or cable.

The two primary types of pattern generators are fixed test and variable pattern devices. As the name implies, fixed test pattern generators transmit a predefined and nonalterable test message. In comparison, a variable pattern generator provides the operator with the ability to enter the test message to be transmitted. The latter device can be used as a simulator, because the operator, as an example, could enter a polling sequence into the transmit buffer of the equipment and connect it to a port on a controller to simulate the operation of a terminal.

Originally, pattern generators were developed to check the operation of circuits connecting teletypewriter equipment. Early pattern generators used the sentence:

```
"THE QUICK BROWN FOX JUMPS OVER THE LAZY DOG 1234567890 TEST DE. . ."
```

where:

"TEST DE" means "test from" and includes the sender's identifier at the end of the message.

In examining the preceding pattern generator message, note that it includes all 26 letters of the alphabet in the first 33 characters, plus the 10 digits. Thus, it was viewed as a comprehensive test of the electromechanical operation of teletypewriter equipment.

Although early pattern generators were standalone devices, today most pattern generators are manufactured as an additional capability built into a protocol analyzer. By providing the operator with the ability to enter different types of patterns, pattern generators can be used with the capability of the protocol analyzer to exercise code converters, simulate polling sequences, and initiate other digitally activated sequences.

Figure 6-8 illustrates the insertion of a pattern generator between a multiplexer channel and an attached computer. By sending a predefined message, the composition of the composite high speed channel can be examined to determine whether the multiplexer at the computer center is operating correctly. At the remote site, the terminal's correct reception of the test message can be used to show that the network segment is operative or the data flow can be monitored at the indicated points in an attempt to isolate a hardware problem.

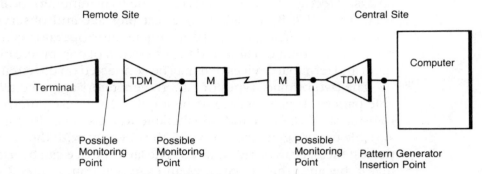

Figure 6-8. Using a pattern generator.

Bit Error Rate Tester

The bit error rate tester is more commonly known by its abbreviation—BERT. BERTs are used to inject a known data sequence into a transmission device and examine for errors the received sequence at the same device or at a remote device. By using a BERT, the operator can check the performance level of communications hardware and line facilities.

Normally, BERT testing capability is built into another device, such as a "sophisticated" breakout box or a protocol analyzer. The bit error rate test results in the device computing the bit error rate (BER), which is

$$BER = \frac{\text{bits received in error}}{\text{number of bits transmitted}}$$

The BER provides an indication of end-to-end channel performance. As an example, at 1200 bps, a typical voice grade circuit might have an error rate of 1 bit per 10^5 bits.

Test Patterns and Runs

Most BERT devices permit the operator to select several different types of test patterns, including alternate MARK and SPACE, all MARK, all SPACE, or pseudo random bit sequences. Depending on the type of equipment the BERT is to test, one test pattern can be more appropriate to use than another test pattern. As an example of this, consider the use of a BERT to test the operation of a frequency shift keying (FSK) modem. This type of modem places one of two frequencies on the circuit—f_1 to represent a MARK and f_2 to represent a SPACE. If you connect a BERT to the digital input of the FSK modem, set the BERT to transmit all MARKs, and use an analog test instrument to examine the resulting frequency of the modulated output, you can determine whether the modem is correctly transmitting MARKs. Similarly, you could set the BERT to transmit all SPACEs to determine whether the FSK modem is correctly modulating spaces. When a BERT is used in this fashion, it is commonly called a modem test set, although some equipment in this category is more sophisticated than a BERT. Modem test sets are covered in more detail in the section titled ''Modem Test Set'' in this chapter.

Pseudo random bit sequences are generated in $2^n - 1$ series, with n normally between 6 and 9. This results in pseudo random bit sequences of 63, 511, 2047, and 4095 bits being generated.

Depending on the type of device, users may be able to run BERT tests continuously or for a predefined time or data block count. For the latter situation, the BERT permits the operator to select a data block size, then transmit a predefined number of such blocks.

The following table lists six of the major selectable parameters of many bit error rate testers. Here the framing parameter category provides for the BERT to be used with character-oriented equipment, such as 212A modems and certain types of multiplexer and front-end processor ports. The error insertion parameter permits the BERT operator to insert a bit error into the data stream. This enables the operator to observe the reaction of equipment to one or more forced bit errors.

BERT Selectable Parameters

Data rate

Framing

Character set—ASCII, EBCDIC, etc.
Data bits—5, 6, 7, 8
Parity—odd, even, none

Data type—asynchronous, synchronous

Test pattern

Test runs

Error insertion

Utilization

In test mode, the BERT simultaneously counts transmit and receive bits, blocks, or characters based on its setting. Then, depending on the capability of the device, it may count and display parity errors and frame errors as well as display the elapsed time since testing began.

As an example of the utilization of a BERT, consider an organization that has a leased line between its central computer site and a remotely located office. Suppose this line has a modem installed at each location to support the transmission of data from the central computer site to several terminals connected to a cluster controller at the remote office.

One of the more common problems associated with the utilization of cluster controllers is poor response time. The cause of this problem can come from one or more areas within a communications system, including the workload on the computer, the number of terminals connected to the cluster controller and their activity, and the occurrence of line hits. The latter situation causes data transmitted between the computer and the cluster controller to be retransmitted, because most communications systems correct errors by retransmitting blocks of data. By using a BERT, the network technician can determine the quality of the circuit and either verify the circuit as the cause of poor response time or eliminate it as the culprit. To test the line, the technician would place the modem at the remote location in its loopback mode of operation by issuing a remote loopback command from the modem at the computer site. If these modems did not have a remote control feature, the technician would call an appropriate person at the remote location and instruct that person which button to push or switch to set. After the remotely located modem is in its loopback mode of operation, the technician at the computer site would connect the BERT to the modem at that location and initiate testing.

Depending on whether one or two BERTs are used for testing, you may be abe to narrow the cause of a transmission impairment to a specific component or facility on an extensive network segment. In Figure 6-9A, the use of one BERT is illustrated. Here, the BERT can be used to test the local modem or both modems and the communications line, depending on the type of modem loopback that occurred. If the local modem is placed in a loopback mode, the BERT only tests that modem. If the remote modem is placed in a loopback mode, the BERT tests both modems and the line. Thus, if errors occur when the remote modem is in a loopback mode, the operator is not sure whether the cause of the errors is the remote modem, the line, or both the remote modem and communications line.

Figure 6-9B illustrates how two BERTs could be used to further isolate the cause of a transmission problem. Here, the BERT at the computer site could be used to test the "local" modem at the computer site. Next, the modem remote to the computer site could be placed in a loopback mode of operation to permit the BERT to test both modems and the line. If the modem connected to the BERT at each site operates correctly, but errors occur when the BERT tests both modems and the line, the line is the culprit. This is because each modem was successfully tested but two modems and the line together could not pass the test.

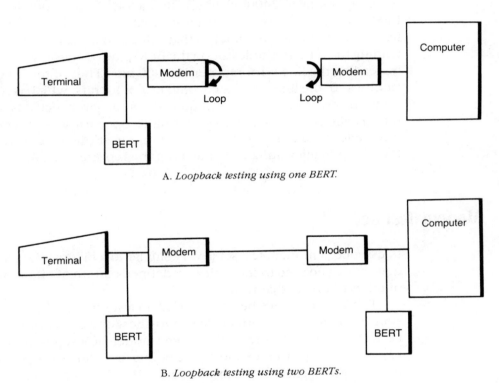

A. *Loopback testing using one BERT.*

B. *Loopback testing using two BERTs.*

Figure 6-9. Using BERT.

Line Quality Determination

Some BERTs include a timer to stop testing automatically after the preset time period is reached. Other BERTs require the operator to observe the test time manually and end the test when the required test duration is reached. Regardless of the type of BERT employed, its utilization provides the operator with the bit error rate (BER) of the line. As previously noted, the BER is simply the number of bits received in error divided by the total number of bits transmitted during the test period. By selecting an appropriate test period based on the data rate of the modems attached to the circuit, the operator can convert the BER into an error rate expressed in a common unit of measurement to which the line quality can be compared.

As an example, consider modems operating at 2400bps. Because line errors are normally expressed as a bit error rate per 100,000 bits transmitted, the BERT operator would first compute the test period required when operating at 2400bps to transmit a total of 100,000 bits. Once the BERT operator computes that a test of 42 seconds duration is required, he or she would set the timer to that value and initiate the test. Then, by reading the bit error indicator on the BERT, the operator would, in effect, be reading the line error rate per 100,000 bits. Thus, if the bit error indicator was 6, the line error rate would be 6×10^6 bits, which is roughly six times the error rate most communications carriers specify as normal for their facilities. In this example, the BERT operator would report a high error rate circuit situation to the communications carrier and request their help in alleviating or eliminating the reported problem.

Modem Test Set

In essence, a modem test set is very similar to a bit error rate tester. Both devices can be used to transmit a predefined pattern of bits and count the number of errors that result.

The key difference between a modem test set and a BERT is the inclusion of LEDs on the former device to show the status of key DTE and DCE control signals. In addition, some modem test sets have positive and negative voltage sources and probe points, enabling the operator to simulate control signals to the modem and view the response of the modem to those signals. Thus, a modem test set can be considered as a combination BERT and breakout box, enabling the operator to transmit data to the modem and denote the line error or modem error rate. In addition, many modem test sets permit a technician to check the operation of the modem's circuits controlling the physical interface and to observe the reaction of the modem to simulated control signals.

Table 6-1 lists some of the applications for which modem test sets can be used, based on different patterns generated by the set. Note that the pattern applications are the same as previously described for a bit error rate tester because both devices are very similar in construction and operation.

Table 6-1. Modem Test Set Pattern Applications

Pattern	Application
Continuous SPACE	Permits the frequency and level of an FSK modem SPACE tone to be measured
Continuous MARK	Permits the frequency and level of an FSK modem MARK tone to be measured
Alternate MARKs and SPACEs	Permits bias distortion and the level of the combined modem tones to be measured
Random	Best for making bit error rate tests due to the generation of all possible bit patterns
START/STOP	Used with character oriented devices such as Racal-Vadic 3400 series, Bell System 212 series, or equivalent modems that require a group of random bits framed by start and stop bits.

The Electrodata modem test set illustrated in Figure 6-10 can be considered a combined bit error rate tester and a limited function active breakout box. This test set contains positive and negative test points, displays the status of the receive data, carrier detect, and clear to send conductors. The test set displays a count of up to 999 bit errors.

Error Counter to Bit Rate Conversion

To convert an error counter number in a modem test set to a bit error rate requires testing for a fixed period of time. Table 6-2 lists the time required for two common bit error rates based on seven distinct data rates.

Table 6-2. Bit Error Rate Versus Test Times

Data Rate (bps)	Bit Error Rate	
	1×10^{-5}	1×10^{-6}
300	5 min 33 sec	55 min 33 sec
600	2 min 47 sec	27 min 47 sec
1200	1 min 23 sec	13 min 53 sec
2400	42 sec	6 min 57 sec
4800	21 sec	3 min 28 sec
9600	11 sec	1 min 44 sec
19.2K	6 sec	52 sec

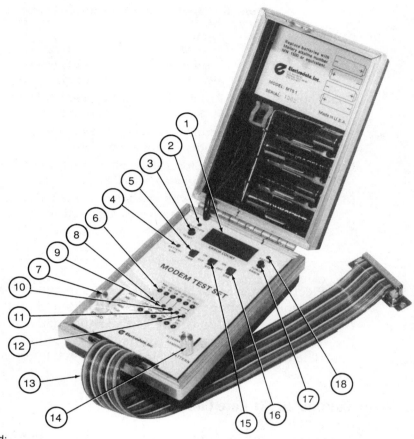

Legend:

1	Error Count Display	10	CD Indicator
2	Overflow Indicator (Error Count Exceeds 999)	11	TEST Test Point Input +
3	RESET Clears Error Count	12	TEST Test Point Input −
4	BATTERY LOW Indicator	13	Ribbon Cable
5	PWR Switch	14	PATTERN Selector
6	Test Points	15	RTS Positive Voltage
7	Sync/Async and Data Rate Selector	16	DTR Positive Voltage
8	Receive Data Indicator	17	FORCE ERROR One Bit per 500 Bits Transmitted
9	CTS Indicator	18	RESYNC

Figure 6-10. Electrodata modem text set.
(photograph courtesy of Electrodata, Inc.)

As an example of the use of Table 6-2, consider the 300 bps data rate for testing purposes. If during a test time of 5 minutes and 33 seconds, exactly 7 bit errors occurred, the bit error rate is 7×10^{-5}.

Testing a Single Modem

To test a single modem with the Electrodata modem test set, the user should first disconnect the modem to be tested from the terminal or computer. Next, the modem should be placed in its analog loopback mode of operation and the test set connected to the modem. After both devices are powered on, the PATTERN switch on the modem test set should be turned to the test pattern that will be used to test the modem. Normally, this switch is set to the RANDOM position. The SPEED switch would be set to its appropriate synchronous or asynchronous data rate. Then the RTS and DTR switches on the modem test set should be turned ON and the RESET switch on the test set should be pressed.

Once the modem test set is operating, it generates a stream of random bits to the modem, where they are modulated, demodulated, and passed back to the test set for validation. If the modem is performing correctly, the error count display should remain at zero.

Block Error Rate Tester

The block error rate tester is another network diagnostic hardware device better known by its acronym—BLERT. The BLERT is used to analyze communications networks that group data into blocks for transmission and on the detection of an error, correct the error by retransmitting the block. Because of this method of error correction, a block error rate tester provides a more realistic indicator of network performance on block-oriented transmission systems than a bit error rate tester.

The primary purpose of a BLERT is to determine the block error rate on a communications circuit. The data obtained from BLERT testing permits the network analyst to improve network performance by adjusting the block size of transmitted data. To understand the relationship between network performance, block error rate, and the size of transmitted data blocks, consider a communications system that has a very low block error rate. This means that very few data blocks have to be retransmitted to correct blocks previously received with one or more bit errors. As the block error rate increases, the number of blocks required to be retransmitted also increases. This results in the data throughput on the circuit decreasing, because a greater proportion of time is now spent correcting transmission errors.

Like BERTs, BLERT capability is incorporated into many protocol analyzers. By using a BLERT, the operator may be able to count block check characters, cyclic redundancy check characters, data frames, and frame errors.

Error-Free Second Tester

The introduction of all-digital communications networks, including AT&T's Digital Dataphone Service (DDS) and British Telecom's Kilostream service, has resulted in the use of error-free seconds to define digital network performance. In an error-free test, received data is analyzed on a per-second basis. If one or more bit errors occurs during a one-second interval, the tester records the second as an errored second. The error-free second percentage is obtained by dividing the errored seconds by the total seconds in the test, multiplying the result by 100, and subtracting the value obtained from 100 percent. Thus,

$$EFS(\%) = 100\% - \frac{\text{Error Seconds}}{\text{Total Seconds}} \times 100$$

Most EFS testers incorporate a V.35 (34 pin) or an RS-449 (37 pin) interface connector for use on digital facilities. Typical data rates supported by most EFS testers are 2.4, 4.8, 9.6, 48.0, and 64.0Kbps; however, some EFS testers can also test T1 carrier facilities and can operate at 1.544Mbps and 2.048Mbps.

Because many communications carriers both specify and guarantee the availability of their high speed digital facilities in terms of errored seconds or error-free seconds, an error-free second tester can be used to validate digital circuit performance claims. In addition, the measurements taken by an error-free tester can be used to request refunds from a communications carrier when circuit performance falls below that guaranteed by the carrier.

Table 6-3 compares the CCITT G.821 error performance recommendation with British Telecom's 64Kbps digital service goal. Table 6-4 illustrates the effect of different error rates at various data rates over a 30-minute period.

Table 6-3. Digital Circuit Error Performance

	% Error Free Seconds	Error Seconds in 8 hour day
CCITT Recommendation G.821 for 64 Kbps Service	98.8	346
British Telecom 64 Kbps Kilostream/Megastream Goal	99.5	144

Table 6-4. Bit Errors in a 30 Minute Period

Data Rate	Error Rate	
(Kbps)	10^{-6}	10^{-3}
64	116	115,200
48	87	86,400
9.6	18	17,280
4.8	9	8,640
2.4	5	4,320

Line Monitor

The original intention of vendors that manufacture line monitors was to provide the operator with a visual picture of line activity, including data and control characters. Over the last decade, many vendors have added a variety of network hardware diagnostic testing features to their line monitors, with breakout box, pattern generator, and BERT and BLERT capability now built into most line monitors. Although a protocol analyzer also provides line monitoring capability and many additional built-in testing features, its data decoding and trapping capabilities, discussed in more detail later in this chapter, usually set it apart from a line monitor.

The major features associated with line monitors are the sources of data that they can monitor and their data selection capability, display control, and interface. Originally, line monitors simply displayed line activity in real time. As data transmission rates increased, operators found it difficult and, in many instances, impossible to examine the line activity as it occurred. This resulted in many manufacturers adding a recording capability to their products. The key benefit of including tape or disk storage was the operators' ability to record line activity to storage. Then operators could play back the recorded data at a lower speed, which increases their ability to visually examine the flow of data traffic that previously occurred on the line.

A second benefit from recording line activity is the operators' ability to forward a tape or disk to another location. This ability enables operators to mail a disk or tape containing recorded line activity to another person for analysis and help.

The data selection capability of a line monitor is based on its code, number of data and stop bits, parity, format, and synchronization character selection capability. Although almost all line monitors permit the operator to select from such codes as ASCII, EBCDIC, and BAUDOT, other line monitors permit the operator also to select EBCD, IPARS, XS-3, and other codes that are not commonly used in transmission systems. Bit selection capability for data ranges from 5 to 8, whereas the stop length element for an asynchronous character can be set to 1, 1.5, or 2 bit elements on most monitors. These two selection parameters, with a parity selection parameter, enable the operator to correctly display asynchronous data.

Common line monitor format selection capability includes asynchronous, synchronous, bit oriented protocol, and bit oriented protocol nonreturn to zero inverted. By selecting an appropriate data format, the operator can select the required asynchronous parameters or the synchronization characters for synchronous data so that the monitor displays data in its correct format.

Recently, some monitors have been introduced with an automatic set-up capability. Monitors with this feature are connected to the line and adjust themselves to correctly display the data being monitored.

The display control of line monitors can include single- or dual-line data presentation and character suppression capability. When the data display is set to a single-line mode of operation, DTE and DCE data traffic are displayed alternately on the same line. In this mode of operation, DCE traffic is underlined for visual identification by the operator.

Because it is essential to maintain a time correlation between DTE and DCE on a full-duplex circuit, most line monitors include a dual-line display capability that enables both sides of a full-duplex line to be displayed in real time. Borrowing the technique used in a single-line mode of operation, the dual-line display mode also underlines DCE data to give the operator an easy way to identify DTE and DCE data sources.

Figure 6-11 illustrates five display settings available on the Digilog 800 protocol analyzer, which can also function as a line monitor. In the full-duplex expanded (FDX) display mode transmit and receive, data are displayed on alternate lines with receive data underlined and spaces used to separate characters. In the FDX compressed display mode, data are displayed without spaces, with transmit and receive data displayed on alternate lines, and received data underlined.

When the display mode of the Digilog 800 is placed in half-duplex (HDX) mode, transmit and receive characters alternate on the same line, with receive characters underlined. The last two display modes of the Digilog 800, SEND and RECEIVE, as their names imply, cause only transmitted data or received data to be displayed.

In examining the two top and two bottom display modes illustrated in Figure 6-11, note that several characters are represented by a pair of small superscript and subscript characters, such as ^C_R and ^L_F. The Digilog 800 and most other line monitors and protocol analyzers use this display technique to denote control characters, which are normally nonprintable characters that are not displayed on conventional terminals and personal computer monitors.

Table 6-5 illustrates how ASCII control characters appear on the Digilog 800 and most other protocol analyzers and line monitors. In comparing Table 6-5 and Figure 6-12, note that the sequence $^C_R{}^L_F$ in Table 6-5 denotes the occurrence of a carriage return character followed by a line feed character.

Table 6-5. ASCII Control Character Display

Control Character	Meaning	Monitor Display	Control Character	Meaning	Monitor Display
NUL	Null	N_U	DEL	Delete	D_L
SOH	Start of Header	S_H	DC1	Device Control 1	D_1
STX	Start of Text	S_X	DC2	Device Control 2	D_2
ETX	End of Text	E_X	DC3	Device Control 3	D_3
EOT	End of Transmission	E_T	DC4	Device Control 4	D_4
ACK	Acknowledgment	A_K	NAK	Negative Acknowledgment	N_K
BEL	Bell	B_L	SYN	Synchronization	S_Y
BS	Backspace	B_S	ETB	End of Transmission Block	E_B
HT	Horizontal Tab	H_T	CAN	Cancel	C_A
LF	Line Feed	L_F	EM	End of Medium	E_M
VT	Vertical Tab	V_T	SUB	Substitute	S_U
FF	Form Feed	F_F	ESC	Escape	E_C
CR	Carriage Return	C_R	FS	File Separator	F_S
SO	Shift Out	S_O	GS	Group Separator	G_S
SI	Shift In	S_I	RS	Record Separator	R_S
			US	Unit Separator	U_S

Some monitors permit the operator to suppress from being displayed one or more defined control characters or all control characters, such suppression being used to enhance the operator's ability to read the data traffic. Other monitors may include both control character and data character suppression capability, with the latter providing operators with a method to focus their attention on the control character flow by suppressing data traffic.

The visual display by line monitors of data and control character traffic makes this device indispensable in a technical control center. Here, the line monitor is normally connected to a patch panel. To visually observe the data flow, a technician in the technical control center patches a potential problem circuit to the monitor.

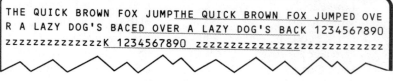

```
T H E    Q U I C K    B R O W N    F O X    J U M P E D
T H E    Q U I C K    B R O W N    F O X    J U M P E D
O V E R    A    L A Z Y    D O G ' S    B A C K    1 2 3 4
O V E R    A    L A Z Y    D O G ' S    B A C K    1 2 3 4
5 6 7 8 9 0         T H E    Q U I C K    B R O W N    F O
5 6 7 8 9 0   CᵣCᵣLꜰ T H E    Q U I C K    B R O W N    F O
```

A. *FDX expanded.*

```
THE QUICK BROWN FOX JUMPED OVER A LAZY DOG'S BACK 1234
THE QUICK BROWN FOX JUMPED OVER A LAZY DOG'S BACK 1234
567890Cᵣ Cᵣ Lꜰ ZZZZZZZZZZZZZZZZZZZZZZZZZZZZZZZZZZZZZZZZZZZZ
567890Cᵣ Cᵣ Lꜰ ZZZZZZZZZZZZZZZZZZZZZZZZZZZZZZZZZZZZZZZZZZZZ
ZZZZZZZZZZZZZZZZZZZZZZZZZZZZZZZZZZZZZZZZZZZZZZZZZZZZZZ
```

B. *FDX compressed.*

```
THE QUICK BROWN FOX JUMPTHE QUICK BROWN FOX JUMPED OVE
R A LAZY DOG'S BACED OVER A LAZY DOG'S BACK 1234567890
ZZZZZZZZZZZZZZK 1234567890 ZZZZZZZZZZZZZZZZZZZZZZZZZZZZ
```

C. *HDX.*

Figure 6-11. Digilog 800

Protocol Analyzer

A protocol analyzer is designed to both monitor and test data communications lines. Also known as a data communications analyzer and data test set, this device is more sophisticated than a line monitor. Normally, the protocol analyzer includes BERT and BLERT test capability, EFS test capability, data trapping, decoding and monitoring capability, and the capability of performing many breakout box functions.

Protocol analyzers interact in one of two modes—monitor or simulate—with a communications system under test. In the monitor mode, the protocol analyzer functions as a passive device, but the data link remains in service. Triggering or trapping capability permits specified sequences of data, control characters, bit patterns, or interface leads to initiate predefined activities. These predefined activities can include displaying information on the monitor, recording data to tape or disk, incrementing or decrementing counters, or doing computations and logging their results. By using the protocol analyzer in a monitor mode, many parameters affecting network performance may be measurable. Examples of measurable parameters could include count measurements of polls, data and protocol characters, and the time duration of predefined activities.

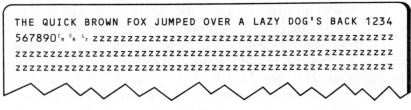

D. *SEND.*

E. *RECEIVE.*

display modes.

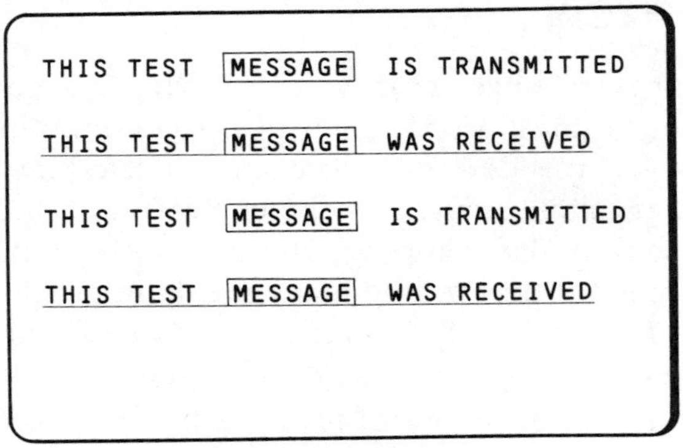

Figure 6-12. Assigning the string MESSAGE to a trap.

Traps and Triggers

A trap or trigger is a user-defined sequence of characters or bits to be matched. Normally, the occurrence of a trap is used to perform such operations as starting or stopping data capture, starting or stopping a timer, incrementing or decrementing a counter, or operating an alarm (audio buzzer). The decoding capability of a monitor refers to how it displays control characters in a character oriented protocol and bit oriented protocol (BOP) data.

Figure 6-12 (shown previously) illustrates a general example of a trap where an occurrence of the string MESSAGE is searched for on either side of the line being monitored. If the string MESSAGE is assigned to a trap, it is recognized whenever it appears in a message.

Figure 6-13 illustrates the Trap Menu on the Digilog 300 protocol analyzer. The options that can be selected for each of the Trap Menu fields are listed and described in Table 6-6. To understand the versatility and utilization of protocol analyzers, we examine how the Digilog 300 Trap Menu can be set to trap predefined data elements and how the resulting trap can be associated with a counter to provide information about the number of times data that matches the trap was encountered.

The Digilog 300 keyboard contains two pairs of keys that can be used to simplify the construction of traps. The first pair of keys, Tab FWD and Tab REV, can be used for rapid positioning of the cursor over the option area for each field. The second pair of keys, FLD SEL FWD (field select forward) and FLD SEL REV (field select reverse), can be used to cycle through the various selection options available for each field. As an example of the use of these keys, consider the "Search" field for Trap 1. By pressing the FLD SEL FWD key after the cursor is positioned on that

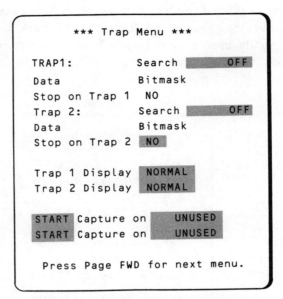

Figure 6-13. Digilog 300 Trap Menu.

field, the options OFF, SEND, RECEIVE, and BOTH would appear in sequence to correspond to each press of the SEL FWD key.

Table 6-6. Digilog 300 Trap Menu Options

Field	Options	Remark
Search	OFF, SEND, RECEIVE, BOTH	Side(s) of line to be searched.
Data	(user-entered)	Up to 8 characters to search for. Don't care entered as X_X.
Bitmask	(user-entered)	1,0 or don't care (X_X).
Stop on Trap	NO, YES	Whether to stop on trap.
Display	NORMAL, REVERSE	How data is to appear in display buffer.
Capture On:		
Leading	START, STOP	Whether to start or stop capturing data on a trap.
Trailing	UNUSED, TRAP1, TRAP2,	When to take action in leading field.

Figure 6-14 illustrates the setup of the Digilog 300 Trap Menu if the operator of that device wants to trap the data sequence "01/033" on the receive side of the line. This protocol analyzer permits users to specify up to 8 data characters or an 8-bit bitmask for a trap, with the bitmask normally used to specify a bit-oriented protocol string, which may be easier to define than trying to determine the data character that has the same bit composition.

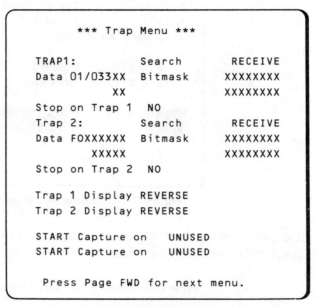

```
            *** Trap Menu ***

TRAP1:          Search       RECEIVE
Data 01/033XX   Bitmask      XXXXXXXX
           XX                XXXXXXXX
Stop on Trap 1  NO
Trap 2:         Search       RECEIVE
Data FOXXXXXX   Bitmask      XXXXXXXX
        XXXXX                XXXXXXXX
Stop on Trap 2  NO

Trap 1 Display  REVERSE
Trap 2 Display  REVERSE

START Capture on    UNUSED
START Capture on    UNUSED

Press Page FWD for next menu.
```

Figure 6-14. Digilog 300 Trap Menu setup.

The double row of X's for the last two character positions in the data field of trap 1 and all eight positions of the bitmask show "don't care" conditions. Normally, don't cares are displayed as ^x_x on the screen. However, when the screen is printed, they appear as a double row of X's.

As shown from the setup of the Trap Menu in Figure 6-14, the Digilog 300 displays in reverse video the data sequence 01/033 when encountered. Because operators might want to simply leave the protocol analyzer attached to the line while they do other things, they could set

The Stop on Trap 1 field to YES to halt the display when the first occurrence of the data to be trapped occurs on the receive side of the line.

Set the START Capture on field to Trap 1 to record the data flow after the first trap is encountered, or associate the trap with a counter if they want to determine how many times the specified sequence 01/033 occurred.

Figure 6-15 illustrates the Digilog 300 protocol analyzer Counter/ Timer Menu after Trap 1 is assigned to Counter 1 and the device is placed in its trap mode of operation for a period of time. When the operator interrupts the trapping operation and examines the Counter/Timer Menu, he or she observes that Trap 1 occurred six times. This shows that the data sequence 01/033 was encountered six times on the receive side of the line.

```
+--------------------------------------------+
|        *** Counter/Timer Menu ***          |
|                                            |
|    Counter 1       TRAP1            6       |
|    Counter 2       TRAP2            0       |
|    Counter 3       OFF             0       |
|    Counter 4       OFF             0       |
|     Reset Counters at RUN         YES      |
|                                            |
|   Time Counter 1 to 2  ON        00mS      |
|   Time Counter 2 to 1  ON        00mS      |
|   Time Counter 1 to 2 OFF        00mS      |
|                                            |
|    Press Page FWD for next menu.           |
+--------------------------------------------+
```

Figure 6-15. Associating traps to counters.

In the preceding trapping example, suppose that the line being monitored is the statistics port of a port selector, which generates connect and cross-connect data messages as users access resources through the device. Some port selectors are constructed with a shelf-port numbering system, such that 01/033 references port 33 on shelf 1. Thus, trapping the sequence 01/033 when the protocol analyzer is monitoring the statistics port of the port selector provides the operator with information about the number of times network users accessed that port during the monitoring period. In fact, by setting appropriate traps for connect and disconnect activity, the protocol analyzer could be used to measure the duration of time users accessed a particular port. Thus, many protocol analyzers can be used to develop statistics about network performance, as well as to observe the data flow on a circuit.

Simulation

In the simulate mode of operation, a protocol analyzer can be used to simulate the activity of a DTE, such as a computer port or terminal device. Figure 6-16 illustrates the insertion of a protocol analyzer between a modem and a control unit to isolate a problem with one of the terminals attached to the control unit.

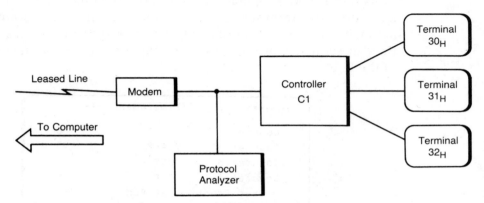

Figure 6-16. Cluster controller system test.

Suppose that the operator using the terminal, which has an address of Hex 30, reports that on entering a screen of data and pressing the Enter key, the terminal "froze." The terminal's inaction could be due to a failure in the terminal; a failure in the controller to which the terminal is connected; or a failure of the modem, leased line, or computer to which the controller is connected.

If the other terminals connected to the controller are operating correctly, the leased line from the controller to the computer and the modems on the line can be eliminated as possible culprits. By inserting a protocol analyzer with simulation capability between the modem and the controller, a polling sequence to the terminal that appeared to fail can be generated. Then, the response to the poll can be examined to shed additional information on the cause of the failure.

If the terminal fails to respond, the controller is possibly causing the problem. To verify this, a line monitor could be attached between the controller and the terminal, which has an address of Hex 30, or the protocol analyzer could be relocated to a position between the controller and the terminal that appeared to fail. If a line monitor is used, the polling flow through the controller can be observed to include the response or lack of response by the terminal. If the simulated poll does not pass through the controller, the controller obviously is the culprit. If the poll passes through the controller and the terminal fails to respond to the poll, a terminal failure is suspect as the cause of the problem.

If a line monitor is not available, the protocol analyzer could be relocated between the controller and the terminal and used to simulate a poll to terminal Hex 30 in the format that the controller uses to poll terminals. By examining the response of the terminal to the simulated poll, the operable condition of the terminal can be determined and corrective action taken to alleviate what the operator considers to be a terminal problem.

Programmability

Some protocol analyzers include a capability that operators use to program the device in "near-BASIC" language. Many vendors marketing equipment with this capability also offer an optional set of library programs that can be obtained for testing, troubleshooting, and capacity planning purposes. To better understand the utility of using a protocol analyzer programming language, we investigate the Digilog Command Language (DCL), which is included as a standard feature in that vendor's series of protocol analyzers.

The Digilog Command Language is very similar to BASIC, including constants, variables, relational operators, expressions, and Boolean logic operators. As an example of some simple DCL statements, consider the following.

```
IF TIMER 1>100, THEN GOTO 10
IF TIMER 1>50 AND CTS=HIGH GOTO 10
```

In the first example, a branch to line 10 occurs if the value of TIMER 1 exceeds 100. In the second example, the branch occurs only if the value of TIMER 1 exceeds 50 and the clear to send (CTS) signal is HIGH.

DCL programs are created by the operator pressing one of two keys to select an instruction (Tab Fwd), then selecting the appropriate parameters (Field Select) from a list of possible values. Only when a trap value, bitmask, or line number branch is required does the operator have to access other keys.

Table 6-7 lists the instructions and the definition of each instruction in the Digilog Command Language.

To obtain an appreciation of the versatility of this language, we next examine several instructions in detail.

Figure 6-17 illustrates the syntax of the DCL COUNTER instruction, which has a mnemonic of CNTR. When the operator places the protocol analyzer in its program mode of operation, the Tab Fwd key is used to cycle through mnemonics of instructions until the CNTR instruction is accessed. Next, the operator uses the FLD SEL (field select) key to select the counter to be set (1 through 6 or ALL) and the setting (INCREMENT, DECREMENT, or RESET).

Table 6-7. Digilog Command Language Instructions

Instruction	Definition
ALARM	Controls the audible alarm.
CALL	Invokes a subroutine.
CAPTURE	Stores specified data in the capture buffer.
COUNTER	Increments, decrements, or resets specified counters or all counters.
CRC	Allows CRC marks to be entered or deleted in messages or string variables.
DEFINE	Defines a string variable.
DISPLAY	Allows an integer or string expression to be displayed anywhere in the upper 16 rows of the Remark page.
EXECUTE	Calls another program with option setup, message, and/or miscellaneous menu.
FRAME	Builds or decodes Level 2 messages.
GOTO	Jumps to a specified line number.
IF	Jumps to a specified line number if a conditional test is met.
INPUT	Displays the specified prompt to show that program is waiting for keyboard input.
LET	Assigns a value to an integer variable.
LEVEL3	Builds or decodes Level 3 messages.
LOOP	Executes a designated set of instructions a specified number of times.
PLOT	Allows display of statistics in graphic or numerical format.
PRESERVE	Retains values of one or more specified variables. Can be used to transfer variable values to another program when using EXECUTE.
PRINT	Prints data to CRT or printer.
RECEIVE	Receives data from the data comm line without trapping.
RECORD	Starts/stops recording of data.
REPLACE	Replaces characters in message or string.
RETURN	Ends a subroutine.
SEND	Transmits a specified message to the data comm line.
SET	Sets three signals (C1, C2, C3) HIGH or LOW.
STOP	Stops program execution and data capture.
TIMER	Starts, stops, or resets value of specified timers or all timers.
WAITFOR	Suspends program execution until trap or timeout occurs.

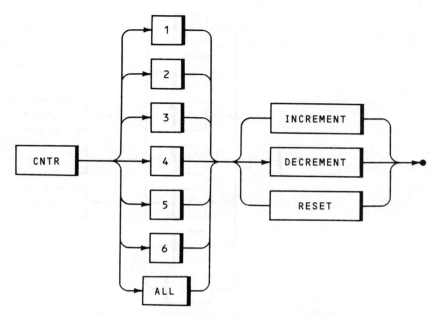

Figure 6-17. The COUNTER instruction, mnemonic: CNTR.
(drawing courtesy of Digilog, Inc.)

Three examples of DCL statements using the COUNTER instruction follow.

```
CNTR ALL RESET
CNTR 2 INCREMENT
CNTR 6 DECREMENT
```

In the first example, all counters are reset when the program line is executed. In the second example, counter 2 is incremented by one when the line containing the statement is executed. Execution of the third example results in the decrement of counter 6 by one.

Figure 6-18 illustrates the syntax of the TIMER instruction, which is similar to the CNTR instruction. As with the previously discussed method for setting the counter field values, the operator first uses the Tab Fwd key to select the TIMER instruction, then uses the Field Select key to select the appropriate values for each of the two timer fields associated with the instruction.

Two examples of statements using the DCL TIMER instruction are listed below.

```
TIMER 5 START
TIMER 1 STOP
```

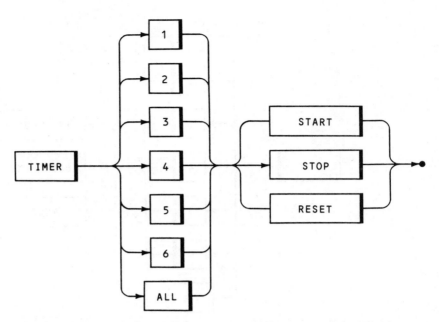

Figure 6-18. The TIMER instruction, mnemonic: TIMER.
(drawing courtesy of Digilog, Inc.)

In the first example, TIMER number 5 starts operating when the program line containing the instruction is executed. In the second example, TIMER 1 stops when the program line containing that instruction is executed.

The RECEIVE instruction illustrated in Figure 6-19 is slightly more complex than the two previously discussed instructions. This instruction is used to obtain data from the communications line without trapping. As shown in Figure 6-19, the operator can enter values for seven fields to complete this instruction. GOOD and BAD refer to messages or characters received with correct parity or in error. By setting appropriate field values, the operator can check a message or, on an individual character basis, either side or both sides of the line and cause the statement to branch to a specific line in the program if a timeout occurs, or the operator can ignore timing out and receive data on a continuous basis. Thus, the DCL statement:

```
RECEIVE ANY MESSAGE ON EITHER SIDE OF THE LINE AND DON'T TIMEOUT
```

would cause the protocol analyzer to continuously gather data from the send and receive buffers whenever the statement is executed.

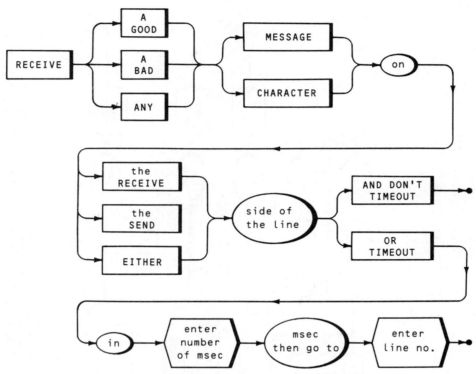

Figure 6-19. The RECEIVE instruction, mnemonic: RECEIVE.
(drawing courtesy of Digilog, Inc.)

Perhaps the most comprehensive instruction in the DCL language is its IF instruction. This instruction can be used to compare one of ten defined functions to one or more conditions, permitting program branches to be effected based on predefined conditions occurring. Figure 6-20 illustrates the general syntax of the DCL IF instruction, with the letters that appear inside circles denoting a continuation reference for a portion of the syntax.

Figure 6-21 illustrates a continuation of the IF instruction for the LEAD, COUNTER, and TIMER comparisons used in the instruction. As an example of the use of Figures 6-20 and 6-21, let us examine using the IF instruction to compare a protocol analyzer counter to a specific value.

From Figure 6-20, the operator first selects the IF statement, then uses the Field Select key to select COUNTER as the value of the first field in the instruction. Selecting COUNTER dictates that the syntax construction follows the rules specified under B on Figure 6-20. Turning to Figure 6-21, under the B continuation syntax, the operator would first select one of six counters. Next, the operator would select a rational operator

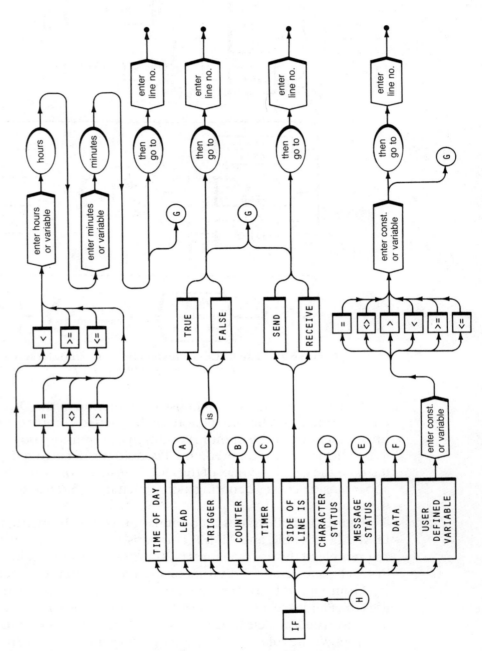

Figure 6-20. The IF instruction, mnemonic: IF.
(drawing courtesy of Digilog, Inc.)

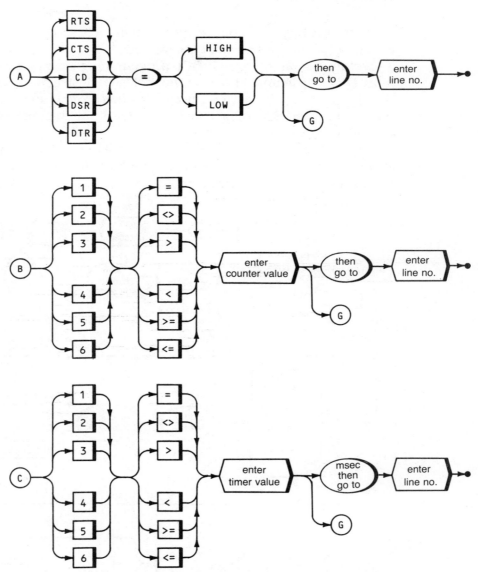

Figure 6-21. The IF instruction (continued).
(drawing courtesy of Digilog, Inc.)

and enter the counter value with which the counter is to be compared and the line number the program should branch to when the operation becomes true. An example of the DCL IF statement using the counter field follows.

```
IF CNTR 3 = 60 GOTO 30
```

In the previous example, the program branches to line 30 if counter 3 equals 60 when the statement is executed.

Before examining several DCL programming examples, look at one more DCL instruction, known as the WAITFOR instruction. This instruction is very versatile because it enables the programmer to construct traps or to have the program wait a period of time before executing the instruction on a referenced line.

Figure 6-22 illustrates a portion of the WAITFOR instruction. Only a small portion of the WAITFOR instruction's capability is used for illustrative purposes.

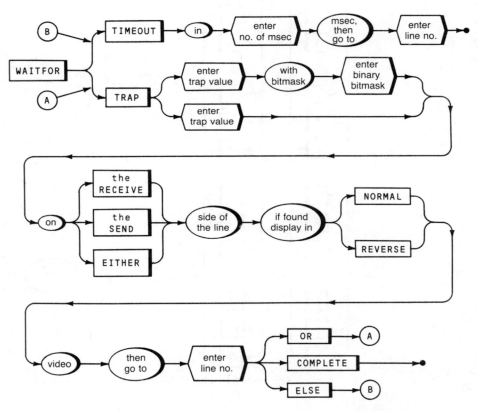

Figure 6-22. WAITFOR Instruction, mnemonic: WAITFOR.
(drawing courtesy of Digilog, Inc.)

As an example of the use of this instruction, consider the following program line.

```
WAITFOR TRAP 'LOGON' ON SEND
side of the line
IF found display in REVERSE
then goto 30 (end)
```

The preceding instruction causes the protocol analyzer to examine the SEND side of the line for the character string LOGON. When this string is encountered, the program displays it in reverse video and branches to line 30. At line 30, the programmer might have a statement to turn on an alarm, initiate the logging of data to disk, or perform some other operation.

To obtain an appreciation of the capability of the Digilog Command Language, examine a few programs constructed to do predefined operations.

Suppose that we desire to count the number of messages and the number of CRC errors within a one-hour period. To do so, we could construct the following program.

```
 1  CNTR ALL RESET
 2  TIMER 1 START
 3  IF TIMER 1 = 60000 MS THEN GOTO 10
 4  RECEIVE ANY MESSAGE ON EITHER SIDE OF THE LINE AND DON'T TIMEOUT
 5  IF MESSAGE STATUS CRC ERROR THEN GOTO 8
 6  CNTR 1 INCREMENT
 7  GOTO 3
 8  CNTR 2 INCREMENT
 9  GOTO 3
10  TIMER 1 RESET
11  CNTR 3 INCREMENT
12  IF CNTR 3 = 60 THEN GOTO 14
13  GOTO 2
14  STOP
```

In this program, CNTR 1 is used to contain the number of good messages, CNTR 2 contains the number of CRC errors, and CNTR 3 is the minute counter for program routine computations.

Line 1 causes all counters to be reset, and line 2 starts the operation of TIMER 1. Because older versions of Digilog protocol analyzers could compute time only in milliseconds (ms), the program must convert milliseconds to minutes and develop a minute counter that can be compared to 60. To accomplish this task, line 3 compares TIMER 1 to 60000 ms and causes a branch to line 10 when the timer reaches a value of 60000. At line 10, TIMER 1 is reset to zero. Next, CNTR 3 is incremented by 1 in line

11 and its value compared to 60 in line 12. If 60 minutes is reached, the program branches to line 14 and ends execution. Otherwise, line 13 is executed, resulting in a branch back to line 2 where TIMER 1 again starts counting in milliseconds.

Until TIMER 1 reaches a value of 60000 ms, line 4 causes data on both sides of the line to be received. Line 5 compares the message status to a CRC error condition and, if a CRC error occurred in the received message, causes a branch to line 8. If a CRC error occurred, line 8 causes CNTR 2 to be incremented, and line 9 results in the program branching back to line 3. If the message status does not show that a CRC error occurred, line 6 is executed, causing CNTR 1 to be incremented. This counter, in effect, counts the number of good messages, whereas CNTR 2 counts the number of bad messages or CRC errors.

As a second example of the DCL's use, consider a need to count the number of occurrences of a particular string. This requirement could be satisfied by the following program.

```
1 CNTR ALL RESET
2 WAITFOR TRAP '02/017' on EITHER
  side of the line ,
  if found display in REVERSE ,
  then goto 3 (end)
3 ALARM ON for 150 msec
4 CNTR 1 INCREMENT
5 GOTO 2
<EOF>
```

The preceding example results in the statistics port of a port selector being searched to determine how many users obtained access to shelf 2, port 17, on the port selector during the time the program was executing. In this program, the WAITFOR instruction is used to trap the string 02/017 on EITHER side of the line. When this string is encountered, it is displayed in reverse video and a branch to line 3 occurs, which causes an audio alarm to sound for 150 milliseconds. Next, line 4 increments CNTR 1, and the program branches back to line 2 where it waits for another occurrence of the string 02/017 to occur.

PC Based Protocol Analyzers

An alternative to conventional protocol analyzers are adapter cards and software designed to convert an IBM PC or compatible personal computer into a sophisticated communications test system.

Figure 6-23 illustrates the Frederick Engineering FELINE adapter board which can be inserted into an IBM PC, XT, AT, or compatible personal computers to obtain a protocol analyzer capability.

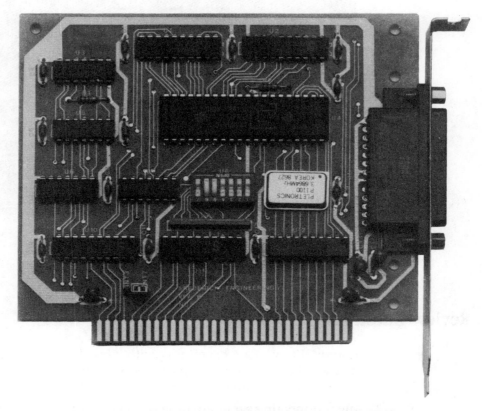

Figure 6-23. Frederick Engineering FELINE adapter board.
(photograph courtesy of Frederick Engineering.)

Because the port on the adapter board uses TTL logic, it must be cabled to a special Frederick Engineering-supplied breakout box, illustrated in Figure 6-24. This breakout box is called the FELINE pod and provides the interface between DTE and DCE.

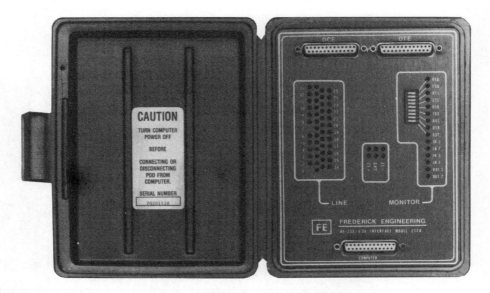

Figure 6-24. Frederick Engineering FELINE pod.
(photograph courtesy of Frederick Engineering.)

Review Questions

1. Assume that you are examining with a breakout box the connector on a serial printer. When the printer is on, pins 5 and 6 show a high voltage. Is the printer a DTE or DCE?

2. After connecting a modem to a computer port, you note that the carrier is not dropping after you enter BYE. You believe the problem is the failure of the computer port to drop DTR. Explain how you could use a breakout box to test your belief.

3. Assume you have a terminal at a remote location that is directly cabled to a multiplexer, as illustrated in Figure 6-25.

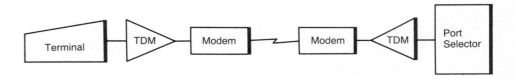

Figure 6-25. Dedicated terminal connection.

If the multiplexer passes the terminal's DTR signal and the port selector operates as a ring start (RI signal) system, how could you use a breakout box to determine the special conductor cabling required between the multiplexer and the port selector?

4. If a bit error rate test at 2.4 Kbps for a duration of 10 seconds results in 4 errors, what is the approximate bit error rate?

5. Under what conditions should you transmit framed data during a BERT?

6. Assume that you are monitoring bisynchronous data using a Digilog 300 test set. How would you use the Trap and Counter Menus illustrated in Figures 6-5 and 6-7 to count the number of NAKs on the line?

7. Assume that your data line monitor has a trigger capability that can be set high or low by a predefined control signal. Assume also that a trigger activation can be assigned to counters and timers. How can you use a data line monitor to count the number of calls and the total call duration?

8. Assume that a port selector generates the sequence XX/YYY SS XX/YYY L_F C_R on the statistics port whenever a connect is attempted. The first XX/YYY denotes the shelf (XX) and port (YYY) on the input, whereas the second sequence of XX/YYY denotes the output destination. If SS is a status code such that

CF = Forced Connect

DF = Forced Disconnect

Write a program in the Digilog Command Language to count CFs and DFs.

Chapter 7

Integral Diagnostic Testing

T HE COMPLEXITY OF COMMUNICATIONS NETWORKS often requires the utilization of expensive diagnostic equipment to isolate the cause of a transmission impairment. Fortunately, many vendors have added to their communications products a variety of testing capabilities that can be used to check the operational state of their equipment. In this chapter, we examine the built-in diagnostic testing capability of modems and multiplexers, focusing attention on how this capability can be used to isolate many network problems without requiring the use of standalone testing equipment. We also look at how the isolation of other problems can be accomplished with low-cost bit error rate testers, modem test sets, or block error rate testers.

Modems

The common type of diagnostic test built into most modems is a self-test. This test is designed to identify faults in the modem's internal circuits and in the components mounted on circuit boards. When a self-test is initiated, the modem disconnects itself from the communications line and ties its transmitter to its receiver, as illustrated in Figure 7-1A. A pattern generator in the modem produces a predefined sequence of bits that are looped through the modem and examined by a pattern comparator, which compares the received data bit stream to the bit stream that the pattern generator generated. If the received bit sequence matches the sequence that the pattern comparator expects, the modem is assumed to be operating correctly. Otherwise, a fault is assumed to have occurred in the modem. This condition usually is shown by the comparator circuitry illuminating a light-emitting diode indicator located next to an error label on the modem's front panel. Many multiport modem vendors permit users to initiate self-tests on an individual port basis, as illustrated in Figure 7-1B.

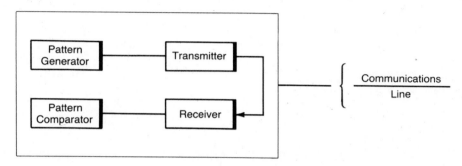

A. *Operation.*

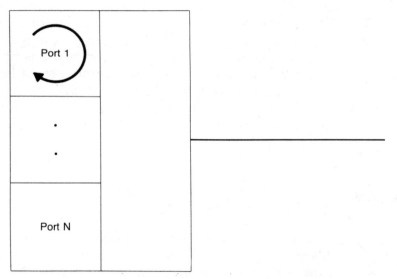

B. *Use with multiport modem.*

Figure 7-1. Modem self-test.

Initiating a specific port self-test permits the user to inhibit data transmission on just one of many ports on the multiport modem, whereas a self-test conducted on the complete modem affects the data being transmitted on each port.

Loopback Tests

Compared with a self-test that is restricted to verifying the correct operation of the internal circuitry of a modem, a series of loopback tests can be employed to check the operation of attached DTEs and the line connecting two modems.

Modems can perform four types of loopback tests. Figure 7-2 illustrates the relative position of the loopback based on the type of test initiated.

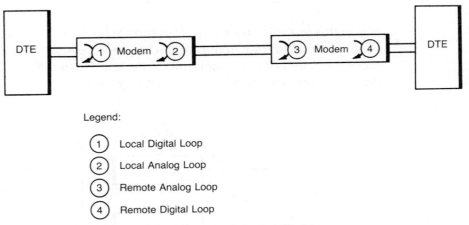

Legend:

(1)   Local Digital Loop

(2)   Local Analog Loop

(3)   Remote Analog Loop

(4)   Remote Digital Loop

Figure 7-2. Modem loopbacks.

The local digital loop test tests the operation of the DTE to determine whether data is leaving the terminal or computer port. When this test is initiated, the transmitter of the local modem is tied to its receiver, and the input from a connected DTE is tied to the receive data output of the DTE. In effect, a digital local loop results in the establishment of two loops because the modulator and demodulator of the modem are tied together also, as illustrated in Figure 7-3.

When a modem is placed in local digital loop mode, data characters transmitted by the attached DTE are echoed without modulation occurring. Thus, this test can be used to check the operation of the local DTE and the cable connecting the DTE to the modem. Because this test bypasses the pattern generator of the modem, an external test device or the DTE must be used to verify the continuity of the cable or correct operation of the DTE.

The local analog loop test checks the digital and analog circuits of the local modem to determine whether they are in working condition.

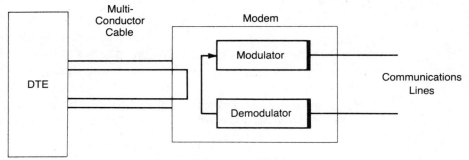

Figure 7-3. Digital loop test.

When this test is initiated, two loops are established, which results in the modem's transmitter being looped to its receiver while the send and receive circuits of the communications line are tied together. Figure 7-4 illustrates the data flow during an analog loop test.

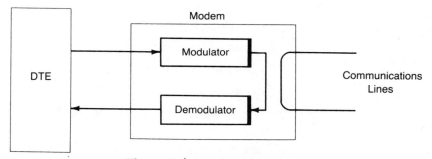

Figure 7-4. Analog loop test.

During an analog loop test, an external device must be connected to the modem to monitor errors. Users could type on the keyboard of a terminal and monitor the echoed response, or they could use a BERT, BLERT, or modem test set to transmit a digital pattern to the modem. This pattern is modulated, demodulated, and routed back to the tester where the test device compares the received data to the transmitted data and displays the number of bit or block errors or the error rate. Because an error on an analog loop test could result from a modem failure or a problem with the cable connecting the DTE to the modem, the user normally combines a digital test with the analog test in an attempt to isolate a problem to a local modem or cable.

As illustrated in Figure 7-2, a remote analog loop test, as its name implies, is done at the remote modem. When this test is initiated, the transmitter of the modem is tied to its receiver, resulting in the bypass of the modulation and demodulation circuits of the remote modem. Because the remote analog loop is equivalent to looping back the circuit, this loop permits a user to test both the local modem and the line.

If a remote analog loop test, using a test set or terminal device, shows the presence of transmission errors, the test itself only suggests that the local modem or transmission line is causing the errors. To more precisely isolate the cause of the transmission impairment, a local analog test should be done. Then, if no errors occur, the circuit is the most probable cause of the transmission impairment.

The remote digital loopback test can be used to check the operation of both modems and the line between the modems. Then, when the result of this loopback test is compared with the result of other modem loopbacks, the operator can isolate a problem to either modem or the circuit between the two modems.

The remote digital loop test results in the remote modem tying its demodulator to its modulator. This causes the analog signal received by the remote modem to be demodulated, then remodulated.

If a remote analog loop is successful but a remote digital loop results in transmission errors, the remote modem's modulator or demodulator probably is the cause of the problem. To verify this, the remote modem could be placed in a self-test mode or in a local analog loopback. Because the pattern generator of most modems is limited to a short, fixed sequence, a self-test alone may not be sufficient to isolate an intermittent problem in a modem. Thus, if intermittent problems have been occurring, the network technician probably should place the modem in analog loopback mode and employ a bit error rate tester or modem test set to conduct a sustained test on the device.

Modem Control

Until the mid- to late-1970s, setting remote modems into a desired loopback mode required the physical presence of a person at the remote site to press a switch or button on that modem. To permit from a central facility the unattended placement of modems into different types of loopbacks, vendors developed two methods of signaling remote modems—in-band and out-band.

In in-band signaling, certain predefined coded sequences are used to place the remote modem into different modes of operation. The in-band signals flow on the same path as the data being transmitted by the modem. A microprocessor in the remote modem continuously scans the received data, examining it for in-band signals to which the modem is designed to react.

In out-band signaling, predefined coded sequences are transmitted on a secondary channel that uses a small portion of bandwidth at the edge of the channel. The frequency band used for signaling on the secondary channel is outside of the frequency band used for transmitting data, hence, it is known as out-of-band signaling or simply out-band signaling.

Because the baud rate is proportional to the bandwidth on a channel, out-band signaling occurs at a fraction of the data rate of in-band signaling, which occurs at the same rate at which the primary channel is transmitting data. Another key difference between in-band and out-band signaling is that in-band signaling interrupts the flow of data on the primary channel, whereas out-band signaling permits data to continue to flow on the primary channel because signaling flow is restricted on the secondary channel.

The differences between the two types of signaling are trivial when placing a remote modem in a loopback mode of operation. This is because once placed in a loopback, data transmission is inhibited. The differences may be more pronounced if the modem's operation is governed by a network management system that periodically sends out status check requests to local and remote modems. When in-band signaling is used, the status check requests each modem to include the modem's address and its response to the check request flow on the primary channel, which interrupts the flow of data. In comparison, when the network management system checks the status of the modems connected to that system and receives their response, the use of out-band signaling does not interfere with the flow of data on the primary channel.

CCITT V.54 Loopbacks

The CCITT promulgates a set of recommendations governing the loopback operations of modems. Known as V.54 loopbacks, the recommendations are intended for use with modems primarily manufactured for international circuits. Under the V.54 loopback recommendations, in-band signaling controls the remote looping and testing of data circuits. Figure 7-5 illustrates the four CCITT V.54 loop locations, which the reader may wish to compare with the conventional modem loopbacks illustrated in Figure 7-2.

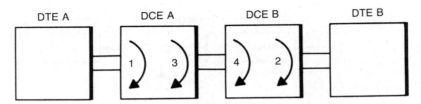

Figure 7-5. CCITT V.54 loop locations.

The V.54 loop 1 test initiates a digital loop on the local modem, connecting the modem's transmitter to its receiver (as illustrated in Figure 7-3). The V.54 loop 3 test is similar to a local analog loop test. When this test is initiated, a modem-side loop is created in the analog circuits of the modem, which connects its transmitter to its receiver. In addition, the circuit between modems is grounded to prevent any other modems on the line from receiving test data as normal data. Figure 7-6 illustrates the V.54 loop 3 test. To monitor errors during this test, an external test device is required because the pattern generator of the modem is not used.

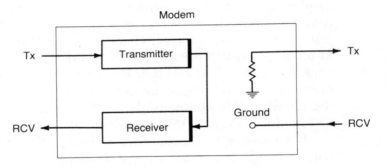

Figure 7-6. V.54 loop 3 test.

The V.54 loop 4 test is essentially the same as a remote analog loopback test (illustrated in Figure 7-4). The V.54 loop 2 test is similar to a remote digital loop test because the remote modem's transmitter is tied to its receiver. When the V.54 loop test is initiated, the remote modem is disconnected from its attached DTE, as illustrated in Figure 7-7. Errors occurring on a loop 2 test can result from the transmission line or either modem, so loop 3 and loop 4 testing results normally are required to isolate the cause of the impairment to either modem or the transmission line.

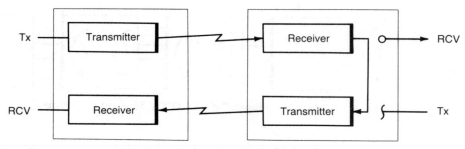

Figure 7-7. V.54 loop 2 test.

Monitoring and Indicator Capability

Many modems include line quality monitoring and interchange circuit condition observation capability. To obtain an understanding of the impairment isolation ability that line quality monitoring provides, we use the features of the Codex 2680 modem for illustrative purposes.

Figure 7-8 illustrates the front panel of a Codex 2680 modem, which has the capability of transmitting data at 19200bps and at several fallback data rates when circuit quality does not permit its primary data rate to be achieved. The control panel includes 13 indicators to permit personnel to monitor modem operations. In addition, by using three movement keys, a selection key, and four function keys, the operator can control both the local and remote modem to initiate tests, display the status of the modems, and configure the modems for a distribution of the line bandwidth among the modem's built-in ports.

The Transmit and Receive Data indicators illuminate to correspond to data activity, whereas the request to send, clear to send, data set ready, data terminal ready, and data carrier detect indicators function in a similar manner to that of most modems' display indicators. What sets this modem apart from many other modems are its receive signal quality, fallback, and network control indicators and an internal built-in eye pattern generator that can be used with an oscilloscope to evaluate telephone line performance.

The receive signal quality indicator flickers when signal quality conditions are marginal, providing the operator with a visual indicator of the circuit's capability to pass a signal between modems. For more information about the condition of the circuit, personnel can use the control panel of the modem to display data about several circuit quality monitoring system (CQMS) parameters. Table 7-1 lists six CQMS parameters that the Codex 2680 modem records and displays on operator request. Thus,

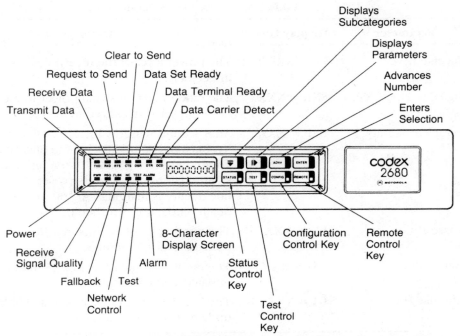

Figure 7-8. Codex 2680 modem control panel. *(reproduction with permission of Codex Corporation).*

from the front panel of the modem, the operator can note a deterioration in received signal quality. Then, from an examination of CQMS parameters, the modem operator can obtain information about six key circuit parameters that the modem monitors.

The fallback indicator automatically illuminates whenever the modem is forced to lower its data transmission rate because of marginal circuit conditions. Thus, this indicator's illumination should be followed by an examination of the modem's CQMS parameters to obtain additional information about the probable cause for the modem operating in its fallback rate.

To automate modem operations, Codex, like several other modem manufacturers, markets network control systems. Several of these systems can be used to interface the firm's 2600 series modems to include the 2680. Using software and hardware sold by Codex, an IBM PC AT or compatible personal computer can be used to control up to several hundred modems from a central site. When a 2680 modem is connected to a Codex network control system, the Network Control indicator on the front panel of the modem illuminates.

Table 7-1. Codex CQMS Parameters

Parameter	Display Form	Description
Receive Level	RL = XXDB	The power level of the received signal is displayed in decibels.
Signal to Noise Ratio	SNR = XXX	The ratio of analog signal power to received analog noise power is displayed in decibels.
Error Probability	ERP = XXX	An 8-second window measure of average line quality. Between 0 and 30, the line quality is considered good; between 30 and 70, the line quality is considered fair to marginal; between 70 and 100, the line quality is marginal. At 100, the receive signal quality indicator is turned off.
Phase Hits	PH = XXX	The number of phase hits in a 15-minute interval, updated every 5 minutes.
Gain Hits	GH = XXX	The number of gain hits in a 15-minute interval, updated every 5 minutes.
Impulse Hits	IH = XXX	The number of impulse hits in a 15-minute interval, updated every 5 minutes.

Eye Pattern Generator

The internal eye pattern generator of the Codex 2680 modem converts equalizer digital inputs into analog voltages that can be displayed on an oscilloscope as an "eye" pattern, with the number of points that appear in the pattern based on the modem's bit and baud rate. The resulting eye pattern display permits performance of a visual analysis of distortions on the telephone line.

To understand the capability of an eye pattern generator in permitting a visual analysis of telephone line distortions, assume a 4800bps/1600 baud modem operating rate as the 8-point eye pattern. This type of modem is better for clarity of illustration than the actual eye pattern produced by high speed modems.

Figure 7-9 illustrates the effect of transmission impairments on an eye pattern for several distinct types of distortion, line hits, loss of signal, and impulse noise conditions. Note that under ideal circuit conditions, the eye pattern should appear as a series of eight distinct points, as illustrated in the lower right corner of Figure 7-9.

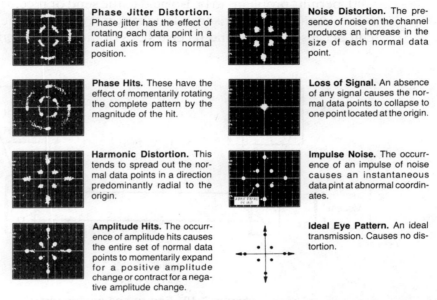

Phase Jitter Distortion. Phase jitter has the effect of rotating each data point in a radial axis from its normal position.

Noise Distortion. The presence of noise on the channel produces an increase in the size of each normal data point.

Phase Hits. These have the effect of momentarily rotating the complete pattern by the magnitude of the hit.

Loss of Signal. An absence of any signal causes the normal data points to collapse to one point located at the origin.

Harmonic Distortion. This tends to spread out the normal data points in a direction predominantly radial to the origin.

Impulse Noise. The occurrence of an impulse of noise causes an instantaneous data pint at abnormal coordinates.

Amplitude Hits. The occurrence of amplitude hits causes the entire set of normal data points to momentarily expand for a positive amplitude change or contract for a negative amplitude change.

Ideal Eye Pattern. An ideal transmission. Causes no distortion.

Figure 7-9. Effect of transmission impairments on an eye pattern.
(reproduction with permission of Codex Corporation.)

Testing Strategy

An effective testing strategy is the key for isolating the cause of most transmission impairments. To be efficacious in determining the cause of the problem, the strategy should incorporate a logical step-by-step approach that examines both the equipment and the line facilities.

One of the first, if not *the* first, tests that should be done between modems is a test for continuity. The continuity test confirms the establishment of a path between two points and can range from simply applying a test tone on the line and listening for it at the other end to using a BERT, modem test set, or BLERT to obtain a figure of merit while confirming continuity. Once continuity is verified the modem self-test feature can be invoked at each end of the transmission path to verify the operational state of those devices. Next, local and remote analog and digital loopback tests can be employed to attempt to isolate the cause of a transmission impairment. If test equipment and trained personnel located at each end of a point-to-point line are having trouble, an end-to-end analog test should be considered as a substitute for a remote analog loopback test. This is because the end-to-end test, as illustrated in Figure

7-10, permits problems to be isolated to the send or receive side of a four-wire circuit. In comparison, a loopback test examines the complete circuit because transmit and receive sides of the line are tied together.

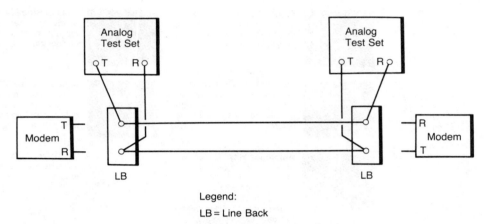

Legend:

LB = Line Back

Figure 7-10. End-to-end analog test.

Figure 7-11 illustrates the employment of an analog tester on a circuit that has been looped around.

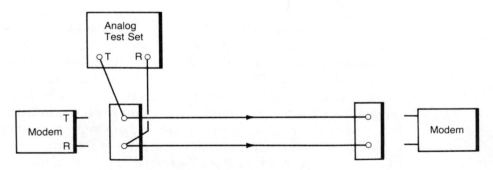

Figure 7-11. Loop around test.

If analog test equipment or the modem's analog line parameter displays show that the communications line is within acceptable limits, the next step in a testing strategy normally is to do digital testing. In digital testing, a variety of devices, including BERT, BLERT, and pattern generators, can be used because they all have the common function of generating a predefined sequence of bits and comparing the looped-back data to the data that was transmitted. Figure 7-12 illustrates the use of a BERT for local and remote loopbacks and two BERTs for doing end-to-end tests in each direction.

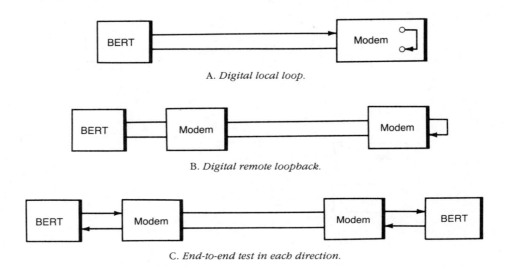

A. *Digital local loop.*

B. *Digital remote loopback.*

C. *End-to-end test in each direction.*

Figure 7-12. Digital testing methods.

When errors occur at the same point in a transmission sequence or appear to be occurring in a predictable manner, there is a high degree of probability that the software or DTE is at fault. When this situation occurs, protocol testing, including the use of a data simulator, may be warranted to verify the results of monitoring.

Figure 7-13 illustrates how protocol testing can be employed to isolate the cause of a transmission impairment. In Figure 7-13A, a monitor is used to examine the data flow between the terminal and the computer. In Figure 7-13B and C, two methods by which a protocol analyzer can be used as a data simulator are illustrated. In Figure 7-13B, the protocol analyzer was assumed to be at the terminal site and directly connected to the terminal. In Figure 7-13C, the protocol analyzer was assumed to be located at the other end of the line, distant from the terminal.

In the setup illustrated in Figures 7-13B and C, the protocol analyzer can be used in a variety of ways to correspond to the method of communications between the terminal and the computer. If the terminal is a remote batch device, the protocol analyzer can be coded to receive data blocks from the terminal, then issue negative or positive acknowledgments based on the results of a cyclic redundancy check done by the analyzer on the received data. If the terminal is an interactive device connected to the computer on a multidrop circuit, the protocol analyzer can

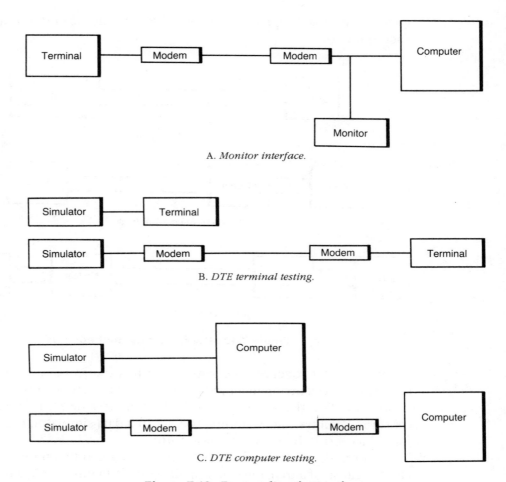

A. *Monitor interface.*

B. *DTE terminal testing.*

C. *DTE computer testing.*

Figure 7-13. Protocol testing options.

be used to simulate polls to the terminal using its line address. Then, based on the terminal response, the analyzer can select the terminal and transfer a predefined screen of information for the operator to examine.

Figure 7-13B and C illustrate how a protocol analyzer functioning as a simulator can be used also to test the computer port. In Figure 7-13B, the protocol analyzer is assumed to be colocated with the computer and is directly connected to a port on that device. Then, the protocol analyzer operator could simulate the operation of a terminal device to the computer and also observe the computer port's response to the simulated terminal, including both data and control characters. In Figure 7-13C, assume that the protocol analyzer is located at the terminal site and is used to check the response of the computer to simulated terminal traffic and to determine the operational status of the modems and leased line connecting the two locations. The operational status of the modems and leased line normally can be checked by using the BERT capability built into many protocol analyzers and by conducting the local and remote loopbacks previously discussed in this chapter.

Multiplexers

Many multiplexers include an array of monitoring features and diagnostic aids for examining the individual components of the device. These monitoring features and diagnostic aids normally are built into the multiplexer's central logic unit, composite channel adapter, and individual channel adapter cards.

Central Logic Unit

The central logic unit is the key component of modern multiplexers, governing the method employed to scan each channel adapter for data, then multiplex the data streams from individual channels into a frame that is passed to the composite adapter for transmission on a high speed line. Normally included on the central logic unit are LEDs that illuminate to show the state of power to the central logic and whether it failed a continuous test of its logic by test circuitry and generated a logic alarm. Because multiplexers normally operate in pairs, many are designed to report the status of their logic to the master unit on the line. This permits the master unit to display its status, which is called primary, and the status of the slave, which is normally called remote logic.

Table 7-2 lists the possible problems that many multiplexer central logic unit indicators can denote and the corrective actions that should be considered to alleviate these problems. One additional problem not listed in the table for both power and logic alarms is the failure of an LED to illuminate. Although rare, an LED can burn out. This possibility should be considered before taking action to replace a multiplexer component.

Table 7-2. Multiplexer Central Logic Indicators

Trouble Indicator	Problem Fault	Corrective Action
Power Indicator Off	Disruption of AC power	Check power source
	AC plug disconnected	Check AC plug is connected to power source
	Internal power supply	Replace power supply malfunctioned
Logic Alarm:		
Primary	Defective central logic	Replace defective central logic board
Remote	Defective remote central logic	Replace remote defective central logic board

Composite Channel Adapter

Installed in many multiplexers is the composite channel adapter, which is a special card that governs the interface of the device to the high speed line. Two buffers in this adapter are used to clock framed data onto the line and receive data being transmitted on the line to the multiplexer. Thus, most composite adapters include LEDs to display the state of the transmit and receive clocks.

Because the composite channel adapter is normally cabled to a modem, the adapter typically displays the state of EIA control signals, including data set ready (DSR), carrier detect (CD), clear to send (CTS), data terminal ready (DTR) and request to send (RTS). Other indicators included on many multiplexer composite adapters show the state of synchronization between multiplexers connected on a circuit (sync loss) and the detection of a transmission error between multiplexers (line error) because of the multiplexer's use of cyclic redundancy checking, which causes a previously transmitted frame to be retransmitted and the occurrence of flow control. The latter is the response of statistical multiplexers to a composite data flow into the device exceeding its capability to transmit data through the composite adapter onto the high speed line. When this situation occurs, because of the simultaneous activity of many data sources, the buffer in the multiplexer eventually overflows and data is lost. To prevent this situation from occurring, the multiplexer carries out flow control, in effect turning off the flow of data until the multiplexer can transmit the buffered data onto the high speed line thereby is emptied to a predefined level, the multiplexer turns off flow control, permitting data sources connected to the multiplexer to resume transmission.

Table 7-3 lists six commonly found indicators included on the composite channel adapter of multiplexers, a description of the problem they indicate, and corrective action one can consider implementing. In addition to the trouble indicators listed in Table 7-3, as previously mentioned, many composite channel adapters also display the state of key interchange circuits. When this capability is included in the composite adapter, the state of the physical interface between the adapter and an attached modem can be readily observed without using a breakout box.

Table 7-3. Multiplexer Composite Channel Adapter Indicators

Trouble Indicator	Problem Fault	Corrective Action
Tx CLK	Transmit clock not being supplied	Check central and remote modems, telephone line, and central logic
Rx CLK	Receive clock not being supplied	Check central and remote modems, telephone line, and central logic
Carrier Loss	Carrier detector control signal not received	Same as above
Sync Loss	High speed line malfunction or modem reequalization	Check modem and line
Line Error	Hit on high speed line resulted in error in received message	If light on for extended time, check telephone line parameters
Flow Control	Traffic increasing beyond the capacity of the multiplexer to accommodate	Check channel loading and usage

Individual Channel Adapters

The individual channel adapters of most multiplexers are manufactured as dual or quad port cards. Each of these cards is designed to provide an interface between several data sources and the internal logic of the multiplexer. The indicators on individual channel adapters can include LEDs to denote data activity on each of the ports on the adapter, key physical interface interchange circuit states, and such error conditions as a clocking or framing error for a synchronous adapter card and a received parity error for an asynchronous adapter card.

By carefully examining multiplexer indicators, many problems are easily isolated and rectified. Unfortunately, not all problems lend themselves to the simple observation of indicators. In such situations, a variety of self-tests, built-in loopback tests, or the event reporting log of some devices may be required to obtain additional information about the cause of a problem.

Loopback Tests

Both internal and external loopback tests are supported by many multiplexers. Internal loopback tests permit a predefined data pattern to be generated either on a channel basis or at the composite level on an end-to-end basis to the multiplexer at the other end of the line. At that location, the multiplexer loops back the data to the first multiplexer, where it is examined in the multiplexer's pattern comparator. If the received data matches the pattern transmitted, a green LED is illuminated or an appropriate message is transmitted on the system console port. If the received pattern does not match the transmitted pattern, a red LED is illuminated or an error message is transmitted on the system console.

In an external loopback, specific channels or ports on the multiplexer have their transmit and receive sides tied together, in effect causing data transmitted to a specific multiplexer port to be echoed back to the data transmission source. Normally, the external loopback is used to test the operation of devices cabled to the multiplexer and the cable. In comparison, the internal loop is used to check the operation of a specific channel or port and the composite channel adapter. Figure 7-14 illustrates the flow of data in internal and external multiplexer loopbacks.

Event Reports

Many multiplexers have a circular log that can be directed to a printer. This log contains system generated event reports, including information about inbound and outbound errors, buffer overflows, link failures, and link initialization. Inbound errors are errors that occur on the receive side of the line and are determined by the local multiplexer performing a cyclic redundancy check (CRC) on received frames or blocks of data. Outbound errors are errors occurring on the transmit side of the line,

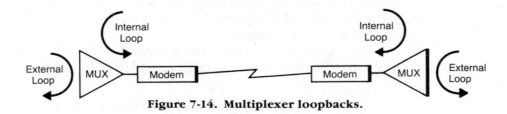

Figure 7-14. Multiplexer loopbacks.

which are reported to the local multiplexer by the remote multiplexer after it receives the transmitted data and as a result of performing a CRC check determines that an error has occurred.

Normally, inbound and outbound errors should differ due to several factors, including the relationship of inbound to outbound data traffic. If a remote batch terminal is transmitting the contents of a reel of data to a computer system, the transmit side of the line has a greater portion of occupancy than the receive side of the line, over which short acknowledgments flow. If impulse hits or other impairments occur at random, they have a higher probability of affecting the side of the line with the higher data transmission occupancy. Only when the ratio of inbound to outbound errors greatly favors one over the other can this data possibly serve as an indicator that one of the multiplexers is failing or there is a level problem with one side of the 4-wire circuit. For illustrative purposes, Table 7-4 lists four events that might occur and their meaning.

Table 7-4. Sample Multiplexer Event Report

Event	Meaning
HH:MM:SS NODE N INBOUND LINE OPEN LINK X	Broken circuit
HH:MM:SS NODE N LOCAL INIT-SYSTEM RESET	System has to be initialized locally
HH:MM:SS NODE N LOCAL INIT-BUFFER OVERFLOW	Local system buffer overflowed resulting in system initialization
HH:MM:SS NODE N REMOTE INIT-BUFFER OVERFLOW	Remote system buffer overflowed resulting in system initialization

Representative Equipment

To illustrate the capability of modern multiplexer systems to isolate problems, we examine the system diagnostic capability of the Infotron

Systems Corporation 990 network processor. First marketed in the mid-
1980's, the 990 today represents the state-of-the-art in multiplexer vendor diagnostic capability.

Selecting the diagnostic options menu on the Infotron 990 multiplexer displays the menu illustrated in Figure 7-15.

```
The following SYSTEM DIAGNOSTICS are available:

<S>  Single Character Test Pattern
<B>  Barber Pole Test Pattern
<M>  Message to/from Channel
<D>  Round Trip Delay
<L>  Loop a Channel
<U>  Unloop a Channel
<T>  Loop Table
<C>  Read/Write Control Signals
<R>  Read Control Signals
```

Figure 7-15. Infotron 990 system diagnostics menu.

Single Character Test Pattern

This test transmits a low speed (one CPS) sequence of test characters to a
specified channel from a system console. Because the operator must set a
channel loopback path before initiating the test, each received character
at the console can be compared with the transmitted character. The letters G (good) and B (bad) are used to show the status of the received test
character so that the console operator can note the state of the flow of
data through one channel on one multiplexer to another channel on a
second multiplexer and back to the first multiplexer.

To isolate problems to a channel adapter on the local multiplexer or
to the remote system, the operator can use the loop command to selec-
tively loop different channels before initiating the single character test
pattern. Thus, to test the operation of a channel on the local multiplexer,
the console operator first places that channel into a loopback mode of
operation.

Similarly, to do an end-to-end test from a channel on the local multiplexer to a channel on the remote multiplexer and back to the local device, the console operator sets the appropriate channel on the remote
multiplexer into a loopback mode of operation. Then, after the appropriate loopback is initiated, the console operator can execute the single
character test pattern.

Barber Pole Test Pattern

This test pattern is generated only for asynchronous channels and consists of five lines of recurrent ASCII characters as shown below.

```
0123456789:;<=>@ABCDEFGHIJKLMNOPQRSTUVWXYZ[\]^_'abcdefghijklmno
123456789:;<=>@ABCDEFGHIJKLMNOPQRSTUVWXYZ[\]^_'abcdefghijklmno0
23456789:;<=>@ABCDEFGHIJKLMNOPQRSTUVWXYZ[\]^_'abcdefghijklmno01
3456789:;<=>@ABCDEFGHIJKLMNOPQRSTUVWXYZ[\]^_'abcdefghijklmno012
456789:;<=>@ABCDEFGHIJKLMNOPQRSTUVWXYZ[\]^_'abcdefghijklmno0123
```

The barber pole test is similar to the use of a pattern generator, permitting a check of the character set while providing a pattern which when displayed permits the operator to easily identify errors. Normally, the barber pole test is directed to a specific channel on a local or remote multiplexer, which in turn is cabled to a terminal device. Then the terminal operator can observe the results of the test and relay the results to the console operator.

Message to/from Channel

This test option permits an operator to communicate with any asynchronous channel. Messages include C for conversation, R for receiving a message, and T for transmitting a message. By using this feature, the central site operator can direct test messages to other users and receive their observations of those tests.

Round Trip Delay

This test is used to measure the elapsed time in 20 msec increments from when a test character is transmitted to a specified channel until it is received back at the operator's console. By using this test, inordinate delay times due to flow control, line hits causing retransmissions, or other problems can be determined.

Like the barber pole test pattern, the round trip delay test requires the console operator to use first the Loop a Channel command to establish a loopback path along the channel path. Here, only one loopback is set, with the loopback located at a remote channel determining the worst case round trip delay. Because most synchronous protocols have timeout limits, the results of this test can be used as a guide to either modify the current synchronous timeout value to a higher value to alleviate timeouts or to investigate upgrading the transmission rate to reduce delays through the multiplexer.

When many or all data sources are active and exceeding the data rate of the high speed line, data is buffered into the multiplexer's RAM, causing a delay to occur until the data reaches the high speed line. In Chapter 8, we examine the statistical multiplexer tables that can be used to determine the delay time through the device due to the data rate into the multiplexer.

Channel Loops

By using the set of three loop commands, the operator can enable and disable loopback modes of operation and display a list of channels operating in loopback. The Loop a Channel option enables the console operator to place a local or remote channel in a loopback mode. The opposite effect is achieved by the Unloop a Channel command, which restores a looped channel to its normal operation. The third loop command, Loop Table, results in the display of all channels set for loopback.

Read/Write Control Signals

This command permits the console operator to examine (read) and to set (write) the control signal levels of a specified channel. Control signals that are readable and setable are based on the type of device to which the channel is connected. If the channel is connected to a DTE, the multiplexer channel simulates a DCE, enabling it to examine and alter the BSY, RTS, and DTR control signals on the inbound side of the channel and the RI, CD, DSR, and CTS signals on the outbound side of the channel. If the channel is connected to a DCE, the channel simulates a DTE. In this situation, inbound control signals that can be observed or changed include RI, CD, DSR, and CTS, whereas outbound control signals that can be observed or changed are BSY, RTS, and DTR.

Changing the state of key RS-232 control signals enables an operator to connect a channel with an external device that uses unconventional control signals. In such cases, this feature can alleviate the need to fabricate cables that require the strapping of different conductors together to obtain nonstandard control signals.

Troubleshooting Guidelines

In many ways, troubleshooting can be considered as a mixture of art and science. Like art, a high degree of innovation and creativity is required to isolate communications problems that are usually slightly or completely different from preceding and succeeding problems. Like science, the basic successful approach attempts to define the problem as explicitly as possible and to develop a list of symptoms that may provide information about the cause of the problem. Often, the list of symptoms may permit the probable cause of the problem to be isolated to a defective DTE or DCE, the transmission media, or software. Then, to validate the isolation of the problem to a specific cause, the indicators on DTEs and DCEs, their self-testing and loopback modes of operation, and the use of available test equipment and other hardware or software diagnostics should be considered.

In Table 7-5, the reader finds a list of error symptoms for three distinct categories of errors and the probable cause of each error. As noted in Table 7-4, certain error symptoms can be associated with a variety of causes, whereas other types of errors may point to a specific device or facility. By using the data presented in Table 7-5 as a guide, you should be able to structure a testing program to explicitly isolate the cause of the problem.

Table 7-5. Transmission Errors and Probable Causes

Error Symptom	Cause
I. *Data Related Errors*	
a. Polling sequence that times out at same address	computer, software, or terminal
b. Error occurs at same place in message	computer, software, or terminal
c. Any format or application dependent error	computer, software, or terminal
d. Dropped character(s)	multiplexer, computer, software, or terminal
II. *Periodic Errors*	synchronous modem which gains or loses a bit and retrains
III. *Random Errors*	telephone line noise

Once the user recognizes a communications problem exists, thought should be given to carrying out backup procedures based on the criticality of the operation affected and an estimate of the time required to restore service (if it is possible to make the latter estimate, based on prior experience or the ability to isolate the cause of a communications failure to the replacement of a component that has to be ordered or shipped to a distant location). Once the problem is resolved, the communications facility should be tested to verify the resolution of the problem before informing end-users that they can resume operations. Then, after a resumption in service has occurred, verify that the need for a previously carried out backup procedure has ended. Otherwise, many end-users in the organization may continue to use expensive backup facilities, such as direct distance dialing or value added carriers, long after the cause of the problem is resolved and the method of primary communications can be resumed.

Review Questions

1. Using the analog and digital loopback tests, illustrate how you can isolate a link failure to a modem or the line.

2. What are the key differences between in-band and out-band modem signaling?

3. Three times in sequence a tape-to-tape transmission between a remote batch terminal and a mainframe computer aborted roughly 112 minutes into the transmission. What is your educated guess about the source of the problem? What equipment would you use to isolate the cause of the problem?

4. Assume bisynchronous data is multiplexed via a satellite link. Because of delays in multiplexing data statistically and the satellite hop delay time, it appears that BISYNC timeouts are occurring. How could you confirm this, using the round trip delay test on the multiplexer?

Chapter 8

Capacity Planning

CAPACITY PLANNING as related to data communications is a broad term that can be reasonably defined as "the observation and/or measurement of line and equipment utilization used to adjust existing and planned facilities." In certain instances, the visual observation of line and/or equipment utilization may be sufficient for the network manager or analyst to determine that a facility requires modification. In other cases, the use of specialized equipment may be necessary to observe and record data traffic over a period of time before being able to develop a conclusion about the necessity of modifying an existing facility.

In this chapter, we first examine examples of statistics generated by modern multiplexers and port selectors. Next, we review the trapping and programmability capability of protocol analyzers to obtain traffic measurement data that may not be retrievable from the use of other communications equipment or from statistical reports produced by a computer system. Then, using the preceding information as a base, we investigate the field of traffic engineering and its applicability to the data communications equipment sizing process.

Equipment Aids

Most modern multiplexers are based on the incorporation of microprocessor technology that has been used to develop, then provide a wide range of statistics on demand. In certain cases, the statistics can be directed as "raw information" to a specific RS-232 port on the multiplexer or to the command console of the device where it can be printed or displayed. Other multiplexers may include a network management system that operates on the raw information to generate hourly, daily, weekly, or other periodic time-based reports, charts, and graphs on the console of the console operator.

When statistics are generated, the multiplexer reports different types of activity in the form of percentages or ratios at predefined intervals of time. Some multiplexers generate statistics at 5- or 10-minute intervals, whereas other devices may permit the interval to be adjusted by commands issued from the command console.

The following list shows seven of the more common statistics generated by multiplexers. The percentage of multiplexer loading can be considered as a measurement of the actual operation of the device. As this percentage increases towards unity, it serves as an indicator that the multiplexer is reaching its saturation level and that additional multiplexer facilities may be required.

Typical Multiplexer Statistics and Ratios

Multiplexer loading: % of time device not idle

Buffer utilization: % of buffer storage in use

Number of negative acknowledgments received

$$\text{Traffic density} = \frac{nonidle\ bits}{\text{total bits}}$$

$$\text{Error density} = \frac{NAKs\ received}{\text{frames transmitted}}$$

$$\text{Compression efficiency} = \frac{total\ bits\ received}{\text{total bits compressed}}$$

$$\text{Statistical loading} = \frac{number\ of\ actual\ characters\ received}{\text{maximum number which could be received}}$$

The buffer utilization percentage provides an indication of the data flow into statistical multiplexers and the probable degree of flow control issued by the multiplexers. Buffer utilization increases as line activity into a multiplexer from many low- to medium-speed devices begins to exceed the data rate at which the multiplexer transfers composite information onto the high-speed circuit connecting multiplexers. When the buffer utilization reaches a predefined level, the multiplexer automatically implements flow control to inhibit additional data entering the device, in effect providing the multiplexer with the opportunity to empty its buffer to another, predefined lower level. When that level is reached, the multiplexer disables flow control, permitting transmission to resume from low- to medium-speed data sources into the multiplexer. The three methods that can be used to implement flow control are discussed later in this chapter when the efficiency of statistical multiplexers is examined.

The number of negative acknowledgments received over a period of time can be used as an indicator of end-to-end circuit and equipment quality. Because the quantity of data actually transmitted between statistical display intervals can vary, a comparison of error density is normally more significant.

The traffic density provides an indication of the high-speed line's use between multiplexers. Here, a low ratio shows that data traffic through the multiplexers has room to grow before it is necessary to upgrade the transmission rate on the circuit between multiplexers or to obtain a second multiplexing system. Conversely, a high ratio shows that the multiplexers may not be able to service additional traffic before it is necessary to increase the data transmission rate between devices or to install a second system to service the additional workload.

Multiplexer Flow Control

For multiplexers that incorporate data compression, statistics about compression efficiency can be used to better size the number of ports serviced by the multiplexers. Normally, statistical multiplexers are sized using a 3:1 to 4:1 service ratio for asynchronous transmission. This means that for each bps output onto the high-speed line, 3 to 4bps on the input side of the devices can be serviced. If the multiplexer compresses data and has a compression efficiency of 2, the service ratio used for determining the number of ports and data rate per port should be doubled. As an example of the use of the compression efficiency, consider Figure 8-1. In Figure 8-1A, a conventional time-division multiplexer servicing four 2400bps data sources is illustrated. Because the aggregate input data flow into the multiplexer is 4 times 2400bps, or 9600bps, it must output data onto the high-speed composite line at that data rate or higher to successfully transfer multiplexed data onto the composite line.

In Figure 8-1B, the use of a statistical time division multiplexer with an assumed service ratio of 4:1 is illustrated. Through the process of transmitting data onto the high-speed line only when data is input into the multiplexer, the device uses the inactivity of many data sources to service active data sources. Thus, on average, the STDM can service 4 times the data input into a conventional time division multiplexer or 16 lines operating at 2400bps.

When all 16 data sources become active, the input data rate into the multiplexer is 16 × 2400bps or 38,400bps. If the multiplexer is con-

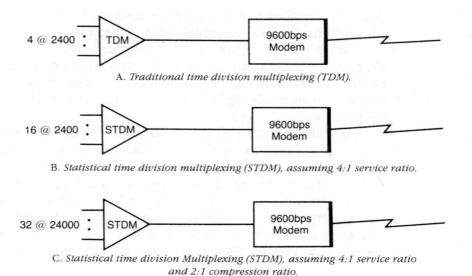

A. *Traditional time division multiplexing (TDM).*

B. *Statistical time division multiplexing (STDM), assuming 4:1 service ratio.*

C. *Statistical time division Multiplexing (STDM), assuming 4:1 service ratio and 2:1 compression ratio.*

Figure 8-1. Multiplexer data source servicing comparison.

nected to a 9600bps modem, the input data flow into the multiplexer is 4 times the rate at which the data is transferred to the modem, causing the multiplexer's buffer to rapidly fill. The longer this situation persists, the more data flows into the buffer, until the buffer eventually overflows unless the multiplexer implements flow control. Thus, flow control is the method whereby a statistical time division multiplexer enables and disables data flow into the device to prevent its buffer from overflowing.

The three methods of flow control implemented in most statistical multiplexers include inband signaling, outband signaling, and clock modification. Inband signaling is the issuance of XOFF and XON signals from the multiplexer to the attached terminal or computer port. Because the XOFF and XON characters are transmitted on pin 2, this method of flow control is also called inband signaling. Outband signaling is the raising and lowering of the clear-to-send (CTS) control signal. Here, the statistical multiplexer lowers the CTS signal to inhibit data flow into the device, whereas it raises that control signal when it is able to process data. Because the CTS signal is a control signal and not data on pin 2, it is also known as outband signaling.

The first two methods of flow control only work with asynchronous terminals and computer ports. For synchronous devices, neither method works because such devices could inhibit transmission in the middle of a data block, which could result in a false timeout occurring. To prevent this, most vendors modify the synchronous clock rate to correspond to the buffer level of occupancy in the multiplexer. That is, when the buffer is filled to a predefined level, the statistical multiplexer may halve the clock rate provided to synchronous devices. Then, when the buffer is emptied to a lower predefined level, the clock rate is restored to its original value.

In part C of Figure 8-1, the use of an STDM with a 4:1 service ratio and a 2:1 compression efficiency is illustrated. Because a 2:1 compression efficiency means that because of compression 1 bit is not transmitted for every 2 bits, in effect the high-speed line has half the load it was sized for, as shown in Figure 8-1B. Thus, because of a 2:1 compression efficiency, the number of inputs into the STDM can be doubled, as shown in Figure 8-1C.

Sizing Problems

The major problem associated with the use of statistical multiplexers is a result of improper sizing. When too many data sources become active, the multiplexer rapidly implements and disables flow control. As flow control is toggled on and off, the data flow between terminals and computer ports and the statistical multiplexer is affected.

The effect of too many active data sources serviced by a statistical multiplexer usually can be observed on a terminal's display. Here, the data flow to the terminal appears to stop at random locations on the display for random time durations. In actuality, the implementation of flow control causes the display of data to stop, whereas the disabling of flow control by the multiplexer causes the display of data to resume.

If too many data sources supported by a statistical multiplexer remain active, the flow of data through the device encounters significant time delays. Not only does this reduce the performance level of individual terminal devices, but also normally results in user complaints. Later in this chapter, we examine how the use of statistical reports produced by many multiplexers can be employed to determine the delay time through the device. Then, the network manager may be able to implement corrective action before the end-user realizes a problem is occurring.

Status Reports

Some multiplexer systems can generate a report every X minutes for each site in the network. This report provides the character input rate per second averaged over the prior X minutes. In addition, some multiplexers also provide the peak character input rate over any one second period in the prior X minutes and a transmit buffer utilization report. Figure 8-2 illustrates a typical line status report that can be displayed on the command console of some statistical multiplexers.

```
HH:MM:SS LOCAL HS LINE 9600 BPS
       CHANNEL INPUTS: 10 MIN AVG    896 CPS
                        1 SEC PEAK 1225 CPS

HH:MM:SS REMOTE HS LINE 9600 BPS
       CHANNEL INPUTS: 10 MIN AVG    741 CPS
                        1 SEC PEAK  802 CPS
```

Figure 8-2. Statistical multiplexer line status report.

By using the line status report, the network analyst can obtain an indication of the capability of the multiplexer to service the data sources attached to the device based on the data rate of the high-speed line connecting multiplexers together. From Figure 8-2, the 10-minute average of 896CPS for the local multiplexer is equivalent to 7168bps or an approximate 74.6 percent (7168/9600) utilization of the outbound high-speed (HS) line capacity. Similarly, the remote high-speed (HS) outbound line portion operating at 9600bps, which is inbound to the local multiplexer, has a 10-minute average occupancy of 61.75 percent (5928/9600). Assuming a full-duplex line is used between the multiplexers and operates at 9600bps, the composite average utilization of the line is roughly 68 percent for the 10-minute period. By observing the 10-minute averages produced by the line status report during peak organizational operation times, such as before lunch and in the late afternoon, the network analyst can determine whether the data rate on the line should be increased or whether a second line linking the two multiplexers should be installed.

An example of a typical multiplexer transmit buffer report is illustrated in Figure 8-3. This report displays the number of characters in 1000-byte increments that are awaiting transmission. By comparing the buffer content to the data transmission rate of the high-speed line, an approximate delay time can be determined. As an example of the preceding, consider the local transmit buffer filled with 2K of characters. If the operating rate of the line between multiplexers is 9600bps, the delay is

$$\frac{2K \times 1000 \; \frac{characters}{K} \times \frac{8 \; bits}{character}}{9600 \; bps} = 1.66 \; seconds$$

From the preceding, it is taking approximately 1.7 seconds for characters entering the multiplexer to be placed onto the high-speed line to the remote multiplexer. In the reverse direction, the data in Figure 8-3 shows that a delay of .83 seconds occurs because 1K of characters in the remote unit's transmit buffer are waiting for transmission to the local multiplexer located on the opposite end of the circuit.

```
HH:MM:SS LOCAL XMIT BUFFER  02K CHAR

HH:MM:SS REMOTE XMIT BUFFER 01K CHAR
```

Figure 8-3. Multiplexer transmit buffer report.

Representative Hardware

The Racal-Milgo OMNIMUX 82, 162, and 322 multiplexers gather statistics for both local and remote units at 5-minute intervals. These statistics can be read by connecting an asynchronous ASCII terminal or the serial port on a personal computer to a supervisory port on the multiplexer or via a control front panel on a multiplexer. The following lists and describes the eight types of statistics gathered by this multiplexer series.

Racal-Milgo OMNIMUX Statistics

Total Link Utilization	Percentage of available bandwidth used by all channels
Peak Utilization	Maximum percentage of the link or channel used in the preceding 30-minute period
Asynchronous Link Utilization	Percentage of the aggregate link used by all the asynchronous channels
Synchronous Link Utilization	Percentage of the aggregate link used by all the synchronous channels
Channel Utilization	Percentage of asynchronous or synchronous utilization on a per-channel basis
Number of Retransmissions	Total number of retransmissions requested by the OMNIMUX because of bad data reception on the link

Control Utilization	Number of flow controls issued by an asynchronous channel during a 5-minute period
Overflows	Number of characters lost by an asynchronous channel in a five-minute period. Caused by improper flow control selection or no flow control selection

Operation

The RS (read statistics) command can be issued by a supervisory terminal operator to initiate a 5-minute statistical update report feature of the multiplexer. The format of the RS command is:

$$RS \begin{Bmatrix} L \\ R \\ S \\ A \\ B \end{Bmatrix} N$$

where:

    L = for the local unit

    R = for the remote unit, if only one remote

    A = for the remote unit attached to link A

    B = for the remote unit attached to link B

    S = for all units in the multiplexer system

    N = reporting interval in minutes (1-5) or a default of 5

    Figure 8-4 illustrates the format of a sample report generated in response to the issuance of an RS S command, where two OMNIMUX multiplexers are connected via one high-speed line.

    In this figure, the peak asynchronous and synchronous line utilization represents the highest percentage in the preceding 30 minutes. By examining the statistical display, you get an indication of the efficiency of each multiplexer channel and of the composite high-speed data lines. This information can be used to determine the general usage, quality, and efficiency of a selected channel or composite line.

```
COMMAND: RS S

DISPLAY:

    UNIT=LOCAL        RET   AU    AP    SU    SP    TU

    LINK              XXX   XX%   XX%   XX%   XX%   XX%

    CH   FL   OF   CU   PU   CH   FL   OF   CU   PU
    01   XX   XX   XX   XX   02   XX   XX   XX   XX
    03   XX   XX   XX   XX   04   XX   XX   XX   XX
    05   XX   XX   XX   XX   06   XX   XX   XX   XX
    07   XX   XX   XX   XX   08   XX   XX   XX   XX
    13   -    -    XX   XX   14   -    -    XX   XX
    15   -    -    XX   XX   16   -    -    XX   XX
    13   -    -    XX   XX   14   -    -    XX   XX
    15   -    -    XX   XX   16   -    -    XX   XX

    UNIT=REMOTE       RET   AU    AP    SU    SP    TU

    LINK              XXX   XX%   XX%   XX%   XX%   XX%

    CH   FL   OF   CU   PU   CH   FL   OF   CU   PU
    01   XX   XX   XX   XX   02   XX   XX   XX   XX
    03   XX   XX   XX   XX   04   XX   XX   XX   XX
    05   XX   XX   XX   XX   06   XX   XX   XX   XX
    07   XX   XX   XX   XX   08   XX   XX   XX   XX
    09   XX   XX   XX   XX   10   XX   XX   XX   XX
    11   XX   XX   XX   XX   12   XX   XX   XX   XX
    13   -    -    XX   XX   14   -    -    XX   XX
    15   -    -    XX   XX   16   -    -    XX   XX
```

Legend:

RET—Number of Retransmission Requests	TU—Total Link Utilization (Percentage)
AU—Async Utilization of the Link	CH—Channel Number
AP—Peak Async Utilization of the Link	FL—Number of Flow Controls
SU—Sync Utilization of the Link	OF—Number of Overflows
SP—Peak Sync Utilization of the Link	CU—Channel Utilization

Figure 8-4. Racal-Milgo OMNIMUX statistical display.

Port Selector Statistics

A port selector can be considered to operate as a dynamic data switch, permitting data sources from multiplexer channels, local directly connected terminals, and dial-in rotaries to contend for access to ports on the device. The selector's ports can be connected to computer ports, multiplexer channels, and even other directly cabled local terminals. Figure 8-5 illustrates a typical port selector configuration.

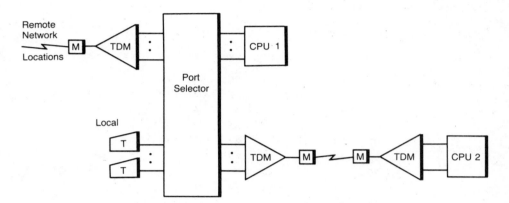

Figure 8-5. Port selector employment.

By using a keyboard controlled routing feature, network users prompted for a destination by the port selector can control their final routing through the device. In the example illustrated in Figure 8-5, two routing classes on the port side of the port selector are shown with one class assigned to the ports directly cabled to a local computer (CPU1), whereas the second class is assigned to ports on a multiplexer that are routed to a distant computer (CPU2). Thus, a common network can terminate at the port selector and provide users with the ability to access two or more computer systems.

As the focal point of network activity the statistics provided by port selectors can be employed to modify channel usage to correspond to changes in network activity.

Questions that port selectors can answer include what resources (classes) have the most activity, what resources (classes) have the least activity, are too many channels allocated to a port class, are too few channels allocated to a port class, are users being placed into queues too often, and do users know what they are supposed to know about the method required to access different classes? To answer these questions, most port selectors are designed to generate activity records that identify and time and date stamp each port selector operation. Figure 8-6 illustrates the typical format of a port selector record.

Normally, port selector activity records are either recorded onto a fixed disk built into the system or directed as output to an RS-232 port. In the latter situation, the records can be displayed on an ASCII terminal in

Activity Indicator	Line	Port	Time	Day

Common Activity Indicators

C   Connect
CF   Forced Connect
D   Disconnect
DF   Forced Disconnect
Fn   Failures to Connect (up to 10)
T   Timeout
Qnn Queued Position nn

Figure 8-6. Port selector activity record.

real time to correspond to the actions of the port selector or stored on the fixed disk of a personal computer for later analysis.

Some port selector vendors market optional network analysis software that operates on IBM PC or compatible personal computers. This software uses the activity records to generate statistical tables and charts for predefined time periods based on operator defined queries.

Examples of such queries could be a display of the number of users queued for access to a particular class between 8AM and 5PM or a graph of the number of users connected to Class 2 between 12 noon and 4PM. In the first example, by examining the number of users in a queue waiting for access to a particular port, the network manager can decide whether additional ports between the port selector and the destination class to which end-users are requesting access should be increased to lower the amount of queuing. As a result of the second query, the network manager could compare the number of users on Class 2 with the number of ports routed to that class. If over a period of time, the number of users on the class is significantly fewer than the number of ports routed to the class, a reduction in the number of ports to Class 2 is warranted. Figure 8-7 illustrates two of the more useful graphical displays generated by port selector network management software programs.

Figure 8-8 illustrates a sequence of seven port selector records generated over a short period of time. The activity indicator in the first record shows a connection between line 10 and port 23 was established at 20 seconds after 8:35AM. The 127 in the record is the Julian day of the year, allowing different types of port selector activity to be accumulated over extended periods of time and the activity during one period to be compared with the activity that occurred in another period of time.

In the third record listed in Figure 8-8, note that the activity indicator is a D, which denotes a disconnect. From the line and port fields, note that line 10 was disconnected from port 23, which in effect is the discon-

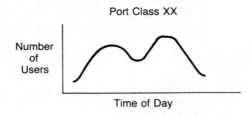

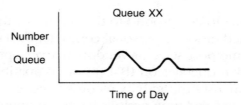

Figure 8-7. Port selector graphical displays.

```
C     L10   P23   08:35:20   127
C     L15   P18   08:36:15   127
D     L10   P23   08:37:10   127
F1    L16         08:38:20   127
Q1    L16         08:38:21   127
D     P18         08:39:30   127
C     L16   P18   08:39:31   127
```

Figure 8-8. Typical port selector record generation.

nection of the connection establishment noted in the first record. By subtracting the time of disconnect from the time of connection, the duration of this session is determined, enabling the occupancy of individual ports to be determined.

In the fifth record, the activity indicator F1 is used to show a specific type of failure to connect. Here, F1 could denote a request to access a nonexistent class, the failure to enter a routing, class, or another reason that the end-user accessing the port selector on line 16 could not be successfully cross-connected through the system. By examining the types of failures to connect, the network manager or analyst may find patterns that require corrective action by the distribution of modified standard operating procedures or other documents to clarify items previously taken for granted.

Using Communications Test Equipment

Test equipment with triggering capability based on RS-232/V.24 circuits can be used to obtain traffic measurement data. In certain situations, the use of communications test equipment may represent the only mechanism by which the network manager can obtain accurate information about network activity.

As an example of the use of test equipment, consider the network segment illustrated in Figure 8-9. In this illustration, the hunt or rotary group enables network users to dial the low telephone number assigned to the group. If that number is busy, the incoming call is bumped to the next available telephone line.

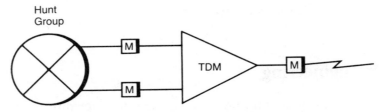

Figure 8-9. Network segment.

One of the more frequent problems associated with hunt groups is determining the activity on individual business lines, which may be useful for modifying a network segment. As an example, if one or more "high" rotary numbers are never accessed, there is excess capacity in the form of one or more telephone company business lines, modems, and time division multiplexer channels. Because the telephone company does not supply call transaction data on normal business lines and most multiplexers do not record port occupancy data, the use of a protocol analyzer to count calls and call duration on high number lines or a hunt group represents perhaps the only mechanism available to the network manager to obtain this information.

Most protocol analyzers can be programmed to count both the number of calls and call duration occurring on an individual line basis. To count calls, the protocol analyzer could be programmed to recognize both ring indicator (RI) and carrier detect (CD) signals, with the latter used to prevent wrong number calls from being counted. To count the call duration, RI and CD becoming active can be used to turn on a second counter, while CD or data terminal ready (DTR) becoming inactive can be used to stop the counter.

Some protocol analyzers double as a performance analyzer to measure line utilization and answer questions that enable you to manage your network more efficiently. Typical questions protocol analyzers can answer include:

What is the peak utilization during a period?

What is the average utilization over a time period?

What are the average and peak response times and when does the peak response time occur?

By using protocol analyzers, the network manager obtains another mechanism to determine the data traffic occurring over one or more lines. Then, as we observe in the following section of this chapter, this information can be used in the traffic engineering process to size communications equipment.

Traffic Engineering

The goal of traffic engineering is to determine the most favorable level of service and to minimize total organizational costs, based on the sizing of network components. Although this goal is like motherhood and apple pie, it is difficult to achieve. To understand the difficulties associated with minimizing total organizational costs, consider Figure 8-10, which contains a generalized graph showing the relationship between the level of network service and the total cost associated with providing a defined level of service.

To better appreciate the significance of the relationship between the level of service and network cost illustrated in Figure 8-10, assume that this illustration refers to a network consisting of a pair of multiplexers connecting a remote location to a central computer site via a leased line facility. At the remote site, assume also that users access the individual multiplexer channels by dialing an N position rotary with N business lines connected to N dial-in modems, which in turn are connected to N multiplexer channels.

When preparations are made to install a multiplexer system to service remote users, a key question requires answering, "What level of service should be provided to remote users?" Here, the level of service is equivalent to determining the value of N. That is, how many positions on the rotary, how many business lines, how many dial-in modems, and how many multiplexer channels are required?

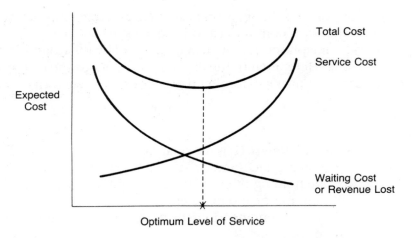

Figure 8-10. Level of service versus network cost.

As the value of N increases, the service cost associated with N increases, as shown by the curve labeled Service Cost in Figure 8-10. Because the level of service is inversely proportional to the number of remote users dialing the rotary and receiving a busy signal, we can reasonably expect end-user waiting time to decrease as the level of service increases. In addition, a degree of lost productivity is associated with end-users encountering busy signals. Thus, some waiting cost is associated with each busy signal. Unfortunately, it is often difficult to place a precise dollar amount on waiting cost, because some users do other operations and redial the system later in the day, whereas other users may continuously retry the busy rotary group.

If the waiting cost can be reasonably estimated, a curve similar to that illustrated in Figure 8-10 shows a decreasing waiting cost as the level of service increases. By adding the service cost and waiting cost, the true total cost of the system is obtained. The minimum point on the total cost line represents the best level of service and is the design goal of traffic engineering.

Traffic Measurements

The application of traffic engineering to telephone networks dates back to the early 1900's and the famous Danish mathematician Erlang. Today, many of the ideas developed to size the number of trunks between telephone company central offices are applicable to the sizing of the number of ports or channels on multiplexers, concentrators, port selectors, and other data communications devices.

Telephone activity can be defined by the calling rate and the holding time. Here, total traffic (T) is the product of the calling rate per hour (C) and the average holding time per call (D), such that

$$T = C * D$$

A call hour (CH) is the quantity represented by one or more calls having an aggregate duration of one hour. Thus, five calls per hour with an average holding time of 20 minutes per call would result in an aggregate call duration of 100 minutes.

In traffic engineering, the preferred unit of measurement is the erlang where

$$1 \text{ erlang} = 60 \text{ call-minutes}$$

As an example of the use of the erlang, consider a rotary group consisting of 20 dial-in lines. If the activity of all lines was monitored and a call intensity of 10 erlangs determined over the group, one-half of the lines would be busy at the time of measurement.

Grade of Service

One of the most important ideas in traffic engineering relates to the grade of service that networks are designed to provide. The grade of service represents the probability that a call will be blocked, with a grade of service of unity meaning that there is no service. A grade of service of zero means that the end-user requesting access to a facility will always gain access. An example of the latter situation would be a network that has one telephone number for each remote terminal user.

Like probability figures, a grade of service is expressed as a percentage. Thus, a .05 grade of service is equivalent to 1 call in 20 encountering a busy signal.

The Erlang Traffic Formula

The probability that T trunks are busy when a traffic intensity of E erlangs is offered to those trunks can be determined by the following formula, more formally known as the Erlang B distribution.

$$P(T,E) = \frac{E^T/T!}{\displaystyle\sum_{n=0}^{T} (E^N/n!)}$$

where:

$$\sum_{n=0}^{T} (E^N/n!) = 1 + E + (E^2/2!) + (E^3/3!) + \ldots (E^T/T!)$$

and

$$T! = T * (T\text{-}1) * (T\text{-}2) \ldots 3 * 2 * 1$$

In Table 8-1, you find an extraction of an Erlang B distribution that results from using a computer to calculate the traffic formula. The formula is based on considering multiplexer ports or channels functioning similarly to telephone trunks when a traffic load is presented to the device. As an example of the use of this table, consider a load of 6 erlangs on a 10 channel device. Here, the probability that all channels are busy is .043, which is the grade of service of the device. This means that a multiplexer, rotary, port selector, or any other device with 10 channels, ports, or lines that has a traffic load of 6 erlangs presented to it has a 4.3 percent probability of not being able to service the access request. By increasing the number of channels to 11, the grade of service is reduced to .022. Decreasing the number of channels to 9 raises the probability of users encountering a busy signal to 7.5 percent.

Sizing Problem

Assume that during the busy hour, we expect an average of 6 terminals to require access to a remote multiplexer. Suppose that we want to size the multiplexer to ensure that at most only 1 out of every 100 calls to the device encounters a busy signal. How many ports should be installed in the multiplexer?

The traffic intensity offered to the multiplexer is 6 erlangs, whereas the grade of service required is .01. By checking the list near the beginning of this chapter (the one describing eight types of statisics gathered by a multiplexer series), you see that a .01 grade of service under the 6 erlang load column requires 13 channels. Thus, 13 ports should be installed to minimize users encountering a busy signal in one out of every 100 access requests.

Table 8-1. Erlang B Distribution Extracts

Probability All Channels Busy When Call Attempted
(Load in Erlangs)

Channels	5.5	6.0	6.5
1	.846	.857	.866
2	.699	.720	.737
3	.561	.590	.615
4	.435	.469	.499
5	.324	.360	.393
6	.229	.264	.299
7	.152	.185	.217
8	.094	.121	.150
9	.054	.075	.097
10	.029	.043	.059
11	.144	.022	.034
12	.006	.011	.018
13	.002	.005	.008
14	.001	.002	.004
15	.000	.001	.002

Poisson Formula

A second formula commonly used in the sizing process is the Poisson formula. The general model or formula for computing the number of arrivals per unit time at a service location based on the Poisson formula is given by the following equation.

$$P(r) = \frac{e^{-\lambda}(\lambda)^r}{r!}$$

where:

r = number of arrivals .

P(r) = probability of arrivals

λ = mean arrival rate

e = base of the natural logarithm (2.71828)

r! = r factorial = r * (r − 1) * (r − 2) . . . 3 * 2 * 1

The probability of an arrival rate being fewer than or equal to some specific number, n, is the sum of the probabilities of the arrival rate being 0, 1, 2 . . n. Thus, the probability that the arrival rate is n becomes

$$P(r \leq n) = \sum_{r=0}^{n} \frac{e^{-\lambda} * \lambda^r}{r!}$$

Because $P(r \leq n) + P(r > n) = 1$, one can easily find the probability that $r > n$ once the probability of $r \leq n$ is known. In addition, by using mathematics beyond the scope of this book, the probability of $r \leq n$ can be expressed in terms of r and n as well as E erlangs of traffic as follows:

$$P(r \geq n) = e^{-E} \sum_{r=n+1}^{\infty} \frac{E^r}{r!}$$

In Appendix A, you can find the listing of a computer program, and two tables generated by the execution of the program, each listing the probability that all channels are busy when a call is attempted. The calculations are based on different traffic levels in erlangs and the number of channels in a system. The first set of tables is based on the Erlang B distribution. The second set of tables is based on the Poisson distribution.

In general, the Poisson formula produces a more conservative sizing at a lower traffic intensity than the Erlang formula. This is because the Poisson formula assumes that lost calls are held or retired immediately after a busy signal is encountered. In comparison, the Erlang formula assumes that lost calls are cleared. When reading the tables in Appendix A, note that at higher traffic intensities, the results are reversed, with the Erlang formula producing a more conservative sizing. The difference between formulas is at most 1 or 2 channels at traffic intensities up to 30 erlangs, making the use of either formula sufficient for most sizing requirements. For traffic intensities beyond 30 erlangs, the use of an appropriate formula should be based on whether the organization's usage follows a held call or cleared call concept.

Review Questions

1. The average buffer utilization of a statistical multiplexer during a prime shift was 95% during the month. What problems are users

probably experiencing and what steps could be taken to alleviate those problems?

2. Assume that you can place a 4800bps RJE data stream through a port on a multiport modem or a port on a statistical multiplexer as illustrated in Figure 8-11.

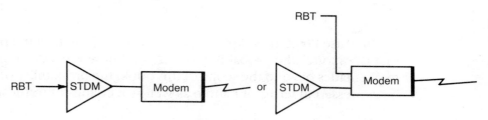

Figure 8-11. Servicing a remote batch terminal (RBT).

How could you use the compression efficiency, statistical loading, and buffer utilization statistics of a statistical multiplexer during a test to determine which configuration is most appropriate?

3. Assume that the transmit buffer of a statistical multiplexer contains 4K characters on the average and its standard deviation is 2K characters. Also assume that the multiplexer is connected to a 9.6Kbps modem and services a bisynchronous data source that has a 2-second timeout setting. What problem can be expected to occur and how could it be alleviated?

4. A line status report obtained from a statistical multiplexer shows that the average utilization of the transmit side of a high-speed line during the month was 1600CPS. If the line is connected to a 14.4Kbps modem, what problem can be expected to occur if it is not already occurring? What can the network manager do to resolve the problem?

5. The terminal population at a remote location is 18 devices, of which one-third can be expected to require access to a multiplexer during the busy hour. If we desire to size the multiplexer to ensure that at most only 1 out of every 20 calls encounters a busy signal, how many ports should be installed in the multiplexer?

References

Data Communications Equipment Sizing Program and Tables[1,2]

Notice: Although precaution was taken during the preparation of this reference to ensure its accuracy, it is distributed on an "as is" basis by Gilbert Held and 4-Degree Consulting, which assume no responsibility for errors or omissions and assume no liability or responsibility for damages or liabilities alleged to be caused by the use of this reference.

The following program was developed for use on a Hewlett Packard HP 3000 minicomputer and written in HP BASIC.

```
10 REM ***************************************************************
20 REM                     PROGRAM SEGMENT TO PRINT
30 REM                     COVER PAGE.
40 REM ***************************************************************
50 MARGIN 132
60 PRINT CTL(199),TAB(45);&
   "DATA COMMUNICATION EQUIPMENT SIZING TABLES"
70 PRINT CTL(199),TAB(57);"TABLES BASED UPON:"
80 PRINT CTL(48)
90 PRINT
100 PRINT TAB(55),"1)ERLANG B DISTRIBUTION"
110 PRINT TAB(55),"2)POISSON DISTRIBUTION"
120 PRINT
130 PRINT TAB(57),"PREPARED BY:"
140 PRINT TAB(57),"4-DEGREE CONSULTING"
150 PRINT TAB(57),"4736 OXFORD ROAD"
160 PRINT TAB(57),"MACON, GA.  31210"
170 PRINT TAB(57),"912/477-0293"
```

---

[1] Tables based on Erlang B Distribution and Poisson Distribution.
[2] © 1983 by Gilbert Held/4-Degree Consulting.

```
180 PRINT CTL(199)
190 PRINT TAB(31),"NOTICE"
200 PRINT TAB(35),"ALTHOUGH PRECAUTION WAS TAKEN DURING ";
210 PRINT "THE PREPARATION OF THIS"
220 PRINT TAB(31),"REFERENCE TO ENSURE ITS ACCURACY, IT IS  ";
230 PRINT "DISTRIBUTED ON AN ";
240 PRINT '34"AS IS"'34
250 PRINT TAB(31),"BASIS BY GILBERT HELD AND 4-DEGREE ";
260 PRINT "CONSULTING, WHICH ASSUME NO "
270 PRINT TAB(31),"RESPONSIBILITY FOR ERRORS OR OMISSIONS ";
280 PRINT "AND ASSUME NO LIABILITY OR"
290 PRINT TAB(31),"RESPONSIBILITY FOR ANY DAMAGES OR ";
300 PRINT "LIABILITIES ALLEGED TO BE "
310 PRINT TAB(31),"CAUSED BY THE USE OF THIS REFERENCE."
320 PRINT CTL(48)
330 PRINT
340 PRINT TAB(31),"COPYRIGHT 1983 BY GILBERT HELD/4-DEGREE CONSULTING"
350 PRINT CTL(193)
360 REM ******************************************************************
370 REM                      PROGRAM SEGMENT TO PERFORM
380 REM                      CALCULATIONS USING ERLANG B
390 REM                      DISTRIBUTION.
400 REM                      A IS THE OFFERED LOAD IN ERLANGS,
410 REM                      S IS THE NUMBER OF PORTS, DIAL
420 REM                      IN LINES OR TRUNKS.
430 REM ******************************************************************
440 DIM A[80],B[55,80]
450 C=0
460 FOR I=5 TO 400 STEP 5
470     C=C+1
480     A=I/10
490     A[C]=A
500     FOR S=1 TO 55
510        X=S
520        REM ******************************************************************
530        REM                   SUBROUTINE WILL COMPUTE S FACTORIAL
540        REM                   VALUE. F IS THE FACTORIAL VALUE
550        REM                   RETURNED.
560        REM ******************************************************************
570        GOSUB 1350
580        REM ******************************************************************
590        REM                   N IS THE NUMERATOR, D IS THE
600        REM                   DENOMINATOR OF THE ERLANG TRAFFIC
610        REM                   FORMULA.
620        REM ******************************************************************
```

```
630        N=(A**S)/F
640        D=1
650        FOR D1=1 TO S
660          X=D1
670          GOSUB 1350
680          D=D+(A**D1)/F
690        NEXT D1
700        B[S,C]=N/D
710      NEXT S
720 NEXT I
730 REM ***************************************************************
740 REM                        PROGRAM SEGMENT TO PRINT ERLANG B
750 REM                        DISTRIBUTION TABLES.
760 REM ***************************************************************
770 FOR I=1 TO 71 STEP 10
780    PRINT CTL(49)
790    PRINT
800    PRINT TAB(56);"ERLANG B DISTRIBUTION"
810    GOSUB 1440
820    PRINT
830 NEXT I
840 REM ***************************************************************
850 REM                        PROGRAM SEGMENT TO PERFORM
860 REM                        CALCULATIONS USING POISSON
870 REM                        DISTRIBUTION.
880 REM                        A IS THE OFFERED LOAD IN ERLANGS,
890 REM                        S IS THE NUMBER OF PORTS, DIALS
900 REM                        IN LINES OF TRUNKS.
910 REM ***************************************************************
920 C=0
930 FOR J=5 TO 400 STEP 5
940    C=C+1
950    A=J/10
960    A[C]=A
970    K=0
980    FOR S=0 TO 54
990      K=K+1
1000     X1=0
1010     FOR X=0 TO S
1020       REM ***********************************************************
1030       REM                   SUBROUTINE WILL COMPUTE S FACTORIAL
1040       REM                   VALUE. F IS THE FACTORIAL VALUE
1050       REM ***********************************************************
1060       REM ***********************************************************
1070       GOSUB 1350
```

```
1080      REM ***********************************************************
1090      REM                        X1 IS THE RESULT OF THE POISSON
1100      REM                        PROBABILITY FORMULA.
1110      REM ***********************************************************
1120      X1=X1+(A**X)/(F*2.71828**A)
1130    NEXT X
1140    B[K,C]=1-X1
1150    B[X,C]=ABS(B[K,C])
1160  NEXT S
1170 NEXT J
1180 REM ***************************************************************
1190 REM                          PROGRAM SEGMENT TO PRINT
1200 REM                          POISSON DISTRIBUTION TABLES.
1210 REM ***************************************************************
1220 FOR I=1 TO 71 STEP 10
1230    PRINT CTL(49)
1240    PRINT
1250    PRINT TAB(56);"POISSON DISTRIBUTION"
1260    GOSUB 1440
1270 NEXT I
1280 STOP
1290 REM ****************END MAIN PROGRAM*******************************
1300 REM ***************************************************************
1310 REM                          SUBROUTINE TO COMPUTE FACTORIAL
1320 REM                          S VALUE. X IS THE REPRESENTATIVE
1330 REM                          VARIABLE FOR S.
1340 REM ***************************************************************
1350 F=1
1360 IF X=0 THEN 1410
1370 FOR F1=X TO 1 STEP -1
1380    F=F*F1
1390 NEXT F1
1400 RETURN
1410 F=1
1420 RETURN
1430 REM ***************************************************************
1440 REM                          SUBROUTINE TO PRINT ERLANG B
1450 REM                          DISTRIBUTION TABLES, OR
1460 REM                          POISSON DISTRIBUTION TABLES.
1470 REM ***************************************************************
1480 PRINT
1490 PRINT TAB(33);"PROBABILITY ALL CHANNELS BUSY WHEN";
1500 PRINT " CALL ATTEMPTED (GRADE OF SERVICE)"
1510 PRINT
1520 PRINT "CHANNEL";TAB(56);"TRAFFIC IN ERLANGS"
```

```
1530 PRINT
1540 PRINT USING 1550;A[I],A[I+1],A[I+2],A[I+3],A[I+4],A[I+5],A[I+6],A&
     [I+7],A[I+8],A[I+9]
1550 IMAGE 12X,10(DD.DDD,6X)
1560 PRINT
1570 FOR S=1 TO 55
1580   IF B[S,I+9]<=.000001 THEN 1610
1590   PRINT USING 1600;S,B[S,I],B[S,I+1],B[S,I+2],B[S,I+3],B[S,I+4],B&
     [S,I+5],B[S,I+6],B[S,I+7],B[S,I+8],B[S,I+9]
1600   IMAGE XDDD,6X,10(D.DDDDDD,4X)
1610 NEXT S
1620 RETURN
```

Erlang B Distribution

Probability All Channels Busy When Call Attempted (Grade of Service)

Traffic in Erlangs

Channel	.500	1.000	1.500	2.000	2.500	3.000	3.500	4.000	4.500	5.000
1	.333333	.500000	.600000	.666667	.714286	.750000	.777778	.800000	.818182	.833333
2	.076923	.200000	.310345	.400000	.471698	.529412	.576471	.615385	.648000	.675676
3	.012658	.062500	.134328	.210526	.282167	.346154	.402110	.450704	.492901	.529661
4	.001580	.015385	.047957	.095238	.149916	.206107	.260271	.310680	.356712	.398343
5	.000158	.003067	.014183	.036697	.069731	.110054	.154112	.199067	.243021	.284868
6	.000013	.000511	.003533	.012085	.028234	.052157	.082484	.117162	.154166	.191847
7	.000001	.000073	.000757	.003441	.009983	.021864	.039608	.062749	.090170	.120519
8	.000000	.000009	.000142	.000859	.003110	.008132	.017033	.030420	.048272	.070048
9	.000000	.000001	.000024	.000191	.000863	.002703	.006581	.013340	.023567	.037458
10	.000000	.000000	.000004	.000038	.000216	.000810	.002298	.005308	.010494	.018385
11	.000000	.000000	.000000	.000007	.000049	.000221	.000731	.001926	.004275	.008287
12	.000000	.000000	.000000	.000001	.000010	.000055	.000213	.000642	.001600	.003441
13	.000000	.000000	.000000	.000000	.000002	.000013	.000057	.000197	.000554	.001322
14	.000000	.000000	.000000	.000000	.000000	.000003	.000014	.000056	.000178	.000472
15	.000000	.000000	.000000	.000000	.000000	.000001	.000003	.000015	.000053	.000157
16	.000000	.000000	.000000	.000000	.000000	.000000	.000001	.000004	.000015	.000049
17	.000000	.000000	.000000	.000000	.000000	.000000	.000000	.000001	.000004	.000014
18	.000000	.000000	.000000	.000000	.000000	.000000	.000000	.000000	.000001	.000004
19	.000000	.000000	.000000	.000000	.000000	.000000	.000000	.000000	.000000	.000001

Channel	5.500	6.000	6.500	7.000	7.500	8.000	8.500	9.000	9.500	10.000
1	.846154	.857143	.866667	.875000	.882353	.888889	.894737	.900000	.904762	.909091
2	.699422	.720000	.737991	.753846	.767918	.780488	.791781	.801980	.811236	.819672
3	.561840	.590164	.615234	.637546	.657510	.675462	.691679	.706395	.719803	.732064
4	.435835	.469565	.499939	.527345	.552138	.574635	.595112	.613809	.630933	.646663

	10.500	11.000	11.500	12.000	12.500	13.000	13.500	14.000	14.500	15.000
5	.324059	.360400	.393910	.424719	.453016	.479008	.502906	.524908	.545201	.563952
6	.229022	.264922	.299099	.331330	.361541	.389752	.416041	.440516	.463299	.484515
7	.152503	.185055	.217365	.248871	.279209	.308165	.335633	.361584	.386037	.409041
8	.094897	.121876	.150100	.178822	.207455	.235570	.262869	.289158	.314326	.338318
9	.054814	.075145	.097803	.122101	.147397	.173141	.198888	.224300	.249130	.273208
10	.029265	.043142	.059772	.078741	.099544	.121661	.144608	.167963	.191379	.214582
11	.014422	.022991	.034115	.047717	.063557	.081288	.100511	.120821	.141839	.163232
12	.006566	.011365	.018144	.027081	.038206	.051406	.066464	.083087	.100953	.119739
13	.002770	.005218	.008990	.014373	.021566	.030665	.041647	.054393	.068705	.084339
14	.001087	.002231	.004157	.007135	.011421	.017221	.024662	.033785	.044544	.056819
15	.000398	.000892	.001798	.003319	.005678	.009101	.013783	.019868	.027437	.036497
16	.000137	.000334	.000730	.001450	.002655	.004530	.007269	.011052	.016030	.022302
17	.000044	.000118	.000279	.000597	.001170	.002127	.003621	.005817	.008878	.012949
18	.000014	.000039	.000101	.000232	.000487	.000945	.001707	.002900	.004664	.007142
19	.000004	.000012	.000034	.000085	.000192	.000398	.000763	.001372	.002327	.003745
20	.000001	.000004	.000011	.000030	.000072	.000159	.000324	.000617	.001104	.001869
21	.000000	.000001	.000003	.000010	.000026	.000061	.000131	.000264	.000499	.000889
22	.000000	.000000	.000001	.000003	.000009	.000022	.000051	.000108	.000215	.000404
23	.000000	.000000	.000000	.000001	.000003	.000008	.000019	.000042	.000089	.000176
24	.000000	.000000	.000000	.000000	.000001	.000003	.000007	.000016	.000035	.000073
25	.000000	.000000	.000000	.000000	.000000	.000001	.000002	.000006	.000013	.000029
26	.000000	.000000	.000000	.000000	.000000	.000000	.000001	.000002	.000005	.000011
27	.000000	.000000	.000000	.000000	.000000	.000000	.000000	.000001	.000002	.000004
28	.000000	.000000	.000000	.000000	.000000	.000000	.000000	.000000	.000001	.000001
Channel	10.500	11.000	11.500	12.000	12.500	13.000	13.500	14.000	14.500	15.000
1	.913043	.916667	.920000	.923077	.925926	.928571	.931034	.933333	.935484	.937500
2	.827392	.834483	.841017	.847059	.852660	.857868	.862722	.867257	.871503	.875486
3	.743318	.753681	.763252	.772118	.780353	.788020	.795176	.801870	.808145	.814038
4	.661156	.674545	.686947	.698464	.709184	.719185	.728535	.737295	.745516	.753247
5	.581314	.597423	.612400	.626352	.639375	.651554	.662964	.673674	.683744	.693227

continued

Erlang B Distribution continued

Traffic in Erlangs

Channel	10.500	11.000	11.500	12.000	12.500	13.000	13.500	14.000	14.500	15.000
6	.504288	.522736	.539969	.556089	.571189	.585355	.598663	.611184	.622980	.634111
7	.430664	.450984	.470084	.488045	.504946	.520863	.535869	.550029	.563406	.576057
8	.361123	.382756	.403251	.422655	.441021	.458406	.474867	.490459	.505238	.519256
9	.296424	.318714	.340049	.360426	.379856	.398367	.415990	.432765	.448730	.463929
10	.237366	.259580	.281122	.301925	.321951	.341185	.359626	.377285	.394181	.410341
11	.184723	.206085	.227143	.247766	.267857	.287353	.306210	.324407	.341933	.358792
12	.139142	.158894	.178765	.198567	.218150	.237397	.256222	.274560	.292371	.309626
13	.101030	.118515	.136545	.154901	.173390	.191852	.210158	.228205	.245912	.263222
14	.070435	.085186	.100851	.117210	.134058	.151210	.168505	.185803	.202993	.219983
15	.046988	.058797	.071770	.085729	.100489	.115865	.131684	.147788	.164038	.180316
16	.029914	.038852	.049054	.060413	.072792	.086040	.099998	.114507	.129420	.144602
17	.018141	.024523	.032118	.040900	.050805	.061734	.073568	.086174	.099414	.113153
18	.010471	.014765	.020107	.026543	.034079	.042683	.052291	.062814	.074145	.086169
19	.005754	.008476	.012024	.016488	.021928	.028375	.035823	.044236	.053554	.063695
20	.003011	.004640	.006866	.009796	.013520	.018110	.023610	.030035	.037376	.045593
21	.001503	.002425	.003746	.005566	.007983	.011087	.014951	.019631	.025158	.031539
22	.000717	.001211	.001954	.003027	.004516	.006509	.009091	.012338	.016311	.021051
23	.000327	.000579	.000976	.001577	.002448	.003665	.005308	.007454	.010178	.013543
24	.000143	.000265	.000468	.000788	.001273	.001981	.002977	.004329	.006112	.008394
25	.000060	.000117	.000215	.000378	.000636	.001029	.001605	.002419	.003532	.005011
26	.000024	.000049	.000095	.000174	.000306	.000514	.000833	.001301	.001966	.002883
27	.000009	.000020	.000041	.000078	.000142	.000248	.000416	.000674	.001055	.001599
28	.000004	.000008	.000017	.000033	.000063	.000115	.000201	.000377	.000546	.000856
29	.000001	.000003	.000007	.000014	.000027	.000052	.000093	.000163	.000273	.000442
30	.000000	.000001	.000003	.000005	.000011	.000022	.000042	.000076	.000132	.000221
31	.000000	.000000	.000001	.000002	.000005	.000009	.000018	.000034	.000062	.000107
32	.000000	.000000	.000000	.000001	.000002	.000004	.000008	.000015	.000028	.000050
33	.000000	.000000	.000000	.000000	.000001	.000001	.000003	.000006	.000012	.000023
34	.000000	.000000	.000000	.000000	.000000	.000001	.000001	.000003	.000005	.000010

Channel	15.500	16.000	16.500	17.000	17.500	18.000	18.500	19.000	19.500	20.000
35	.000000	.000000	.000000	.000000	.000000	.000000	.000000	.000001	.000002	.000004
36	.000000	.000000	.000000	.000000	.000000	.000000	.000000	.000000	.000001	.000002
1	.939394	.941176	.942857	.944444	.945946	.947368	.948718	.950000	.951220	.952381
2	.879231	.882759	.886086	.889231	.892207	.895028	.897705	.900249	.902671	.904977
3	.819582	.824809	.829743	.834409	.838828	.843018	.846998	.850781	.854384	.857817
4	.760530	.767401	.773893	.780038	.785861	.791388	.796639	.801635	.806394	.810931
5	.702172	.710621	.718615	.726187	.733370	.740192	.746679	.752855	.758742	.764358
6	.644627	.654576	.664000	.672939	.681427	.689497	.697177	.704495	.711475	.718140
7	.588035	.599387	.610158	.620390	.630118	.639379	.648202	.656617	.664651	.672328
8	.532561	.545201	.557219	.568655	.579546	.589929	.599835	.609293	.618333	.626980
9	.478403	.492191	.505334	.517869	.529831	.541255	.552171	.562609	.572599	.582165
10	.425790	.440561	.454685	.468192	.481114	.493481	.505322	.516665	.527537	.537963
11	.374991	.390547	.405479	.419809	.433559	.446754	.459418	.471576	.483252	.494468
12	.326311	.342421	.357959	.372934	.387357	.401245	.414612	.427480	.439865	.451788
13	.280090	.296489	.312400	.327814	.342729	.357148	.371079	.384531	.397517	.410050
14	.236699	.253087	.269105	.284723	.299922	.314689	.329019	.342911	.356369	.369398
15	.196522	.212573	.228404	.243963	.259209	.274114	.288656	.302822	.316603	.329997
16	.159933	.175308	.190638	.205852	.220886	.235695	.250239	.264490	.278427	.292033
17	.127263	.141627	.156141	.170711	.185258	.199718	.214034	.228161	.242063	.255714
18	.098764	.111815	.125208	.138842	.152623	.166471	.180314	.194092	.207755	.221260
19	.074563	.086057	.098070	.110500	.123248	.136225	.149348	.162544	.175749	.188908
20	.054630	.064411	.074851	.085860	.097344	.109213	.121379	.133761	.146288	.158892
21	.038759	.046779	.055545	.064989	.075034	.085598	.096600	.107957	.119593	.131436
22	.026582	.032902	.039993	.047817	.056324	.065451	.075129	.085284	.095843	.106734
23	.017598	.022376	.027890	.034137	.041094	.048727	.056986	.065815	.075152	.084930
24	.011238	.014698	.018814	.023609	.029093	.035256	.042078	.049523	.057547	.066097
25	.006919	.009319	.012265	.015801	.019958	.024756	.030198	.036273	.042958	.050222
26	.004108	.005702	.007723	.010226	.013256	.016850	.021035	.025822	.031213	.037195
27	.002353	.003368	.004698	.006397	.008518	.011109	.014208	.017847	.022046	.026813

continued

Erlang B Distribution continued

Traffic in Erlangs

Channel	15.500	16.000	16.500	17.000	17.500	18.000	18.500	19.000	19.500	20.000
28	.001301	.001921	.002761	.003869	.005296	.007091	.009300	.011966	.015121	.018792
29	.000695	.001059	.001568	.002263	.003186	.004382	.005898	.007779	.010065	.012794
30	.000359	.000564	.000862	.001281	.001855	.002622	.003624	.004902	.006500	.008457
31	.000179	.000291	.000458	.000702	.001046	.001520	.002158	.002996	.004072	.005427
32	.000087	.000146	.000236	.000373	.000572	.000854	.001246	.001775	.002475	.003380
33	.000041	.000071	.000118	.000192	.000303	.000466	.000698	.001021	.001461	.002044
34	.000019	.000033	.000057	.000096	.000156	.000247	.000380	.000570	.000837	.001201
35	.000008	.000015	.000027	.000047	.000078	.000127	.000201	.000310	.000466	.000686
36	.000004	.000007	.000012	.000022	.000038	.000063	.000103	.000163	.000252	.000381
37	.000001	.000003	.000006	.000010	.000018	.000031	.000052	.000084	.000133	.000206
38	.000001	.000001	.000002	.000005	.000008	.000015	.000025	.000042	.000068	.000108
39	.000000	.000001	.000001	.000002	.000004	.000007	.000012	.000020	.000034	.000056
40	.000000	.000000	.000000	.000001	.000002	.000003	.000006	.000010	.000017	.000028
41	.000000	.000000	.000000	.000000	.000001	.000001	.000002	.000004	.000008	.000014
42	.000000	.000000	.000000	.000000	.000000	.000001	.000001	.000002	.000004	.000006
43	.000000	.000000	.000000	.000000	.000000	.000000	.000000	.000001	.000002	.000003
44	.000000	.000000	.000000	.000000	.000000	.000000	.000000	.000000	.000001	.000001

Channel	20.500	21.000	21.500	22.000	22.500	23.000	23.500	24.000	24.500	25.000
1	.953488	.954545	.955556	.956522	.957447	.958333	.959184	.960000	.960784	.961538
2	.907178	.909278	.911286	.913208	.915047	.916881	.918503	.920128	.921689	.923191
3	.861093	.864222	.867213	.870077	.872820	.875450	.877973	.880397	.882727	.884968
4	.815263	.819402	.823361	.827152	.830784	.834268	.837612	.840825	.843913	.846885
5	.769722	.774850	.779758	.784458	.788964	.793287	.797439	.801428	.805265	.808957
6	.724509	.730602	.736435	.742025	.747386	.752533	.757476	.762228	.766800	.771201
7	.679669	.686698	.693431	.699887	.706082	.712032	.717750	.723249	.728541	.733638
8	.635257	.643186	.650789	.658083	.665088	.671818	.678290	.684517	.690513	.696290

9	.591332	.600123	.608559	.616660	.624444	.631929	.639131	.646065	.652745	.659185
10	.547967	.557573	.566800	.575669	.584199	.592408	.600313	.607929	.615270	.622351
11	.505247	.515611	.525580	.535173	.544410	.553307	.561881	.570149	.578126	.585824
12	.463269	.474326	.484978	.495243	.505139	.514682	.523889	.532775	.541356	.549644
13	.422146	.433819	.445085	.455961	.466461	.476602	.486397	.495862	.505011	.513857
14	.382007	.394207	.406008	.417422	.428464	.439144	.449476	.459474	.469149	.478515
15	.343003	.355624	.367867	.379737	.391244	.402398	.413207	.423684	.433838	.443680
16	.305301	.318224	.330800	.343030	.354917	.366466	.377683	.388576	.399152	.409419
17	.269090	.282176	.294962	.307441	.319609	.331464	.343009	.354246	.365179	.375814
18	.234575	.247671	.260528	.273130	.285465	.297525	.309305	.320803	.332020	.342954
19	.201975	.214911	.227685	.240269	.252644	.264793	.276705	.288370	.299784	.310942
20	.171516	.184111	.196633	.209046	.221320	.233430	.245356	.257083	.268597	.279890
21	.143420	.155485	.167579	.179656	.191677	.203607	.215419	.227088	.238596	.249926
22	.117886	.129236	.140724	.152295	.163902	.175504	.187062	.198546	.209929	.221188
23	.095082	.105544	.116253	.127151	.138183	.149301	.160460	.171622	.182753	.193823
24	.075115	.084543	.094321	.104388	.114689	.125171	.135783	.146482	.157228	.167983
25	.058021	.066308	.075030	.084133	.093563	.103265	.113189	.123286	.133511	.143823
26	.043746	.050834	.058419	.066458	.074903	.083704	.092811	.102175	.111750	.121490
27	.032147	.038034	.044451	.051370	.058752	.066557	.074742	.083260	.092067	.101116
28	.022995	.027734	.033006	.038796	.045083	.051838	.059027	.066612	.074553	.082807
29	.015995	.019688	.023885	.028590	.033796	.039489	.045649	.052247	.059252	.066629
30	.010812	.013594	.016830	.020535	.024720	.029386	.034524	.040121	.046156	.052603
31	.007099	.009125	.011538	.014364	.017626	.021337	.025504	.030125	.035194	.040696
32	.004527	.005953	.007692	.009779	.012242	.015104	.018385	.022095	.026239	.030814
33	.002804	.003774	.004987	.006477	.008277	.010418	.012923	.015815	.019108	.022811
34	.001688	.002325	.003143	.004173	.005448	.006998	.008853	.011040	.013582	.016496
35	.000988	.001393	.001927	.002616	.003490	.004578	.005909	.007514	.009418	.011646
36	.000562	.000812	.001150	.001596	.002176	.002916	.003843	.004984	.006369	.008022
37	.000311	.000461	.000668	.000948	.001322	.001809	.002435	.003222	.004199	.005391
38	.000168	.000255	.000378	.000549	.000782	.001094	.001503	.002031	.002700	.003534
39	.000088	.000137	.000208	.000309	.000451	.000645	.000905	.001248	.001693	.002261
40	.000045	.000072	.000112	.000170	.000254	.000371	.000531	.000748	.001036	.001411

continued

Erlang B Distribution *continued*

Traffic in Erlangs

Channel	20.500	21.000	21.500	22.000	22.500	23.000	23.500	24.000	24.500	25.000
41	.000023	.000037	.000059	.000091	.000139	.000208	.000305	.000438	.000619	.000860
42	.000011	.000018	.000030	.000048	.000075	.000114	.000170	.000250	.000361	.000511
43	.000005	.000009	.000015	.000024	.000039	.000061	.000093	.000140	.000206	.000297
44	.000002	.000004	.000007	.000012	.000020	.000032	.000050	.000076	.000114	.000169
45	.000001	.000002	.000004	.000006	.000010	.000016	.000026	.000041	.000062	.000094
46	.000000	.000001	.000002	.000003	.000005	.000008	.000013	.000021	.000033	.000051
47	.000000	.000000	.000001	.000001	.000002	.000004	.000007	.000011	.000017	.000027
48	.000000	.000000	.000000	.000001	.000001	.000002	.000003	.000005	.000009	.000014
49	.000000	.000000	.000000	.000000	.000001	.000001	.000002	.000003	.000004	.000007
50	.000000	.000000	.000000	.000000	.000000	.000000	.000001	.000001	.000002	.000004
51	.000000	.000000	.000000	.000000	.000000	.000000	.000000	.000001	.000001	.000002

Channel	25.500	26.000	26.500	27.000	27.500	28.000	28.500	29.000	29.500	30.000
1	.962264	.962963	.963636	.964286	.964912	.965517	.966102	.966667	.967213	.967742
2	.924636	.926027	.927369	.928662	.929911	.931116	.932281	.933407	.934497	.935551
3	.887126	.889204	.891207	.893139	.895004	.896805	.898546	.900229	.901857	.903433
4	.849747	.852504	.855162	.857726	.860202	.862593	.864904	.867139	.869301	.871395
5	.812513	.815940	.819245	.822434	.825514	.828489	.831365	.834146	.836838	.839444
6	.775441	.779529	.783472	.787277	.790953	.794504	.797938	.801260	.804476	.807589
7	.738550	.743286	.747857	.752269	.756532	.760652	.764637	.768492	.772225	.775840
8	.701860	.707232	.712419	.717427	.722267	.726946	.731473	.735854	.740096	.744206
9	.665395	.671389	.677177	.682769	.688175	.693403	.698462	.703359	.708103	.712700
10	.629184	.635782	.642157	.648318	.654276	.660041	.665621	.671025	.676261	.681336
11	.593259	.600441	.607383	.614097	.620593	.626880	.632969	.638867	.644585	.650128
12	.557654	.565398	.572888	.580135	.587151	.593945	.600527	.606907	.613093	.619094
13	.522413	.530692	.538705	.546464	.553980	.561262	.568322	.575168	.581809	.588253
14	.487584	.496366	.504875	.513120	.521113	.528863	.536380	.543675	.550754	.557629

15	.453221	.462472	.471444	.480146	.488589	.496782	.504735	.512458	.519958	.527244
16	.419388	.429066	.438464	.447589	.456451	.465060	.473424	.481551	.489450	.497129
17	.386157	.396215	.405995	.415504	.424751	.433743	.442487	.450993	.459266	.467316
18	.353611	.363993	.374106	.383954	.393544	.402882	.411974	.420827	.429447	.437842
19	.321842	.332486	.342875	.353010	.362896	.372537	.381938	.391103	.400038	.408749
20	.290956	.301789	.312388	.322752	.332881	.342776	.352441	.361878	.371092	.380085
21	.261067	.272009	.282745	.293270	.303580	.313675	.323553	.333216	.342665	.351903
22	.232305	.243264	.254054	.264664	.275087	.285317	.295352	.305189	.314826	.324264
23	.204807	.215683	.226434	.237044	.247502	.257798	.267925	.277876	.287647	.297236
24	.178717	.189401	.200013	.210531	.220939	.231221	.241367	.251366	.261211	.270895
25	.154185	.164562	.174927	.185252	.195516	.205699	.215784	.225757	.235608	.245325
26	.131356	.141308	.151313	.161339	.171359	.181349	.191287	.201154	.210936	.220618
27	.110367	.119776	.129307	.138925	.148598	.158296	.167994	.177669	.187300	.196872
28	.091332	.100089	.109036	.118138	.127357	.136663	.146024	.155415	.164811	.174191
29	.074339	.082346	.090609	.099091	.107756	.116569	.125497	.134510	.143581	.152684
30	.059433	.066612	.074106	.081880	.089897	.098122	.106522	.115065	.123720	.132460
31	.046610	.052912	.059575	.066567	.073857	.081411	.089197	.097181	.105333	.113622
32	.035812	.041219	.047016	.053179	.059683	.066498	.073594	.080942	.088509	.096266
33	.026928	.031454	.036382	.041696	.047379	.053409	.059760	.066407	.073320	.080472
34	.019796	.023488	.027574	.032050	.036907	.042131	.047704	.053605	.059811	.066297
35	.014218	.017149	.020451	.024128	.028181	.032606	.037392	.042527	.047993	.053771
36	.009970	.012234	.014831	.017774	.021074	.024733	.028751	.033123	.037839	.042887
37	.006825	.008524	.010510	.012804	.015421	.018373	.021666	.025304	.029286	.033605
38	.004559	.005798	.007276	.009016	.011037	.013357	.015990	.018945	.022230	.025845
39	.002972	.003851	.004920	.006203	.007722	.009499	.011550	.013892	.016537	.019493
40	.001891	.002497	.003249	.004170	.005281	.006605	.008162	.009971	.012049	.014409
41	.001175	.001581	.002095	.002738	.003530	.004491	.005642	.007003	.008595	.010433
42	.000713	.000978	.001320	.001757	.002306	.002985	.003814	.004812	.006001	.007397
43	.000422	.000591	.000813	.001102	.001472	.001940	.002521	.003235	.004100	.005134
44	.000245	.000349	.000489	.000676	.000919	.001233	.001630	.002128	.002741	.003488
45	.000139	.000202	.000288	.000405	.000562	.000767	.001032	.001369	.001794	.002320
46	.000077	.000114	.000166	.000238	.000336	.000466	.000639	.000862	.001149	.001511

continued

Erlang B Distribution *continued*

Traffic in Erlangs

Channel	25.500	26.000	26.500	27.000	27.500	28.000	28.500	29.000	29.500	30.000
47	.000042	.000063	.000094	.000137	.000196	.000278	.000387	.000532	.000721	.000963
48	.000022	.000034	.000052	.000077	.000112	.000162	.000230	.000321	.000443	.000602
49	.000012	.000018	.000028	.000042	.000063	.000093	.000134	.000190	.000266	.000368
50	.000006	.000009	.000015	.000023	.000035	.000052	.000076	.000110	.000157	.000221
51	.000003	.000005	.000008	.000012	.000019	.000028	.000043	.000063	.000091	.000130
52	.000001	.000002	.000004	.000006	.000010	.000015	.000023	.000035	.000052	.000075
53	.000001	.000001	.000002	.000003	.000005	.000008	.000011	.000007	.000004	.000003

Channel	30.500	31.000	31.500	32.000	32.500	33.000	33.500	34.000	34.500	35.000
1	.968254	.968750	.969231	.969697	.970149	.970588	.971014	.971429	.971831	.972222
2	.936572	.937561	.938520	.939450	.940352	.941227	.942078	.942904	.943707	.944487
3	.904959	.906438	.907872	.909262	.910612	.911921	.913193	.914429	.915630	.916798
4	.873423	.875388	.877293	.879141	.880934	.882675	.884366	.886009	.887606	.889160
5	.841969	.844416	.846789	.849091	.851325	.853494	.855601	.857648	.859639	.861575
6	.810606	.813531	.816367	.819119	.821790	.824383	.826903	.829352	.831733	.834048
7	.779343	.782740	.786035	.789231	.792335	.795349	.798278	.801125	.803893	.806585
8	.748190	.752053	.755800	.759438	.762969	.766400	.769733	.772974	.776125	.779191
9	.717157	.721480	.725674	.729746	.733700	.737542	.741276	.744906	.748437	.751873
10	.686258	.691033	.695667	.700167	.704538	.708785	.712914	.716929	.720835	.724636
11	.655506	.660724	.665791	.670711	.675492	.680139	.684657	.689051	.693327	.697488
12	.624917	.630570	.636059	.641392	.646575	.651614	.656515	.661282	.665922	.670439
13	.594510	.600586	.606488	.612224	.617801	.623224	.628500	.633633	.638631	.643497
14	.564305	.570791	.577095	.583224	.589184	.594982	.600625	.606117	.611465	.616674
15	.534325	.541208	.547900	.554409	.560742	.566905	.572904	.578746	.584436	.589980
16	.504597	.511859	.518925	.525801	.532493	.539009	.545355	.551536	.557559	.563429
17	.475150	.482774	.490196	.497422	.504460	.511316	.517996	.524505	.530851	.537037

18	.446019	.453983	.461741	.469301	.476667	.483848	.490847	.497672	.504328	.510821
19	.417242	.425521	.433594	.441466	.449143	.456630	.463934	.471059	.478012	.484798
20	.388863	.397430	.405791	.413952	.421917	.429692	.437282	.446910	.451926	.458990
21	.360931	.369754	.378375	.386798	.395027	.403067	.410922	.418597	.426095	.433423
22	.333503	.342545	.351392	.360047	.368513	.376792	.384889	.392807	.400550	.408121
23	.306641	.315861	.324897	.333749	.342419	.350909	.359220	.367357	.375322	.383118
24	.280415	.289766	.298948	.307958	.316796	.325463	.333960	.342288	.350449	.358445
25	.254902	.264333	.273612	.282735	.291702	.300509	.309157	.317645	.325973	.334143
26	.230189	.239640	.248962	.258150	.267199	.276105	.284865	.293477	.301940	.310253
27	.206367	.215774	.225080	.234277	.243358	.252315	.261144	.269840	.278401	.286825
28	.183535	.192827	.202052	.211198	.220254	.229211	.238060	.246797	.255415	.263911
29	.161797	.170899	.179972	.189000	.197970	.206869	.215687	.224414	.233044	.241570
30	.141258	.150090	.158936	.167777	.176594	.185373	.194101	.202765	.211357	.219866
31	.122021	.130503	.139044	.147622	.156217	.164810	.173386	.181929	.190427	.198869
32	.104184	.112236	.120393	.128633	.136932	.145270	.153628	.161988	.170334	.178654
33	.087834	.095377	.103075	.110902	.118832	.126844	.134915	.143026	.151159	.159297
34	.073037	.080004	.087172	.094513	.102003	.109618	.117333	.125129	.132984	.140881
35	.059838	.066172	.072747	.079539	.086522	.093672	.100966	.108380	.115893	.123484
36	.048250	.053910	.059844	.066033	.072451	.079076	.085885	.092854	.099962	.107186
37	.038252	.043216	.048479	.054024	.059832	.065881	.072150	.078618	.085261	.092058
38	.029788	.034054	.038634	.043514	.048681	.054116	.059802	.065719	.071846	.078163
39	.022765	.026355	.030260	.034473	.038986	.043786	.048859	.054189	.059758	.065548
40	.017062	.020017	.023275	.026838	.030703	.034864	.039311	.044032	.049015	.054244
41	.012534	.014909	.017568	.020517	.023760	.027295	.031120	.035228	.039611	.044256
42	.009020	.010884	.013005	.015392	.018054	.020996	.024221	.027727	.031512	.035568
43	.006357	.007786	.009437	.011324	.013461	.015858	.018520	.021454	.024659	.028136
44	.004387	.005456	.006711	.008169	.009845	.011753	.013905	.016308	.018969	.021891
45	.002965	.003744	.004675	.005775	.007060	.008546	.010245	.012171	.014334	.016742
46	.001962	.002517	.003191	.004002	.004963	.006093	.007406	.008916	.010636	.012578
47	.001272	.001657	.002134	.002717	.003420	.004260	.005251	.006408	.007747	.009280
48	.000807	.001069	.001399	.001808	.002311	.002920	.003651	.004519	.005537	.006721
49	.000502	.000676	.000898	.001179	.001530	.001963	.002490	.003126	.003884	.004778

continued

Erlang B Distribution *continued*

Traffic in Erlangs

Channel	30.500	31.000	31.500	32.000	32.500	33.000	33.500	34.000	34.500	35.000
50	.000306	.000419	.000566	.000754	.000994	.001294	.001666	.002121	.002672	.002418
51	.000183	.000255	.000349	.000473	.000574	.000348	.000212	.000128	.000078	.000047

Channel	35.500	36.000	36.500	37.000	37.500	38.000	38.500	39.000	39.500	40.000
1	.972603	.972973	.973333	.973684	.974026	.974359	.974684	.975000	.975309	.975610
2	.945247	.945985	.946705	.947405	.948087	.948752	.949399	.950031	.950647	.951249
3	.917935	.919040	.920116	.921165	.922186	.923180	.924150	.925096	.926018	.926918
4	.890671	.892141	.893572	.894966	.896325	.897648	.898938	.900196	.901424	.902621
5	.863458	.865291	.867076	.868814	.870507	.872158	.873766	.875336	.876866	.878360
6	.836301	.838495	.840630	.842710	.844737	.846712	.848638	.850516	.852348	.854137
7	.809206	.811756	.814240	.816659	.819017	.821315	.823556	.825741	.827874	.829955
8	.782175	.785080	.787910	.790666	.793352	.795970	.798524	.801014	.803445	.805817
9	.755217	.758473	.761644	.764734	.767746	.770682	.773546	.776340	.779065	.781726
10	.728336	.731940	.735450	.738870	.742205	.745456	.748627	.751721	.754740	.757688
11	.701541	.705487	.709332	.713080	.716733	.720296	.723772	.727163	.730473	.733705
12	.674838	.679123	.683299	.687369	.691338	.695209	.698986	.702671	.706269	.709782
13	.648237	.652856	.657357	.661746	.666026	.670201	.674275	.678251	.682133	.685924
14	.621749	.626695	.631516	.636218	.640804	.645279	.649646	.653909	.658072	.662137
15	.595383	.600650	.605785	.610795	.615682	.620451	.625106	.629652	.634091	.638428
16	.569152	.574733	.580175	.585486	.590668	.595726	.600665	.605488	.610199	.614802
17	.543071	.548956	.554699	.560303	.565773	.571114	.576330	.581425	.586403	.591268
18	.517155	.523336	.529369	.535258	.541009	.546626	.552113	.557474	.562714	.567835
19	.491421	.497887	.504201	.510367	.516390	.522274	.528025	.533645	.539139	.544511
20	.465890	.472628	.479212	.485644	.491930	.498073	.504078	.509950	.515691	.521307
21	.440583	.447581	.454421	.461108	.467645	.474037	.480288	.486402	.492383	.498235
22	.415526	.422768	.429850	.436778	.443555	.450184	.456671	.463018	.469229	.475309
23	.390748	.398215	.405524	.412678	.419680	.426534	.433244	.439813	.446244	.452542

24	.366279	.373952	.381469	.388832	.396044	.403108	.410028	.416806	.423446	.429951
25	.342155	.350013	.357717	.365269	.372673	.379931	.387046	.394019	.400855	.407556
26	.318417	.326433	.334300	.342021	.349598	.357031	.364323	.371476	.378493	.385375
27	.295110	.303254	.311259	.319124	.326850	.334437	.341888	.349203	.356384	.363433
28	.272281	.280523	.288635	.296616	.304466	.312185	.319772	.327229	.334556	.341754
29	.249987	.258290	.266476	.274543	.282489	.290312	.298012	.305587	.313040	.320368
30	.228286	.236611	.244834	.252953	.260962	.268861	.276646	.284315	.291869	.299307
31	.207246	.215547	.223767	.231898	.239937	.247878	.255718	.263453	.271083	.278605
32	.186934	.195165	.203336	.211439	.219467	.227414	.235275	.243046	.250722	.258301
33	.167427	.175534	.183608	.191637	.199612	.207526	.215371	.223142	.230832	.238439
34	.148801	.156730	.164654	.172559	.180436	.188273	.196061	.203794	.211464	.219065
35	.131135	.138828	.146547	.154277	.162005	.169718	.177407	.185060	.192671	.200230
36	.114506	.121904	.129361	.136861	.144389	.151929	.159471	.167001	.174511	.181989
37	.098989	.106033	.113171	.120385	.127658	.134975	.142320	.149680	.157044	.164400
38	.084649	.091283	.098046	.104919	.111884	.118923	.126021	.133163	.140335	.147524
39	.071540	.077713	.084048	.090527	.097131	.103841	.110641	.117514	.124446	.131421
40	.059701	.065370	.071231	.077268	.083460	.089791	.096243	.102798	.109441	.116156
41	.049151	.054282	.059632	.065184	.070922	.076828	.082884	.089074	.095380	.101788
42	.039888	.044459	.049270	.054306	.059552	.064993	.070612	.076393	.082319	.088374
43	.031881	.035886	.040143	.044642	.049371	.054316	.059463	.064797	.070302	.075963
44	.025077	.028524	.032227	.036182	.040378	.044807	.049457	.054314	.059366	.064597
45	.019399	.022310	.025474	.028890	.032553	.036458	.040595	.044956	.049529	.054301
46	.014750	.017160	.019813	.022710	.025852	.029237	.032860	.036716	.040795	.045090
47	.011018	.012973	.015153	.017564	.020210	.023092	.026212	.029565	.033149	.036956
48	.008083	.009636	.011391	.013358	.015543	.017953	.020591	.023458	.026554	.029877
49	.005822	.007030	.008414	.009986	.010165	.006242	.003832	.002353	.001447	.000890
50	.001472	.000896	.000546	.000333	.000203	.000125	.000077	.000047	.000029	.000018

Poisson Distribution

Probability All Channels Busy When Call Attempted (Grade of Service)

Traffic in Erlangs

Channel	.500	1.000	1.500	2.000	2.500	3.000	3.500	4.000	4.500	5.000
1	.393469	.632120	.776870	.864665	.917915	.950213	.969802	.981684	.988891	.993262
2	.090204	.264241	.442174	.593994	.712702	.800851	.864111	.908422	.938900	.959572
3	.014387	.080301	.191152	.323323	.456186	.576809	.679152	.761896	.826421	.875347
4	.001751	.018988	.065642	.142875	.242422	.352767	.463366	.566529	.657703	.734973
5	.000172	.003659	.018575	.052652	.108820	.184735	.274553	.371161	.467895	.559505
6	.000014	.000594	.004455	.016562	.042019	.083916	.142384	.214867	.297068	.384037
7	.000001	.000083	.000925	.004532	.014185	.033507	.065286	.110672	.168947	.237814
8	.000000	.000010	.000169	.001095	.004245	.011902	.026736	.051131	.086584	.133369
9	.000000	.000000	.000027	.000236	.001138	.003801	.009871	.021361	.040255	.068090
10	.000000	.000000	.000003	.000045	.000275	.001100	.003312	.008129	.017090	.031825
11	.000000	.000000	.000000	.000007	.000059	.000290	.001017	.002837	.006666	.013692
12	.000000	.000000	.000001	.000000	.000010	.000069	.000286	.000912	.002402	.005450
13	.000000	.000000	.000001	.000001	.000000	.000014	.000073	.000271	.000802	.002015
14	.000000	.000000	.000001	.000001	.000002	.000001	.000016	.000074	.000249	.000694
15	.000000	.000000	.000001	.000001	.000002	.000001	.000002	.000017	.000071	.000223
16	.000000	.000000	.000001	.000001	.000002	.000002	.000002	.000002	.000017	.000065
17	.000000	.000000	.000001	.000001	.000002	.000002	.000003	.000002	.000002	.000016

Channel	5.500	6.000	6.500	7.000	7.500	8.000	8.500	9.000	9.500	10.000
1	.995913	.997521	.998497	.999088	.999447	.999665	.999797	.999877	.999925	.999955
2	.973436	.982649	.988724	.992705	.995299	.996981	.998067	.998766	.999214	.999501
3	.911623	.938031	.956964	.970364	.979743	.986246	.990717	.993768	.995836	.997231
4	.798300	.848796	.888150	.918234	.940854	.957620	.969891	.978773	.985140	.989664
5	.642481	.714942	.776327	.827008	.867937	.900367	.925636	.945036	.959737	.970747
6	.471079	.554319	.630957	.699290	.758562	.808763	.850402	.884309	.911471	.932914
7	.313961	.393695	.473474	.550287	.621843	.686624	.743821	.793218	.835050	.869858

Channel	10.500	11.000	11.500	12.000	12.500	13.000	13.500	14.000	14.500	15.000
8	.190511	.256017	.327239	.401283	.475358	.547037	.614401	.676101	.731335	.779778
9	.105640	.152759	.208423	.270905	.338029	.407449	.476892	.544345	.608173	.667178
10	.053774	.083920	.122611	.169500	.223587	.283372	.347023	.412588	.478170	.542067
11	.025247	.042617	.066834	.098516	.137756	.184110	.236634	.294007	.354667	.416956
12	.010984	.020088	.033874	.053345	.079235	.111919	.151333	.196987	.248005	.303219
13	.004447	.008824	.016021	.026995	.042660	.063792	.090912	.124221	.163564	.208438
14	.001681	.003625	.007095	.012807	.021558	.034175	.051406	.073845	.101857	.135529
15	.000594	.001396	.002950	.005712	.010254	.017251	.027420	.041460	.059985	.083452
16	.000196	.000505	.001154	.002402	.004602	.008225	.013828	.022030	.033466	.048734
17	.000059	.000171	.000425	.000953	.001953	.003712	.006607	.011100	.017720	.027035
18	.000015	.000053	.000146	.000357	.000784	.001589	.002997	.005313	.008921	.014271
19	.000001	.000014	.000045	.000125	.000297	.000645	.001292	.002420	.004277	.007179
20	.000003	.000001	.000011	.000039	.000104	.000247	.000529	.001050	.001955	.003447
21	.000004	.000003	.000000	.000010	.000032	.000088	.000205	.000433	.000852	.001581
22	.000004	.000004	.000004	.000000	.000006	.000028	.000074	.000169	.000353	.000692
23	.000004	.000005	.000005	.000004	.000002	.000006	.000023	.000061	.000138	.000289
24	.000004	.000004	.000005	.000005	.000005	.000002	.000004	.000018	.000049	.000113
25	.000004	.000004	.000005	.000005	.000006	.000005	.000002	.000003	.000013	.000040
26	.000004	.000004	.000005	.000005	.000006	.000005	.000005	.000003	.000000	.000010

Channel	10.500	11.000	11.500	12.000	12.500	13.000	13.500	14.000	14.500	15.000
1	.999972	.999983	.999990	.999994	.999996	.999998	.999999	.999999	1.000000	1.000000
2	.999683	.999800	.999873	.999920	.999950	.999968	.999980	.999987	.999992	.999995
3	.998165	.998789	.999204	.999478	.999659	.999777	.999855	.999906	.999939	.999961
4	.992853	.995084	.996636	.997708	.998445	.998950	.999293	.999526	.999683	.999789
5	.978906	.984895	.989253	.992400	.994654	.996260	.997396	.998195	.998754	.999143
6	.949619	.962480	.972274	.979659	.985177	.989266	.992273	.994468	.996060	.997208
7	.898367	.921385	.939730	.054177	.965432	.974113	.980746	.985772	.989550	.992368
8	.821488	.856807	.886264	.910495	.930174	.945971	.958516	.968380	.976064	.981998
9	.720585	.768013	.809408	.844971	.875082	.900241	.921004	.937944	.951620	.962553
10	.602864	.659487	.711203	.757606	.798567	.834187	.864735	.890600	.912240	.930146

continued

Poisson Distribution *continued*

Traffic in Erlangs

Channel	10.500	11.000	11.500	12.000	12.500	13.000	13.500	14.000	14.500	15.000
11	.479258	.540108	.598267	.652768	.702922	.748316	.788771	.824317	.855138	.881534
12	.361270	.420729	.480197	.538399	.594235	.646832	.695544	.739958	.779867	.815246
13	.258030	.311298	.367047	.424030	.481019	.536891	.590662	.641538	.688915	.732386
14	.174644	.218703	.266953	.318459	.372158	.426950	.481748	.535548	.587468	.636778
15	.112105	.145949	.184733	.227969	.274960	.324862	.376722	.429558	.482398	.534341
16	.068328	.092597	.121697	.155577	.193962	.236386	.282200	.330634	.380831	.431904
17	.039599	.055917	.076391	.101284	.130682	.164499	.202446	.244075	.288785	.335870
18	.021854	.032183	.045742	.062958	.084153	.109527	.139112	.172791	.210276	.251133
19	.011503	.017679	.026161	.037408	.051841	.069825	.091612	.117348	.147032	.180520
20	.005783	.009282	.014309	.021272	.030584	.042660	.057862	.076496	.098767	.124772
21	.002780	.004664	.007494	.011590	.017297	.025003	.035081	.047899	.063775	.082961
22	.001278	.002244	.003763	.006057	.009389	.014072	.020435	.028835	.039613	.053096
23	.000562	.001035	.001812	.003039	.004895	.007613	.011449	.016703	.023689	.032734
24	.000235	.000456	.000836	.001465	.002453	.003963	.006174	.009318	.013650	.019454
25	.000091	.000191	.000369	.000677	.001181	.001985	.003207	.005010	.007584	.011154
26	.000031	.000075	.000154	.000299	.000545	.000957	.001604	.002598	.004066	.006174
27	.000007	.000025	.000059	.000125	.000240	.000443	.000772	.001299	.002104	.003301
28	.000002	.000005	.000018	.000048	.000098	.000195	.000356	.000625	.001051	.001705
29	.000006	.000003	.000002	.000014	.000035	.000080	.000156	.000289	.000505	.000850
30	.000007	.000006	.000005	.000001	.000008	.000029	.000063	.000126	.000232	.000408
31	.000008	.000007	.000007	.000005	.000004	.000007	.000021	.000050	.000100	.000187
32	.000008	.000008	.000008	.000007	.000008	.000003	.000002	.000016	.000039	.000080
33	.000008	.000008	.000009	.000008	.000010	.000007	.000005	.000001	.000011	.000030
38	.000008	.000008	.000009	.000008	.000011	.000009	.000010	.000010	.000010	.000010
39	.000008	.000008	.000009	.000008	.000011	.000009	.000010	.000010	.000010	.000010
40	.000008	.000008	.000009	.000008	.000011	.000009	.000010	.000010	.000010	.000010
41	.000008	.000008	.000009	.000008	.000011	.000009	.000010	.000010	.000010	.000010
42	.000008	.000008	.000009	.000008	.000011	.000009	.000010	.000010	.000010	.000010
43	.000008	.000008	.000009	.000008	.000011	.000009	.000010	.000010	.000010	.000010

	15.500	16.000	16.500	17.000	17.500	18.000	18.500	19.000	19.500	20.000
44	.000008	.000008	.000009	.000008	.000011	.000009	.000010	.000010	.000010	.000010
45	.000008	.000008	.000009	.000008	.000011	.000009	.000010	.000010	.000010	.000010
46	.000008	.000008	.000009	.000008	.000011	.000009	.000010	.000010	.000010	.000010
47	.000008	.000008	.000009	.000008	.000011	.000009	.000010	.000010	.000010	.000010
48	.000008	.000008	.000009	.000008	.000011	.000009	.000010	.000010	.000010	.000010
49	.000008	.000008	.000009	.000008	.000011	.000009	.000010	.000010	.000010	.000010
50	.000008	.000008	.000009	.000008	.000011	.000009	.000010	.000010	.000010	.000010
51	.000008	.000008	.000009	.000008	.000011	.000009	.000010	.000010	.000010	.000010
52	.000008	.000008	.000009	.000008	.000011	.000009	.000010	.000010	.000010	.000010
53	.000008	.000008	.000009	.000008	.000011	.000009	.000010	.000010	.000010	.000010
54	.000008	.000008	.000009	.000008	.000011	.000009	.000010	.000010	.000010	.000010
55	.000008	.000008	.000009	.000008	.000011	.000009	.000010	.000010	.000010	.000010

Channel	15.500	16.000	16.500	17.000	17.500	18.000	18.500	19.000	19.500	20.000
1	1.000000	1.000000	1.000000	1.000000	1.000000	1.000000	1.000000	1.000000	1.000000	1.000000
2	.999997	.999998	.999999	.999999	1.000000	1.000000	1.000000	1.000000	1.000000	1.000000
3	.999975	.999984	.999990	.999993	.999996	.999997	.999998	.999999	.999999	1.000000
4	.999859	.999907	.999938	.999959	.999973	.999982	.999988	.999992	.999995	.999997
5	.999413	.999600	.999728	.999815	.999875	.999916	.999943	.999962	.999975	.999983
6	.998030	.998616	.999032	.999325	.999532	.999676	.999777	.999846	.999895	.999928
7	.994456	.995994	.997119	.997938	.998530	.998957	.999262	.999480	.999635	.999745
8	.986544	.990000	.992610	.994567	.996026	.997107	.997903	.998487	.998912	.999221
9	.971213	.978012	.983309	.987404	.990548	.992944	.994759	.996127	.997150	.997913
10	.944809	.056701	.066259	.973875	.979895	.984619	.988298	.991144	.993333	.995005
11	.903883	.922603	.938125	.950875	.961254	.969633	.976344	.981678	.985888	.989188
12	.846215	.873006	.895925	.915330	.931598	.945112	.956240	.965327	.972690	.978613
13	.771728	.806876	.837900	.864974	.888350	.908330	.925245	.939438	.951244	.960987
14	.682916	.725486	.764253	.799124	.830131	.857401	.881138	.901600	.919076	.933871
15	.584588	.632469	.677454	.719164	.757357	.791920	.822854	.850248	.874269	.895134
16	.482983	.533250	.581975	.628542	.672454	.713344	.750970	.785203	.816021	.843485
17	.384552	.434031	.483513	.532256	.579591	.624945	.667854	.707962	.745031	.778923

continued

Poisson Distribution *continued*

	Traffic in Erlangs									
Channel	15.500	16.000	16.500	17.000	17.500	18.000	18.500	19.000	19.500	20.000
18	.294807	.340649	.387947	.435970	.483997	.531347	.577404	.621634	.663601	.702968
19	.217527	.257643	.300345	.345034	.391059	.437748	.484441	.530510	.575385	.618573
20	.154482	.187742	.224269	.263670	.305458	.349076	.393925	.439385	.484847	.529736
21	.105622	.131822	.161506	.194510	.230557	.269271	.310198	.352817	.396574	.440900
22	.069559	.089217	.112193	.138524	.168139	.200866	.236439	.274494	.314605	.356293
23	.044151	.058231	.075208	.095261	.118489	.144899	.174413	.206851	.241951	.279379
24	.027028	.036675	.048675	.063285	.080711	.101099	.124524	.150972	.180353	.212496
25	.015970	.022305	.030434	.040635	.053165	.068249	.086067	.106734	.130305	.156761
26	.009114	.013108	.018395	.025233	.033883	.044596	.057609	.073113	.091267	.112173
27	.005026	.007448	.010754	.015162	.020905	.028222	.037360	.048545	.061989	.077874
28	.002680	.004094	.006085	.008822	.012493	.017305	.023486	.031255	.040843	.052467
29	.001381	.002177	.003334	.004972	.007235	.010288	.014319	.019524	.026117	.034320
30	.000687	.001120	.001768	.002715	.004063	.005932	.008471	.011837	.016215	.021805
31	.000328	.000556	.000907	.001436	.002212	.003319	.004864	.006969	.009778	.013461
32	.000149	.000265	.000449	.000735	.001167	.001801	.002712	.003985	.005730	.008078
33	.000062	.000119	.000213	.000363	.000596	.000947	.001468	.002214	.003263	.004714
34	.000021	.000049	.000095	.000171	.000293	.000482	.000771	.001194	.001805	.002674
35	.000002	.000016	.000037	.000075	.000137	.000235	.000391	.000624	.000968	.001475
36	.000006	.000000	.000010	.000028	.000059	.000109	.000190	.000314	.000503	.000790
37	.000010	.000006	.000002	.000006	.000021	.000045	.000087	.000151	.000250	.000409
38	.000011	.000009	.000008	.000004	.000003	.000014	.000036	.000067	.000117	.000203
39	.000012	.000010	.000010	.000009	.000005	.000000	.000011	.000025	.000049	.000095
40	.000012	.000011	.000011	.000010	.000009	.000007	.000001	.000005	.000015	.000039
41	.000012	.000011	.000011	.000011	.000011	.000010	.000006	.000005	.000002	.000011
44	.000012	.000011	.000012	.000012	.000012	.000012	.000010	.000012	.000015	.000012
45	.000012	.000011	.000012	.000012	.000012	.000012	.000011	.000013	.000015	.000013
46	.000012	.000011	.000012	.000012	.000012	.000012	.000011	.000013	.000016	.000014
47	.000012	.000011	.000012	.000012	.000012	.000012	.000011	.000013	.000016	.000014
48	.000012	.000011	.000012	.000012	.000012	.000012	.000011	.000013	.000016	.000014

Channel	20.500	21.000	21.500	22.000	22.500	23.000	23.500	24.000	24.500	25.000
49	.000012	.000011	.000012	.000012	.000012	.000012	.000011	.000013	.000016	.000014
50	.000012	.000011	.000012	.000012	.000012	.000012	.000011	.000013	.000016	.000014
51	.000012	.000011	.000012	.000012	.000012	.000012	.000011	.000013	.000016	.000014
52	.000012	.000011	.000012	.000012	.000012	.000012	.000011	.000013	.000016	.000014
53	.000012	.000011	.000012	.000012	.000012	.000012	.000011	.000013	.000016	.000014
54	.000012	.000011	.000012	.000012	.000012	.000012	.000011	.000013	.000016	.000014
55	.000012	.000011	.000012	.000012	.000012	.000012	.000011	.000013	.000016	.000014
1	1.000000	1.000000	1.000000	1.000000	1.000000	1.000000	1.000000	1.000000	1.000000	1.000000
2	1.000000	1.000000	1.000000	1.000000	1.000000	1.000000	1.000000	1.000000	1.000000	1.000000
3	1.000000	1.000000	1.000000	1.000000	1.000000	1.000000	1.000000	1.000000	1.000000	1.000000
4	.999998	.999999	.999999	.999999	1.000000	1.000000	1.000000	1.000000	1.000000	1.000000
5	.999989	.999992	.999995	.999997	.999998	.999999	.999999	.999999	1.000000	1.000000
6	.999951	.999967	.999977	.999985	.999990	.999993	.999995	.999997	.999998	.999999
7	.999822	.999876	.999914	.999941	.999959	.999972	.999981	.999987	.999991	.999994
8	.999445	.999605	.999721	.999803	.999861	.999903	.999932	.999953	.999967	.999977
9	.998478	.998894	.999200	.999423	.999586	.999703	.999788	.999849	.999893	.999925
10	.996275	.997234	.997956	.998495	.998896	.999194	.999413	.999575	.999693	.999779
11	.991759	.993749	.995281	.996453	.997346	.998022	.998532	.998915	.999201	.999413
12	.983343	.987095	.990053	.992370	.994175	.995573	.996650	.997476	.998106	.998584
13	.968965	.975451	.980686	.984884	.988229	.990878	.992964	.994598	.995870	.996856
14	.946293	.956640	.965194	.972215	.977937	.982571	.986301	.989284	.991656	.993532
15	.913095	.928425	.941404	.952306	.961398	.968925	.975116	.980174	.984282	.987598
16	.867724	.888924	.907304	.923107	.936588	.948001	.957593	.965599	.972238	.977707
17	.809593	.837078	.861482	.882959	.901700	.917922	.931857	.943737	.953794	.962252
18	.739493	.773034	.803531	.831001	.855524	.877227	.896279	.912872	.927215	.939524
19	.659657	.698315	.734312	.767498	.797804	.825229	.849831	.871719	.891037	.907958
20	.573518	.615732	.655985	.693968	.729452	.762282	.792383	.819736	.844387	.866423
21	.485226	.529019	.571783	.613085	.652555	.689895	.724880	.757357	.787240	.814505
22	.399036	.442306	.485577	.528351	.570166	.610613	.649342	.686067	.720569	.752697

continued

Poisson Distribution *continued*

	Traffic in Erlangs									
Channel	20.500	21.000	21.500	22.000	22.500	23.000	23.500	24.000	24.500	25.000
23	.318722	.359535	.401330	.443616	.485905	.527727	.568653	.608295	.646322	.682461
24	.247139	.283961	.322577	.362566	.403475	.444841	.486211	.527142	.567232	.606118
25	.185994	.217834	.252028	.288270	.326197	.365409	.405486	.445990	.486495	.526593
26	.135856	.162287	.191356	.222889	.256647	.292332	.329604	.368083	.407372	.447069
27	.096324	.117422	.141184	.167567	.196459	.227686	.261019	.296169	.332815	.370603
28	.066308	.082528	.101233	.122490	.146303	.172618	.201324	.232246	.265161	.299802
29	.044333	.056356	.070556	.087072	.105999	.127383	.151223	.177454	.205963	.236586
30	.028799	.037405	.047813	.060203	.074728	.091507	.110624	.132109	.155951	.182090
31	.018184	.024139	.031514	.040499	.051275	.064002	.078822	.095834	.115109	.136676
32	.011164	.015152	.020209	.026516	.034253	.043595	.054713	.067749	.082830	.100052
33	.006667	.009255	.012614	.016903	.022284	.028928	.037009	.046686	.058116	.071440
34	.003873	.005502	.007666	.010494	.014124	.018705	.024401	.031367	.039768	.049764
35	.002189	.003184	.004537	.006346	.008723	.011790	.015687	.020554	.026547	.033826
36	.001203	.001793	.002614	.003740	.005252	.007246	.009836	.013139	.017292	.022441
37	.000641	.000982	.001467	.002147	.003082	.004342	.006016	.008196	.010993	.014535
38	.000329	.000521	.000799	.001200	.001763	.002537	.003590	.004989	.006822	.009193
39	.000162	.000267	.000422	.000651	.000981	.001445	.002090	.002964	.004133	.005679
40	.000073	.000130	.000214	.000342	.000531	.000801	.001186	.001718	.002444	.003426
41	.000028	.000058	.000102	.000172	.000277	.000431	.000655	.000970	.001410	.002018
42	.000005	.000021	.000044	.000081	.000138	.000223	.000351	.000533	.000791	.001160
43	.000005	.000002	.000013	.000033	.000064	.000109	.000181	.000282	.000431	.000649
44	.000011	.000007	.000001	.000008	.000025	.000048	.000087	.000143	.000225	.000352
45	.000013	.000011	.000009	.000004	.000005	.000016	.000038	.000067	.000111	.000183
46	.000014	.000013	.000012	.000010	.000005	.000000	.000012	.000026	.000049	.000089
47	.000015	.000014	.000014	.000013	.000010	.000008	.000001	.000005	.000015	.000038
48	.000015	.000014	.000015	.000014	.000012	.000012	.000008	.000006	.000002	.000011
50	.000015	.000015	.000015	.000015	.000014	.000015	.000013	.000014	.000015	.000010
51	.000015	.000015	.000015	.000015	.000014	.000015	.000014	.000015	.000017	.000014
52	.000015	.000015	.000015	.000015	.000014	.000016	.000014	.000016	.000018	.000016

Channel	25.500	26.000	26.500	27.000	27.500	28.000	28.500	29.000	29.500	30.000
53	.000015	.000015	.000015	.000015	.000015	.000016	.000016	.000021	.000033	.000058
54	.000015	.000015	.000016	.000016	.000019	.000029	.000056	.000143	.000398	.001123
55	.000015	.000017	.000023	.000043	.000108	.000324	.000998	.003079	.009337	.027735
1	1.000000	1.000000	1.000000	1.000000	1.000000	1.000000	1.000000	1.000000	1.000000	1.000000
2	1.000000	1.000000	1.000000	1.000000	1.000000	1.000000	1.000000	1.000000	1.000000	1.000000
3	1.000000	1.000000	1.000000	1.000000	1.000000	1.000000	1.000000	1.000000	1.000000	1.000000
4	1.000000	1.000000	1.000000	1.000000	1.000000	1.000000	1.000000	1.000000	1.000000	1.000000
5	1.000000	1.000000	1.000000	1.000000	1.000000	1.000000	1.000000	1.000000	1.000000	1.000000
6	.999999	.999999	.999999	.999999	1.000000	1.000000	1.000000	1.000000	1.000000	1.000000
7	.999996	.999997	.999998	.999999	.999999	.999999	1.000000	1.000000	1.000000	1.000000
8	.999984	.999989	.999992	.999995	.999996	.999998	.999998	.999999	.999999	1.000000
9	.999947	.999963	.999974	.999982	.999987	.999991	.999994	.999996	.999997	.999998
10	.999841	.999886	.999919	.999942	.999959	.999971	.999979	.999986	.999990	.999993
11	.999571	.999687	.999773	.999835	.999881	.999915	.999939	.999956	.999969	.999978
12	.998945	.999218	.999421	.999574	.999687	.999771	.999833	.999878	.999912	.999936
13	.997616	.998200	.998646	.998985	.999242	.999436	.999581	.999690	.999772	.999832
14	.995009	.996164	.997064	.997762	.998300	.998714	.999030	.999271	.999454	.999593
15	.990259	.992383	.994070	.995402	.996450	.997270	.997908	.998403	.998785	.999079
16	.982185	.985830	.988781	.991156	.993058	.994574	.995776	.996724	.997470	.998052
17	.969316	.975181	.980021	.983990	.987229	.989857	.991978	.993682	.995044	.996127
18	.950014	.958895	.966365	.972610	.977800	.982088	.985612	.988492	.990834	.992730
19	.922669	.935370	.946260	.955539	.963393	.970002	.975531	.980130	.983935	.987067
20	.885969	.903177	.918220	.931279	.942542	.952192	.960410	.967368	.973224	.978126
21	.839176	.861328	.881067	.898530	.913871	.927258	.938864	.948862	.957425	.964715
22	.782356	.809514	.834183	.856423	.876326	.894012	.909621	.923307	.935230	.945555
23	.716497	.748279	.777709	.804746	.829395	.851699	.871739	.889620	.905470	.919429
24	.643479	.679057	.712642	.744083	.773281	.800187	.824798	.847146	.867299	.885352
25	.565898	.604066	.640796	.675836	.708984	.740091	.769055	.795822	.820380	.842755
26	.486765	.526076	.564640	.602129	.638258	.672783	.705509	.736287	.765016	.791638

continued

Poisson Distribution *continued*

Traffic in Erlangs

Channel	25.500	26.000	26.500	27.000	27.500	28.000	28.500	29.000	29.500	30.000
27	.409154	.448086	.487019	.525588	.563451	.600297	.635852	.669883	.702199	.732658
28	.335854	.372985	.410836	.449047	.487259	.525127	.562326	.598559	.633566	.667124
29	.269099	.303248	.338734	.375239	.412428	.449956	.487486	.524689	.561256	.596909
30	.210401	.240725	.272848	.306521	.341467	.377378	.413937	.450818	.487699	.524273
31	.160507	.186538	.214648	.244676	.276419	.309638	.344065	.379410	.415369	.451637
32	.119466	.141091	.164897	.190810	.218716	.248454	.279829	.312609	.346538	.381344
33	.086761	.104166	.123696	.145361	.169127	.194917	.222618	.252070	.283084	.315444
34	.061489	.075073	.090611	.108175	.127803	.149493	.173208	.198869	.226361	.255536
35	.042535	.052825	.064824	.078645	.094379	.112084	.131791	.153492	.177145	.202675
36	.028726	.036299	.045300	.055865	.068117	.082157	.098066	.115894	.135663	.157366
37	.018944	.024363	.030928	.038780	.048056	.058881	.071367	.085607	.101670	.119608
38	.012203	.015975	.020634	.026313	.033146	.041266	.050802	.061868	.074568	.088994
39	.007679	.010237	.013456	.017454	.022356	.028287	.035378	.043752	.053529	.064825
40	.004721	.006411	.008578	.011321	.014747	.018969	.024106	.030281	.037614	.046233
41	.002835	.003924	.005347	.007182	.009516	.012446	.016075	.020514	.025877	.032289
42	.001663	.002347	.003258	.004456	.006008	.007991	.010493	.013606	.017432	.022087
43	.000951	.001371	.001941	.002703	.003711	.005021	.006705	.008836	.011500	.014799
44	.000528	.000780	.001128	.001603	.002242	.003088	.004194	.005619	.007431	.009715
45	.000284	.000432	.000639	.000927	.001323	.001857	.002568	.003499	.004703	.006248
46	.000145	.000230	.000351	.000522	.000762	.001091	.001538	.002133	.002914	.003937
47	.000068	.000116	.000185	.000284	.000427	.000625	.000900	.001271	.001767	.002430
48	.000026	.000053	.000092	.000148	.000230	.000348	.000513	.000740	.001047	.001468
49	.000004	.000019	.000040	.000071	.000118	.000186	.000283	.000418	.000605	.000866
50	.000007	.000001	.000012	.000029	.000055	.000093	.000149	.000228	.000338	.000498
51	.000013	.000009	.000003	.000006	.000020	.000041	.000073	.000115	.000071	.000122
52	.000018	.000021	.000036	.000081	.000200	.000510	.001286	.003186	.007822	.018722
53	.000137	.000349	.000917	.002410	.006248	.015946	.040035	.098909	.240667	.576712
54	.003178	.008858	.024271	.065303	.172572	.448158	1.040035	1.098909	1.240667	1.576712
55	.080712	.230108	.643139	1.065303	1.172572	1.448158	2.040035	2.098909	2.240667	2.576712

Channel	30.500	31.000	31.500	32.000	32.500	33.000	33.500	34.000	34.500	35.000
1	1.000000	1.000000	1.000000	1.000000	1.000000	1.000000	1.000000	1.000000	1.000000	1.000000
2	1.000000	1.000000	1.000000	1.000000	1.000000	1.000000	1.000000	1.000000	1.000000	1.000000
3	1.000000	1.000000	1.000000	1.000000	1.000000	1.000000	1.000000	1.000000	1.000000	1.000000
4	1.000000	1.000000	1.000000	1.000000	1.000000	1.000000	1.000000	1.000000	1.000000	1.000000
5	1.000000	1.000000	1.000000	1.000000	1.000000	1.000000	1.000000	1.000000	1.000000	1.000000
6	1.000000	1.000000	1.000000	1.000000	1.000000	1.000000	1.000000	1.000000	1.000000	1.000000
7	1.000000	1.000000	1.000000	1.000000	1.000000	1.000000	1.000000	1.000000	1.000000	1.000000
8	1.000000	1.000000	1.000000	1.000000	1.000000	1.000000	1.000000	1.000000	1.000000	1.000000
9	.999999	.999999	.999999	.999999	.999999	.999999	.999999	1.000000	1.000000	1.000000
10	.999995	.999997	.999998	.999998	.999999	.999999	.999999	.999999	1.000000	1.000000
11	.999984	.999989	.999992	.999994	.999996	.999997	.999998	.999999	.999999	.999999
12	.999954	.999967	.999976	.999983	.999988	.999991	.999994	.999996	.999999	.999998
13	.999877	.999910	.999935	.999952	.999966	.999975	.999982	.999987	.999997	.999993
14	.999697	.999775	.999834	.999877	.999910	.999934	.999952	.999965	.999991	.999981
15	.999305	.999476	.999607	.999706	.999781	.999837	.999879	.999910	.999974	.999951
16	.998506	.998859	.999131	.999340	.999501	.999623	.999717	.999788	.999934	.999882
17	.996985	.997662	.998193	.998608	.998932	.999183	.999377	.999526	.999841	.999729
18	.994256	.995479	.996455	.997231	.997844	.998328	.998707	.999004	.999641	.999414
19	.989631	.991720	.993415	.994782	.995881	.996760	.997461	.998017	.999235	.998802
20	.982207	.985588	.988373	.990658	.992523	.994038	.995264	.996251	.998456	.997675
21	.970886	.976082	.980433	.984059	.987065	.989546	.991583	.993249	.997043	.995703
22	.954443	.962049	.968523	.974004	.978619	.982487	.985712	.988388	.994604	.992416
23	.931647	.942276	.951470	.959378	.966143	.971898	.976771	.980876	.990598	.987187
24	.901417	.915626	.928115	.939029	.948512	.956706	.963749	.969771	.984316	.979230
25	.863001	.881202	.897462	.911897	.924638	.935817	.945572	.954039	.974893	.967625
26	.816133	.838517	.858838	.877169	.893601	.908244	.921216	.932643	.961348	.951379
27	.761153	.787623	.812044	.834425	.854805	.873246	.889833	.904664	.942654	.929508
28	.699046	.729190	.757452	.783767	.808106	.830472	.850895	.869431	.917850	.901158
29	.631393	.664495	.696035	.725871	.753902	.780059	.804309	.826649	.886156	.865720
30	.560242	.595339	.629323	.661987	.693156	.722692	.750494	.776490	.847104	.822950
31	.487904	.523878	.559276	.593843	.627348	.659589	.690400	.719643	.800645	.773052

continued

Poisson Distribution *continued*

Traffic in Erlangs

Channel	30.500	31.000	31.500	32.000	32.500	33.000	33.500	34.000	34.500	35.000
32	.416734	.452417	.488099	.523501	.558356	.592415	.625461	.657295	.687759	.716715
33	.348899	.383188	.418034	.453159	.488286	.523142	.557477	.591051	.623655	.655097
34	.286203	.318156	.351154	.384949	.419277	.453869	.488463	.522798	.556636	.589745
35	.229962	.258862	.289192	.320751	.353313	.386633	.420464	.454546	.488632	.522470
36	.180951	.206344	.233426	.262056	.292060	.323239	.355379	.388244	.421600	.455195
37	.139428	.161120	.184631	.209882	.236763	.265128	.294814	.325625	.357360	.389789
38	.105200	.123230	.143088	.164759	.188191	.213299	.239978	.268084	.297462	.327918
39	.077727	.092319	.108652	.126761	.146649	.168290	.191636	.216599	.243080	.270932
40	.056242	.067750	.080839	.095583	.112031	.130205	.150112	.171716	.194973	.219791
41	.039860	.048708	.058935	.070640	.083904	.098785	.115335	.133564	.153480	.175042
42	.027673	.034311	.042107	.051173	.061608	.073496	.086919	.101927	.118566	.136842
43	.018823	.023684	.029486	.036241	.044355	.053626	.064255	.076315	.089887	.105009
44	.012545	.016023	.020240	.025303	.031315	.038377	.046597	.056064	.066876	.079098
45	.008194	.010626	.013621	.017275	.021683	.026940	.033154	.040416	.048834	.058487
46	.005245	.006907	.008988	.011567	.014727	.018553	.023146	.028593	.035002	.042456
47	.003289	.004402	.005815	.007596	.009812	.012536	.015857	.019854	.024627	.030259
48	.002020	.002749	.003688	.004892	.006414	.008312	.010663	.013532	.017012	.021176
49	.001214	.001682	.002293	.003089	.004113	.005407	.007037	.009054	.011539	.014552
50	.000712	.001006	.001396	.001912	.002586	.003202	.002429	.000469	.007935	.024862
51	.000705	.002188	.005714	.013713	.031336	.069579	.151941	.324262	.679791	1.024862
52	.043918	.101218	.229669	.513713	1.031336	1.069579	1.151941	1.324262	1.679791	2.024862
53	1.043918	1.101219	1.229669	1.513713	2.031336	2.069579	2.151941	2.324262	2.679791	3.024862
54	2.043918	2.101219	2.229669	2.513713	3.031337	3.069579	3.151941	3.324263	3.679791	4.024862
55	3.043918	3.101219	3.229669	3.513714	4.031337	4.069579	4.151941	4.324263	4.679791	5.024862

Channel	35.500	36.000	36.500	37.000	37.500	38.000	38.500	39.000	39.500	40.000
1	1.000000	1.000000	1.000000	1.000000	1.000000	1.000000	1.000000	1.000000	1.000000	1.000000
2	1.000000	1.000000	1.000000	1.000000	1.000000	1.000000	1.000000	1.000000	1.000000	1.000000

n											
3	1.000000	1.000000	1.000000	1.000000	1.000000	1.000000	1.000000	1.000000	1.000000	1.000000	1.000000
4	1.000000	1.000000	1.000000	1.000000	1.000000	1.000000	1.000000	1.000000	1.000000	1.000000	1.000000
5	1.000000	1.000000	1.000000	1.000000	1.000000	1.000000	1.000000	1.000000	1.000000	1.000000	1.000000
6	1.000000	1.000000	1.000000	1.000000	1.000000	1.000000	1.000000	1.000000	1.000000	1.000000	1.000000
7	1.000000	1.000000	1.000000	1.000000	1.000000	1.000000	1.000000	1.000000	1.000000	1.000000	1.000000
8	1.000000	1.000000	1.000000	1.000000	1.000000	1.000000	1.000000	1.000000	1.000000	1.000000	1.000000
9	1.000000	1.000000	1.000000	1.000000	1.000000	1.000000	1.000000	1.000000	1.000000	1.000000	1.000000
10	1.000000	1.000000	1.000000	1.000000	1.000000	1.000000	1.000000	1.000000	1.000000	1.000000	1.000000
11	1.000000	1.000000	1.000000	1.000000	1.000000	1.000000	1.000000	1.000000	1.000000	1.000000	1.000000
12	.999998	.999999	.999999	.999999	1.000000	1.000000	1.000000	1.000000	1.000000	1.000000	1.000000
13	.999995	.999997	.999998	.999999	.999999	.999999	.999999	.999999	.999999	.999999	1.000000
14	.999987	.999990	.999993	.999996	.999999	.999999	.999999	.999999	.999999	.999999	.999999
15	.999964	.999974	.999981	.999989	.999997	.999997	.999998	.999996	.999997	.999998	.999999
16	.999912	.999935	.999952	.999971	.999990	.999990	.999986	.999990	.999992	.999995	.999998
17	.999796	.999846	.999885	.999925	.999965	.999974	.999965	.999974	.999981	.999988	.999995
18	.999553	.999660	.999742	.999827	.999912	.999936	.999917	.999938	.999953	.999970	.999986
19	.999074	.999286	.999451	.999603	.999755	.999804	.999814	.999859	.999893	.999929	.999965
20	.998179	.998578	.998893	.999115	.999336	.999579	.999606	.999698	.999769	.999845	.999920
21	.996590	.997303	.997874	.998283	.998692	.999141	.999205	.999383	.999523	.999674	.999824
22	.993905	.995119	.996104	.996824	.997543	.998330	.998471	.998799	.999060	.999346	.999632
23	.989572	.991543	.993167	.994376	.995585	.996901	.997185	.997763	.998228	.998747	.999266
24	.982883	.985947	.988506	.990449	.992392	.994498	.995034	.996007	.996801	.997701	.998601
25	.972990	.977554	.981417	.984410	.987403	.990632	.991582	.993154	.994451	.995948	.997445
26	.958942	.965466	.971067	.975493	.979919	.984672	.986266	.988703	.990739	.993128	.995517
27	.939761	.948730	.956537	.962832	.969126	.975851	.978395	.982026	.985099	.988766	.992433
28	.914541	.926415	.936895	.945515	.954135	.963298	.967172	.972381	.976847	.982268	.987689
29	.882566	.897725	.911290	.922674	.934058	.946096	.951739	.958947	.965207	.972934	.980660
30	.843425	.862109	.879063	.893580	.908096	.923365	.931251	.940881	.949353	.959987	.970620
31	.797107	.819370	.839854	.857749	.875643	.894363	.904959	.917395	.928477	.942624	.956770
32	.744066	.769738	.793689	.815038	.836386	.858594	.872305	.887849	.901878	.920091	.938304
33	.685223	.713901	.741031	.765707	.790382	.815902	.833018	.851839	.869045	.891761	.914477
34	.621923	.652989	.682788	.710446	.738104	.766539	.787183	.809282	.829744	.848592	.884592

continued

Poisson Distribution *continued*

Traffic in Erlangs

Channel	35.500	36.000	36.500	37.000	37.500	38.000	38.500	39.000	39.500	40.000
35	.555830	.588493	.620263	.650964	.680445	.708586	.735282	.760466	.784086	.806119
36	.488792	.522155	.555058	.587293	.618667	.649017	.678191	.706071	.732558	.757579
37	.422686	.455817	.488948	.521853	.554316	.586140	.617136	.647144	.676020	.703646
38	.359260	.391271	.423731	.456413	.489094	.521563	.553605	.585031	.615562	.645339
39	.300006	.330123	.361088	.392695	.424731	.456986	.489238	.521284	.552921	.583964
40	.246071	.273678	.302461	.332245	.362843	.394065	.425696	.457537	.489376	.521016
41	.198202	.222878	.248964	.276329	.304824	.334290	.364537	.395383	.426625	.458067
42	.156756	.178273	.201339	.225868	.251757	.278889	.307108	.336261	.366170	.396653
43	.121723	.140041	.159950	.181414	.204376	.228764	.254464	.281363	.309314	.338164
44	.092801	.108032	.124817	.143163	.163055	.184467	.207330	.231571	.257085	.283756
45	.069466	.081843	.095673	.110997	.127839	.146211	.166087	.187437	.210198	.234294
46	.051058	.060891	.072034	.084550	.098492	.113906	.130801	.149188	.169041	.190328
47	.036851	.044495	.053277	.063277	.074567	.087219	.101269	.116759	.133701	.152096
48	.026121	.031936	.038711	.046530	.055479	.065643	.077078	.089850	.103999	.119558
49	.018185	.022516	.027634	.030312	.024589	.007307	.032176	.113115	.270095	.564670
50	.060794	.134211	.280451	.569763	.975411	.992693	1.032176	1.113115	1.270095	1.564670
51	1.060794	1.134211	1.280451	1.569763	1.975411	1.992693	2.032176	2.113115	2.270095	2.564670
52	2.060794	2.134211	2.280451	2.569763	2.975411	2.992693	3.032176	3.113115	3.270096	3.564670
53	3.060795	3.134212	3.280452	3.569763	3.975411	3.992693	4.032176	4.113115	4.270096	4.564670
54	4.060795	4.134212	4.280452	4.569763	4.975411	4.992693	5.032176	5.113115	5.270096	5.564670
55	5.060795	5.134212	5.280452	5.569763	5.975411	5.992693	6.032176	6.113115	6.270096	6.564670

Glossary

Attenuation Loss in signal strength as the distance between a transmitter and receiver increases.

Attenuation equalizer A device that adjusts the attenuation distortion on a circuit by introducing a variable gain at frequencies within the passband.

Bandwidth The width of a range of frequencies between two frequencies.

Baud A unit of signaling change.

Bel A unit of power measurement, which results from taking the logarithm to the base 10 of the ratio of power received to power transmitted.

Bit error rate The number of bits received in error divided by the number of bits transmitted.

Breakout box A portable, hand-held tester used primarily for examining the condition of the conductors at the physical interface level.

Buffer utilization The percentage of buffer storage in use.

Cable tester A device used to test the conductors in a data communications cable.

Call hour The quantity represented by one or more calls that have an aggregate duration of one hour.

Carrier frequency The frequency at which a signal that is used to convey information operates.

Circuit loss test A test used to determine the amount of energy lost during a transmission.

Circuit quality monitor test A test that produces a polar plot of the signal amplitude versus signal phase on a circuit. This test uses an oscilloscope and displays the "eye" pattern of a signal.

C-message filter A filter used to remove the test signal placed on the line, which leaves only the noise to be measured.

Compression efficiency Total bits received divided by total bits compressed.

Continuity The flow of a signal from one cable end to the other.

Constellation pattern The set of all possible signal points generated by a modem.

dBm The power level in decibels obtained when a 1mW reference level is used.

dBmeter An instrument used to measure the power output at a point on a circuit.

Decibel One-tenth of a bel.

Decoding The capability of a monitor or protocol analyzer to display control characters in character-oriented protocol and bit-oriented protocol data.

Delay equalizer A device that introduces a delay which is approximately the inverse of the delay on a circuit, which results in a relatively flat delay across the passband.

Dibit encoding The process whereby two bits are used to represent one signal change.

Dropout A sudden, large reduction in the signal level, lasting more than a few milliseconds.

Envelope delay The delay time experienced by certain frequencies in a signal due to filters used on telephone circuits.

Envelope delay test A test that measures the transmission delay over the passband.

Error density NAKs received, divided by frames transmitted.

Frequency shift keying The process of using two separate tones to represent a mark and a space and shifting frequencies to represent binary data.

Gain hit A sudden, uncontrolled increase in the received signal level.

Gain/slope test A test used to determine the loss that is occurring over the passband of a channel.

Grade of service The probability that a call will be blocked.

High pass filter A filter that attenuates all low frequencies, commencing at a cutoff frequency and permitting all high frequencies above the cutoff to pass through the filter.

Impulse noise Irregular spikes of pulses of short duration and relatively high amplitude.

Impulse noise test A test used to measure voltage spikes that are much larger than the average background noise level on a channel.

Interchange circuits The conductors in the cable that connect a DTE to a DCE, two DTEs, or two DCEs.

Line monitor A device that displays transmitted data.

Loading coils Filters placed on a telephone channel that reduce its passband, enabling more voice conversations to be frequency-division multiplexed on a line between telephone company offices.

Low-pass filter A filter that attenuates all high frequencies commencing at a cutoff frequency.

Marginal circuit A circuit where the slight increase in the level of transmission impairments makes the circuit inoperative.

Multiplexer loading The percentage of time that the device is not idle.

Null modem A special cable designed to eliminate the requirement for modems when connecting two DTEs or two DCEs to each other.

Nyquist relationship A principle stating that the rate at which data can be transmitted prior to intersymbol interference occurring must be less than or equal to twice the bandwidth in Hz.

Open *see* Short.

Passband A contiguous portion of an area in the frequency spectrum that permits a predefined range of frequencies to pass.

Pattern generator A data communications testing device that can be used to transmit an easily recognizable test message.

Phase hit A sudden, uncontrolled change in the phase of a received signal.

Phase jitter The unwanted change in phase or frequency of a signal.

Power ratio The ratio of power received to power transmitted.

Protocol analyzer A device designed to both monitor and test data transmission and that normally includes decoding and emulation capability.

Quadrature amplitude modulation The process by which the amplitude and phase of a signal is varied based on the composition of four bits of data to be modulated.

Ring-start A device whose operation is initiated by a ring indicator signal.

Self-test A test of the internal circuitry in a communications device.

Shannon's Law A tenet stating the relationship between the maximum bit rate capacity of a channel of bandwidth W and its signal-to-noise ratio.

Short The failure of a signal entered at one end of a conductor to reach the opposite end.

Signal-to-noise ratio The signal power divided by the noise power.

Signal-to-noise test A test used as an indicator of transmission line quality.

Sizing The process of determining the number of ports on a commuciations hardware device to support a given level of activity.

Statistical loading Number of actual characters received divided by maximum number that could be received.

Stepped frequency response test A test that involves taking readings in 100 Hz increments from 200 to 3500 Hz to obtain an accurate picture of the circuit loss over the passband.

Thermal noise Noise resulting from the movement of electrons, power line induction, and cross-modulation from adjacent circuits.

Tie The connection of two or more conductors so that a signal placed on one produces a signal on all tied conductors.

Traffic density Nonidle bits divided by total bits.

Transmission impairment A level of noise, delay, or distortion that affects data transmission.

Transmission level point The power in dBM that should be measured when a specific test tone signal is transmitted at a location selected as a reference point.

Trap A user-defined sequence of characters or bits to be matched.

Tribit encoding The process whereby three bits are used to represent one signaling change.

Trigger *see* Trap.

White noise *see* Thermal noise.

Zero decibel above reference noise An arbitrary level set equal to −90 dBm, which is designed to represent the lowest level of noise that an average telephone listener can hear.

Zero transmission level The actual measurement less the test tone level, which indicates the departure of a system from its design level.

Abbreviations

AA	auto answer
AL	analog loopback
B	baud rate
BER	bit error rate
BERT	bit error rate tester
BLERT	block error rate tester
CCITT	Consultative Committee for International Telephone & Telegraph
CH	call hour
CLK	clock
CTS	clear to send
dB	decibel
dBm	decibel milliwatt
dBm0	decibel milliwatt zero transmission level
dBrn	decibel above reference noise
dBrnc	decibels above referenced noise C-message weighted
dBrnc0	decibels above referenced noise C-message weighted zero level transmissions
DCD	data carrier detect
DCE	data communications equipment
DSR	data set ready
DTE	data terminal equipment
DTR	data terminal ready
EFS	error free seconds
FSK	frequency shift keying
HS	high speed mode
Hz	hertz
LED	light emitting diode
MR	modem ready
mW	milliwatt (.001 of a watt)
OH	off hook
PTT	post, telephone, and telegraph

QAM	quadrature amplitude modulation	**S/N**	signal-to-noise ratio
RD	receive data	**STDM**	synchronous time division multiplexer
RI	ring indicator	**TD**	transmit data
RSQ	receive signal quality	**TLP**	transmission level point
RTS	request to send	**VF**	voice frequency
SG	signal ground	**W**	bandwidth in Hz

Answers to Questions

Chapter 2

1. $dB = 10 \log_{10} \frac{P1}{P2} = 10 \log_{10} \frac{100}{1}$

   $10 \log_{10} 100 = 10 \cdot 2 = 20dB$

   Because the received power is less than the transmitted power, the power ratio is $-20dB$.

2. Output Signal = Input Signal + Gain

   Output Signal = 12dB + 7dB = 19dB

3. $dB = 10 \log_{10} \frac{P1}{P2} = 10 \log_{10} \frac{.01}{1}$

   Because the 1mW signal was a reference level, we denote the power level as $-20dBm$.

4. Because 0dBrn = $-90dBm$, 30dBrn is equal to $-60dBm$.

5. The zero transmission level equals the actual measurement less the test tone level. Thus,

   dBmO = dBm − TLP

   dBmO = 14 − 16 = −2

   which shows that the system is 2dBm under its design goal.

Chapter 3

1. 2400 baud × 2 bits/baud = 4800 bps
2.   a. From Table 3.1, it is obvious that the amplitude frequency response does not meet the stated limits of the service.
   b. What happens to data transmitted on the service measured depends on the type of modems used.

      If the modems use frequency shift keying with frequencies near the middle of the band, a slight increase in the error rate probably will be experienced. If the modulation technique uses a carrier near the higher portion of the passband, the error rate probably will increase.
   c. British Telecom would verify the readings and adjust attenuation equalizers on the circuit.
3. Normally one would expect the V.33 constellation pattern to be more susceptible to phase jitter increases because the points are closer together. Fortunately, the V.33 modem employs trellis coded modulation, which incorporates an error correction method to reduce the effect of misinterpreted constellation points.

Chapter 4

1. Circuit Y has less loss over the passband because the slope values are less.
2. Increase.
3. Plotting the signal level versus frequency shows that circuit X has the better response.

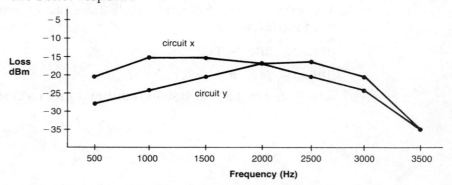

Figure 1. Signal versus frequency plot.

Chapter 5

1. A timeout is occurring at the remote terminal because of the occurrence of a poor signal for a short period of time.

2. If the HS lamp is off, the user is transmitting at the lower data rate of the modem. This might result from an improper speed setting or by the automatic fallback of the modem to a lower data rate when a connection is made to a lower speed modem.

Chapter 6

1. Pins 5 and 6 being on suggest the presence of CTS and DSR, which are associated with modems. Thus, the printer is functioning as a DCE.

2. Insert the breakout box between the computer port and the modem. Have an associate dial the modem, log onto the system, and issue a BYE command. Turn the breakout switch for the DTR connector to the off position to force DTR off and see whether DCD drops.

3. First insert the breakout box between the port selector and the multiplexer port. If the multiplexer passes the DTR (pin 20) signal when the terminal at the remote site turns on, use the breakout box to jumper pin 20 to pin 22 (ring indicator). Doing so forces RI high when the terminal is powered on, providing the required signal to the port selector.

4. From Table 6.4, you see that a 1×10^{-5} error rate at 2.4 Kbps would require 42 seconds. If 4 errors occur in 10 seconds, 4×4.2 results in a bit error rate of 16.8×10^{-5}.

5. Framed data should be transmitted during a bit error rate test when you test character oriented devices, such as some multiplexer ports and modems.

6. The number of NAKs can be determined by setting Trap 1 data to NAK and search to ON, after which Counter 1 is set to Trap 1.

7. Assign Trap 1 to DTR ON and Trap 2 to DCD OFF. Then assign Trap 1 to Counter 1 and Trap 1 to start Timer 1 while assigning Trap 2 to stop Timer 1.

8. DCL Program

```
1  CNTR ALL RESET
2  WAITFOR TRAP "CF" on the RECEIVE
```

```
       side of the line,
       if found display in REVERSE,
       then goto 4 (end)
    3  WAITFOR TRAP "DF" on the RECEIVE
       side of the line,
       if found display in REVERSE,
       then goto 6 (end)
    4  CNTR 1 INCREMENT
    5  GOTO 2
    6  CNTR 2 INCREMENT
    7  GOTO 2
```

Chapter 7

1. To isolate a failure to a modem or line, do the following tests.

   a. Do a self-test on each modem

   b. Do a local analog loop test from each side

   c. Do a remote digital loop test from each side

2. In-band signaling requires the modem to recognize a sequence of characters to go into its "Command Mode." Out-band signaling requires the modem to recognize a frequency near the edge of the frequency spectrum. Because impairments affect an edge frequency more than the center frequencies on the passband, out-band signaling may deteriorate more rapidly.

3. If the transmission appears to abort at the same time, it is highly possible that data is being misinterpreted as an end-of-transmission signal. Users should record the transmission and play back several blocks before the break to determine whether the data was at fault. If so, changing to a transparent protocol or placing the existing protocol in a transparent mode may solve the problem.

4. First set the bisynchronous channel into a loop mode, then run a round trip delay test when the multiplexer is active. Compare the round trip delay time to the bisynchronous timeout setting.

Chapter 8

1. If the statistical multiplexer's buffer utilization averaged 95%, it probably is issuing many XOFF-XON sequences and/or dropping

and raising CTS to prevent buffer overflow. This results in delays that probably make use of the device unsatisfactory to many users. To alleviate this problem, the speed of the high-speed line should be increased or some multiplexer channels should be moved onto a new system.

2 If the compression efficiency, statistical loading, and buffer utilization are all high, the RBT should bypass the multiplexer and be connected to a port on the multiport modem. This results in RBT operations not affecting other multiplexer users to the degree it would if directly input to the multiplexer.

If the compression efficiency is high and statistical loading and buffer utilization are low, the RBT data has a minimal effect on other statistical multiplexer users and can be routed through the multiplexer.

3. For a bisynchronous timeout to occur, the delay must exceed 2 seconds. You can determine the number of characters in the transmit buffer that result in a 2-second or greater delay as follows.

$$\frac{\text{characters} * 8 \text{ bits/character}}{4800 \text{ bps}} = 2 \text{ seconds}$$

or characters > 1200 for a 2-second delay to occur, which results in a bisynchronous timeout.

The standard deviation curve is as shown in the following.

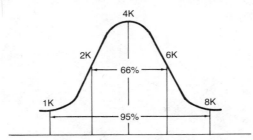

Figure 2 Standard deviation curve.

Based on the preceding, you can expect a bisynchronous timeout to occur over 95% of the time. This problem could be alleviated by setting the timeout to a higher value, increasing the modem data rate, or a combination of both.

4. If the full duplex line is operating at 14.4 Kpbs, the maximum rate that data can be dumped out of the transmit buffer is 1800 cps. If the

average utilization of the transmit side of the line was 1600 cps, it was operating at 88% of its maximum data rate. At this level of operation, the multiplexer is probably toggling XOFF-XON or CTS frequently and may require an increase in the data rate of its high speed line or the installation of a second link.

5. If one-third of the 18 devices in the terminal population can be expected to be active during the busy hour, they provide a call intensity of 6 erlangs. From Table 8.2 a grade of service of .05 for a 6 erlang load requires 10 channels.

INDEX

C Programmer's Guide to NetBIOS

W. David Schwaderer

Network Basic Input/Output System (NetBIOS) has quickly become the standard programming interface used to access local area network (LAN) functions. This book explains how to use the NetBIOS interface with C to create applications for a wide variety of products and applications.

Each principle is explained and illustrated, then used as a building block for the next even more complex principle. Emphasizing the Microsoft® C compiler, examples are clear and complete, revealing the capabilities of the NetBIOS interface.

Topics covered include:

- NetBIOS and IBM® 's LAN Adapters
- Application Services
- NetBIOS Ncb/Mcb Fields
- The IBM LAN Support Program
- NetBIOS Relationships to Other IBM Products
- LAN Data Integrity and Security Issues
- Real-Time LAN Conferencing
- C File Transfer Applications
- Medialess Workstations, RPL, and Redirectors
- A CRC Treatise: CRC-16, CRC General Mechanics, and CRC-32

600 Pages, 7½ x 9¾, Softbound
ISBN: 0-672-22638-3
No. 22638, $24.95

C Programmer's Guide to Serial Communications

Joe Campbell

This book offers a comprehensive examination and unprecedented dissection of asynchronous serial communications. Written for C programmers and technically advanced users, it contains both a theoretical discussion of communications concepts and a practical approach to program design for the IBM® PC and Kaypro environments.

The author introduces a startling advance in the art of programming—the "virtual" UART—which he uses to develop a highly portable C programming library that outperforms costly commercial products.

Topics covered include:

- The ASCII Character Set
- Fundamentals of Asynchronous Technology
- Errors and Error Detection
- Information Transfer
- Modems and Modem Control
- The UART—A Conceptual Model
- Real-World Hardware: Two UARTs
- The Hayes Smartmodem
- Designing a Basic Serial I/O Library
- Portability Considerations
- Timing Functions
- Functions for Baud Rate and Data Format
- RS-232 Control
- Formatted Input and Output
- Smartmodem Programming
- XMODEM File Transfers
- CRC Calculations
- Interrupts

672 Pages, 7½ x 9¾, Softbound
ISBN: 0-672-22584-0
No. 22584, $26.95

Data Communications, Networks, and Systems

Thomas C. Bartee, Editor-in-Chief

Data Communications, Networks, and Systems is the most current publication it its field, written by 11 experts and edited by prominent Harvard University professor Thomas C. Bartee. It presents a comprehensive overview of state-of-the-art communications systems, how they operate, and what new options are open to system users.

Use this reference book to learn the advantages and disadvantages of local area networks; how modems, multiplexers and concentrators operate; the characteristics of fiber optics and coaxial cables; and the forces shaping the structure and regulation of common carrier operations. The book's ten chapters contain a wealth of information—much of which has never before been published—providing an excellent reference tool for all communications professionals.

Topics covered include:

- Transmission Media
- Carriers and Regulation
- Modems, Multiplexers, and Concentrators
- Protocols
- PBX Local Area Networks
- Baseband and Broadband Local Area Networks
- Computer and Communications Security
- Local Area Network Standards

368 Pages, 8 x 10¼, Hardbound
ISBN: 0-672-22235-3
No. 22235, $39.95

Digital Communications

Thomas C. Bartee, Editor-in-Chief

Communications professionals who must stay abreast of state-of-the-art technology will benefit from this comprehensive collection of data.

Nine leading experts have authored chapters on their specialties that reflect the most current information available in their fields.

Digital Communications is organized into nine chapters, each one concentrating on an important technical area. The chapters may be read in order, or separately.

Each chapter provides references that make this an excellent tutorial reference, or introduction to the complex and amazing subject of digital communications.

Topics covered include:

- Fiber-Optic Transmission Technology and System Evolution
- Satellite Communications
- Integrated Services Digital Networks (ISDN)
- Computer-Based Messaging
- Electronic Mail Systems
- Cellular Networks
- Challenges in Communications for Command and Control Systems
- Digital Coding of Speech
- Video Teleconferencing

424 Pages, 7½ x 9¾, Hardbound
ISBN: 0-672-22472-0
No. 22472, $44.95

**Visit your local book retailer, use the order form provided, or call
800-428-SAMS.**

Micro-Mainframe Connection
Thomas Wm. Madron

Focusing on the organizational environment, this book explores the opportunities, technologies, and problems involved in implementing the transfer of data between the mainframe and the micro workstation—more comprehensively than any other book on the market.

Designed to help managers and technical support people design and implement micro-mainframe networks, it gives complete information about features, facilities, and requirements, including cost considerations.

Topics covered include:

■ The Micro-Mainframe Link
■ Features, Facilities, and Problems in the Micro-Mainframe Connection
■ Micros, Mainframes, and Networks
■ Local Area Networks in the Micro-Mainframe Connection
■ Micros as Mainframe Peripherals: Mainframes as Micro Peripherals
■ Micros and IBM® Mainframes in a Synchronous Network
■ Asynchronous Devices in a Synchronous Network: Protocol Conversion
■ File Transfer Protocols
■ Data Extraction, Data Format, and Application Specific File Transfers
■ Making the Micro-Mainframe Connection

272 Pages, 7½ x 9¾, Hardbound
ISBN: 0-672-46583-3
No. 46583, $29.95

The Waite Group's Modem Connections Bible
Curtis and Majhor, The Waite Group

This book describes modems, how they work, and how to hook ten well-known modems to nine name-brand microcomputers. A handy Jump Table shows where to find the appropriate connection diagram and applies the illustrations to eleven more computers and seven additional modems. It also features an overview of communications software, an explanation of the RS-232C interface, and a section on troubleshooting.

Topics covered include:

■ Types of Modems
■ How Modems Work
■ Connecting Equipment
■ The RS-232 Connector
■ The Progress of a Call
■ Full Duplex and Half Duplex Mode
■ Types of Communications Programs
■ Features and Uses
■ Voice/Data Switching
■ How to Read the Charts
■ Jump Table
■ Appendices: Types of Online Services and Costs, The RS-232C Interface, Further Reading, Glossary, Troubleshooting, Communications Software for Microcomputers

192 Pages, 7½ x 9¾, Softbound
ISBN: 0-672-22446-X
No. 22446, $16.95

The Local Area Network Book
E. G. Brooner

Localized computer networks are a versatile means of communication. In this book you'll learn how networks developed and what local networks can do; what's necessary in components, techniques, standards, and protocols; how some LAN products work and how real LANs operate; and how to plan a network from scratch.

Toics covered include:

■ What Is A Network?
■ What Networks Can do for Us
■ Network Components and Techniques
■ Standards and Protocols
■ Some Real Products
■ How Some LAN Products Work
■ Some Real Working Networks
■ How to Plan a Network
■ A Closer Look at Protocols
■ The Future of Networks
■ Appendices: Standards Organizations, Index

128 Pages, 5½ x 8½, Softbound
ISBN: 0-672-22254-X
No. 22254, $7.95

Interfacing to the IBM® Personal Computer
Lewis C. Eggebrecht

The IBM PC's open architecture lends itself to external device interfacing. Learn from the lead designer and architect of the IBM PC how to exploit this capability. Includes design tips and examples, many subroutines for interfacing, and BASIC programs to explain interfacing functions.

Topics covered include:

■ Overview of the IBM Personal Computer System
■ The System Unit Processor Board
■ The 8088 Microprocessor
■ System Unit Bus Operations
■ System-Bus Signal Descriptions
■ System-Bus Timings
■ System-Bus Loading and Driving Capabilities
■ System-Bus Mechanical and Power Characteristics
■ System Interrupts
■ System Direct-Memory Access
■ System Timers and Counters
■ System Memory, I/O Map, and Decoding Techniques
■ Wait-State Generation
■ Digital Input/Output Register Interfacing Techniques
■ Expanding Interrupts on the PC
■ Adding Extended Timing and Counting Functions
■ High-Speed Data Transfer
■ Cards and Ports for Interfacing
■ Interface Signal Conditioning
■ BASIC Language Commands for Interfacing
■ Bus Extension
■ Hardware and Software for Testing Designs

272 Pages, 8 x 9¼, Softbound
ISBN: 0-672-22027-X
No. 22027, $16.95

Visit your local book retailer, use the order form provided, or call
800-428-SAMS.

Understanding Local Area Networks

Stan Schatt

This tutorial on the latest local area network technologies provides an in-depth description of the major LAN's on the market as well as a conceptual framework to help the reader understand how LAN's communicate with mainframe computers.

Another in the highly acclaimed Understanding Series, this book is appropriate for anyone wanting broadly based coverage of local area networks. It details why they are important to business and how they are configured to transmit information from one location to another.

Topics covered include:

- An Overview of Local Area Networks
- The Basics of a Local Area Network
- Gateways
- The IBM PC Network and Token Ring Network
- Novell's Local Area Network Systems
- 3Com's Local Area Networks
- AT&T's STARLAN and ISN
- The Corvus Local Area Network
- Other Networks and Pseudo-Networks
- A Guide to Networkable Software
- Local Area Network Selection and Management

288 Pages, 7 x 9, Softbound
ISBN: 0-672-27063-3
No. 27063, $17.95

Handbook of Computer-Communications Standards Volume 1

William Stallings

This first volume in a three-book series is a comprehensive treatment of computer communications standards, presented within the framework of the OSI model. Intended as an introductory reference for data-processing students and professionals, it provides the background and step-by-step details missing from the actual standards.

Volume 1 introduces the OSI model and its seven-layer architecture. A chapter on each layer illustrates the relevance and value of each standard, analyzes available options, and explains the underlying technology of each.

Topics covered include:

- The OSI Model
- Physical Layer
- Data Link Layer
- Network Layer: Subnetwork Interface
- Network Layer: Internetwork Operation
- Transport Layer
- Session Layer
- Presentation Layer
- Application Layer
- Appendices: Services and Functions of the OSI Layers, Standards Cited in this Book

336 Pages, 6-1/8 x 9-1/4, Hardbound
ISBN: 0-672-22664-2
No. 22664, $34.95

Handbook of Computer-Communications Standards Volume 2

William Stallings

Local network customers, designers, and system managers will welcome this comprehensive volume on the features and architecture necessary in a local network facility. This concise reference discusses critical design issues and explores approaches to meeting user requirements using an effective, step-by-step self-teaching format.

The book begins with a survey of local network technology which introduces the key ingredients and then provides a critical analysis of the alternatives, such as shielded twisted pair versus coaxial cable and baseband versus broadband. The book examines in detail the IEEE 802 standards and the Accredited Standards Committee X3T95 standard.

Topics covered include:

- Local Network Technology
- Local Network Standards
- IEEE 802.2 Logical Link Control
- IEEE 802.3 CSMA/CD
- IEEE 802.4 Token Bus
- IEEE 802.5 Token Ring
- Fiber Distributed Data Interface
- Appendices: The OSI Reference Manual, Encoding of Digital Data for Transmission, Error Detection

256 Pages, 6-1/8 x 9-1/4, Hardbound
ISBN: 0-672-22665-0
No. 22665, $34.95

Handbook of Computer-Communications Standards Volume 3

William Stallings

Designed to meet the needs of students, managers, and data-processing and communications professionals, this third volume in a comprehensive series presents a of the Department of Defense military protocol standards. It identifies the features and structures that are needed to communicate and examines the mechanisms and service of the five military standards.

Beginning with an introduction to the four-layer communications architecture, each chapter discusses separate standard and includes an in-depth comparative analysis of i merits and the options it provides The useful and timely appendices are valuable tools for systems analysts, programmers, systems engineers, network managers, system managers, and communications consultants.

Topics covered include:

- The DOD Communications Architecture
- Internet Protocol
- Transmission Control Protocol
- File Transfer Protocol
- Simple Mail Transfer Protocol
- TELNET
- Appendices: The Open System Interconnection Reference Model, Error Detection

224 Pages, 6-1/8 x 9-1/4, Hardbound
ISBN: 0-672-22666-9
No. 22666, $34.95

Visit your local book retailer, use the order form provided, or call
800-428-SAMS.